T0090655

Praise for Norman Podhoretz's

WHY ARE JEWS LIBERALS?

"Why are Jews liberals? God only knows. But Norman Podhoretz offers as lively and convincing an explanation as we're likely to get from a merely human source. I particularly liked his comparison of today's Jewish liberals to the Church Father Tertullian—one likely to offend both liberals and Tertullianites!"

—William Kristol, editor of *The Weekly Standard*

"Norman Podhoretz has written a characteristically vigorous and well-informed book about one of the most interesting and persistent questions in American politics. He gets right to the heart of the matter, and provides a convincing explanation of why American Jews tend to vote against their own interests, and those of Israel."

—Paul Johnson, author of *A History of the Jews* and *Modern Times*

"This is another uncompromising, hard-hitting, brilliant, and richly provocative Norman Podhoretz book. Nearly every chapter offers a compelling answer to questions you always wanted to ask . . . and then hesitated. Podhoretz's fresh angle for looking at history, especially modernity, brings intellectual excitement of a very high order."

—Michael Novak, winner of the Templeton Prize for
Progress in Religion

"Norman Podhoretz tackles one of the most intractable questions of modern politics: Why do Jews act against their enlightened self-interest in conditions of political freedom? Part of the answer comes in his survey of the historical connection between the Jews and liberalism, the rest in his up-to-date analysis of how liberalism became a proxy for Judaism. Want to know why Jews in overwhelming numbers voted for Barack Obama? Read this wise and insightful book."

—Ruth Wisse, Martin Peretz Professor of Yiddish Literature and
Professor of Comparative Literature, Harvard University

ALSO BY NORMAN PODHORETZ

Norman Podhoretz

WHY ARE JEWS LIBERALS?

Norman Podhoretz, who was the editor in chief of *Commentary* for thirty-five years, is the author of numerous bestselling books, including *Making It*, *Breaking Ranks*, *Ex-Friends*, *My Love Affair with America*, *The Prophets*, and *World War IV*. He holds the Presidential Medal of Freedom, the nation's highest civilian honor.

WHY ARE JEWS LIBERALS?

Norman Podhoretz

VINTAGE BOOKS

A Division of Random House, Inc.

New York

FIRST VINTAGE BOOKS EDITION, OCTOBER 2010

The Library of Congress has cataloged the Doubleday edition as follows:
Podhoretz, Norman.
Why are Jews liberals? / Norman Podhoretz. — 1st ed.
p. cm.
Includes bibliographical references.
1. Jews—Politics and government. 2. Jews—United States—Politics and government.
3. Liberalism—United States. I. Title.
DS140.P63 2009
320.51'3089924073—dc22
2009001357

Vintage ISBN: 978-0-307-45625-0

Author photograph © Leah Munson
Book design by Michael Collica

www.vintagebooks.com

FOR ROGER HERTOG AND PAUL MCHUGH

ACKNOWLEDGMENTS

I am, as always, deeply grateful to my wife, Midge Decter, and to my friend and colleague Neal Kozodoy, both of whom read early drafts of this book and made invaluable suggestions, while also saving me from a number of embarrassing errors. My editor at Doubleday, Gerald Howard, then read what I thought was a final draft but that actually needed more work, which, guided by his incisive queries and challenging comments, I proceeded to do, to the great benefit of what did in the end turn out to be the final draft.

CONTENTS

CONTENTS

WHY ARE JEWS LIBERALS?

INTRODUCTION

Anyone who pays any attention at all to American politics is sure to know that most American Jews are liberals and is also very likely to recognize that there is something anomalous about the fact that they still are. Milton Himmelfarb, who for many years headed the Information and Research Service of the American Jewish Committee, put the anomaly best in a brilliant and deservedly famous epigram: "Jews earn like Episcopalians and vote like Puerto Ricans." The Episcopalians may no longer be the richest group in America or Puerto Ricans the poorest, but the implication of the point still holds. Here is how it is spelled out by Anna Greenberg and Kenneth D. Wald, two close students of the political culture of American Jews:

> Jewish Americans do not exhibit the same political tendencies as other demographically equivalent groups. For instance, we might expect Jewish Americans to become more conservative in their beliefs and voting preferences as succeeding generations attain higher levels of affluence and education. In fact, Jewish Americans are among the most highly educated, professional, and affluent members of the population. . . . But when we compare these Jewish American voters to non-Jews with the same socio-economic status, the Jews remain politically distinctive.[1]

1

By "politically distinctive" Greenberg and Wald mean that

> Jews are clearly on the Left of American politics in their parti-
> san loyalties and voting preferences: they consistently support
> Democratic candidates and identify with the Democratic Party
> at considerably higher rates than non-Jews.[2]

Especially, again, those non-Jews whom they resemble in "socioeconomic status."

In short, Jewish political behavior continues to contradict many
commonplace assumptions. If we go by the most commonplace of all
these assumptions—that people tend to vote their pocket books—we
are forced to conclude that in continuing to vote for the Democrats
Jews have in the last few decades been voting against their own interests. Jewish conservatives, or neoconservatives,* like me, see this as
irrational, but Jewish liberals (which is to say most Jews) take pride in
it as a mark of their refusal to put self-interest (which they equate with
selfishness) above the demands of "social justice."

Nor do they take pride only in where they stand on economic
issues. Some three hundred years ago, surveying the political scene in
the England of his day, Dr. Johnson maintained that it was only a very
small part "of all that human hearts endure" that "laws or kings
[could] cause or cure." In the America of our day, however, it is—or at
least seems to be—very nearly the opposite. With us, government has
become so intrusive that hardly anything escapes its influence. The
practical result is that ideas and attitudes whose full range and depth
are in reality beyond the reach of the ballot box nevertheless keep getting sucked into the political maw. In that realm, too—the realm that
encompasses all the issues involved in what has become known as the

---

* Contrary to the promiscuous and often malicious misuse of this term, it prop-
erly refers to an initially small group of intellectuals—many but by no means all
of them Jewish—who began their political lives somewhere on the Left and who,
in the closing years of the 1960s, began moving toward a conservative position.
Some did so because they had lost faith in the domestic programs of the Great
Society; others (myself included) broke ranks with the radical movement of the
'60s with which they had been associated because they were repelled by the anti-
Americanism that had come to pervade it.

"culture war"—most American Jews are with the Left and against the Right. Greenberg and Wald again:

> Jews identify with groups in American politics traditionally found on the political Left. Jewish Americans support the women's movement more than non-Jews; Jews are also far more likely to call themselves prochoice than prolife. Jews do not support groups traditionally allied with the Republican Party such as the National Rifle Association and the religious Right.[3]

To liberal Jews these positions are a mark of their attachment to yet another high ideal—in this case the ideal of tolerance. But whatever the merits of this claim (which is at the very least compromised by its intolerant exclusion of the Right, and the religious Right most of all), Jewish conservatives like me see nothing here that has much, if anything, to do with being Jewish. That is, we find no warrant either in the Jewish religion or in the socioeconomic condition of the American Jewish community for the stand most Jews continue to take on issues like those on the Greenberg-Wald list (to which I would add the gay rights movement).

As for the attitude of most of our fellow Jews toward the religious Right, it seems to us at least as irrational as the way they vote. Most Jews, including most Jewish liberals, care deeply about the security of Israel, and there is no group in America (not even the Jews themselves) that is more passionate in its support of Israel than the conservative Christian community. Yet instead of forging a political alliance with this community, Jewish liberals look for ways to justify their refusal to do so. At the same time, they are perfectly willing to make common cause with the "mainline" denominations, despite the fact that unfriendliness and even outright hostility to Israel have become pervasive in that sector of the Protestant world.

This attitude toward the conservative Christian community, however, is only one aspect of the largest sense in which the stubborn attachment of American Jews to the liberal community in general and the Democratic Party in particular runs counter to their interest as Jews. For in the last forty years or so, the Left—not only in America but all over the world, and not only in the churches but in every institution it controls—has grown increasingly hostile to Israel, and this hostility has by now metastasized to the point where the difference between "anti-Zionism" and anti-Semitism has become almost invisible to the naked eye. Conversely, the Right, which was always more hospitable than the Left to anti-Jewish ideas and sentiments, has steadily been changing course. Anti-Semites of the traditional kind have become less and less welcome in the precincts of the Right, and so have "anti-Zionists," whether they are, as they always claim, merely critics of Israeli policies, or whether, as is more often the case, they are (knowingly or not) drawing on ancient anti-Semitic canards in their attacks on Israel, or whether they are (knowingly) using anti-Zionism as a respectable cover for a new species of anti-Semitism.

At one time, it seemed reasonable to suppose—and many did so suppose, some in hope and others in fear—that this reversal of roles would lead to a change in the political culture of American Jews. But it was not to be. No wonder, then, that non-Jewish conservatives are puzzled—so puzzled that I cannot remember ever being asked any question as often as I have been asked why so many Jews continue clinging to the Left and why they still vote as heavily as ever for the Democratic Party. Usually I respond by saying that it is a very long and very complicated story. So it is, and I will now take a stab at telling it in the pages that follow.

These pages are divided into two parts. In part 1, I survey the centuries of experience that pushed the Jews of Europe to the Left, and I then try to show how and why this experience carried over to America and how and why it shaped the political attitudes of their descendants (who comprise the vast majority of American Jews today). In this section of the book, I speak for the most part in the impersonal voice of a historian—an amateur, to be sure, but one who has relied on a variety of professional authorities for help and guidance. However, in part 2, which begins with the period in which I myself entered the story to become an active participant in the debates over the politics of the American Jewish community, I shift gears and speak in a different voice: the voice of personal experience. It is also from the perspective of a witness at first hand and a deeply interested party that I examine, and find wanting, the standard answers to the question I am trying to answer in this book. I then conclude with what I believe really explains why American Jews are still committed to liberalism and why this is bad for them both as Americans and as Jews.

PART ONE

HOW THE JEWS BECAME LIBERALS

1

THE "WITNESS" DOCTRINE

The reason the story of how the Jews became liberals is so long is that it begins very far back—all the way back to the birth of Christianity out of the womb of Judaism about two thousand years ago. The earliest Christians (not yet known by that name) were a dissident sect within Judaism. They did not, to begin with, see themselves as belonging to a new religion: they were, rather, Jews who continued observing the laws of Judaism but who differed from most of their fellow Jews in their belief that the Messiah (or the "Christ")* had come in the person of Jesus of Nazareth. It was only with the conversion of Saint Paul a few years after the crucifixion of Jesus that the break with Judaism was initiated.

Paul (né Saul) was himself a Jew ("I also am an Israelite, of the seed of Abraham, of the tribe of Benjamin"[1]), and he sometimes denied that God had now rejected the people He had formerly chosen ("They are beloved for the sake of their forefathers").[2] But he interpreted the coming of Jesus as signifying, and indeed requiring, the abrogation of

---

* "Christ" is an Anglicization of *christos*, the Greek word for "messiah," which is in turn an Anglicization of the Hebrew word *mashiakh*, meaning "anointed one," or king. In the normative Jewish conception of the Messiah, he would be a flesh-and-blood descendant of King David, who would drive the Romans out of the Promised Land and reestablish a monarchy with its seat in Jerusalem whence the Law would go forth and ultimately be accepted by all the peoples of the earth.

the old Law given by God at Mount Sinai to His chosen people, the Jews, and under which they had always lived ("But now," he tells his fellow Jews, "we are delivered from the law").[3]

In the years following Paul's death, a great debate broke out over the relationship between Christianity and Judaism, with the radical theologian Marcion (ca. 85–160) holding that the Hebrew Bible, the Bible of the Jews, the "Old Testament," was not the word of God but the work of the Devil and must therefore be entirely shunned and repudiated. But this idea was declared heretical, and it was Paul's view—namely, that the "Old Testament" had been valid up until the coming of Jesus and remained valid as the prelude to, and the prophetic foreteller of, a "New Testament"—that ultimately prevailed. It followed that the Jews, having refused to accept Jesus as the Messiah sent to them by God for their deliverance from death, had now been superseded as His chosen people by the Christian community (or Church).

But if the Jews were no longer the chosen people, what were they then? Paul asked: "Hath God cast away His people?" and to his own question he answered, "God forbid. . . . God hath not cast away His people which He foreknew."[4] Yet there were also passages in the Letters of Paul that could, and would, be taken as a warrant for regarding those who continued to live by the Law of Judaism as "carnally minded" rather than "spiritually minded," and that this made them enemies of God ("because the carnal mind is enmity against God").[5]

Ominous as this idea was, however, what proved to be even worse for the Jews was the charge made against them in other parts of the New Testament, especially the Gospels of Matthew and John. For there are passages in these books that hold the Jewish people responsible for the crucifixion of the son of God—and not only the Jews living at the time of Jesus's sojourn on earth, but even their descendants unto all the generations that followed ("Then answered all the people and said, His blood be on us, and on our children").[6] Hence the Jewish people as a whole are condemned as the spawn of the Devil ("Ye are of your father the Devil and your will is to do your father's desire").[7]

In a fascinating speculative comment on the ambivalence of the New Testament's conception of the Jews, R. J. Zwi Werblowski, who was for many years the Martin Buber Professor of Comparative Religion at the Hebrew University of Jerusalem, writes:

> Had the Jews disappeared from the stage of history, it would
> have been possible [for Christianity] to relate to them more
> positively as a preparatory phase in the coming of God's king-
> dom. Had the Church severed its ties to its Israelite antecedents
> and completely rejected the "Old Testament" and the "Jewish
> God" (as demanded by Marcion) . . . , then Christianity would
> have been a hostile but essentially separate religion. The Church,
> however, insistently maintained that it was the direct continua-
> tion of that divine action in history of which the election of
> Israel was a major part. Yet the Jews continued to exist.[8]

Because the Jews refused to disappear, what started as ambivalence developed into outright hostility. Marcion may have been excommunicated and his doctrine declared a heresy, but with a little help from the accusations I have just cited from the Gospels of Matthew and John, a version of the Marcionite heresy smuggled its way into the writing and preaching of other early Fathers of the Church like Gregory of Nyssa and John Chrysostom.

The eminent historian Cecil Roth warns against exaggerating how bad conditions were for the Jews in the "Dark Ages," and we do well to take his caution into account. Nevertheless it is beyond dispute that much mob violence against the Jews was triggered in the coming centuries—and, as we shall see, not only in the medieval world—by the anti-Jewish ideas scattered throughout the New Testament, and spread far and wide by the sermons of prelates and priests. There is nothing surprising about this. What may, however, seem surprising, at least at first sight, is how long it took for the image of the Jew as a "Christ-killer" and as the "anti-Christ" to trickle down into the popular mind. As late as the fourth century C.E.,* John Chrysostom complained that Christians who knew no better were living on an equal footing with

---

* I use the neutral designation of C.E.—Christian or Common Era—rather than A.D. (*Anno Domini,* or Year of our Lord)—and B.C.E. (Before the Christian or Common Era)—rather than B.C. (Before Christ).

their Jewish neighbors, who, true to the Pauline characterization of them as "carnally minded," were marked by extravagance, gluttony, and dissolute living, and who, true to the Gospel accounts of their role in the crucifixion of Jesus, were guilty of deicide.[9]

Evidently this vexatious problem of good relations between ordinary Christians and Jews refused to go away, so that it was still eliciting complaints from princes of the Church at the time of Charlemagne (ninth century). "Things have reached a stage," declared Agobard, the Archbishop of Lyon,

> where ignorant Christians claim that the Jews preach better
> than our priests. . . . Some Christians even celebrate the Sabbath
> with the Jews and violate the holy repose of Sunday. . . . Men of
> the people, peasants, allow themselves to be plunged into such a
> sea of errors that they regard the Jews as the only people of
> God, and consider that they combine the observance of a pure
> religion and a truer faith than ours.[10]

But what may seem even more surprising than these friendly relations between Jews and Christians in the early Middle Ages is the reversal of roles between "men of the people" and the princes of the Church that later took place. For there came a time when Jews were often protected from mob violence by the very Catholic authorities whose ideas were the source of it. During the First Crusade (1095–96), when there were horrible massacres in France and Germany of Jewish communities unlucky enough to be living in the path of the Crusaders on their way to the Holy Land, the Bishop of Speyer and the Archbishop of Cologne both used force to stop the killings. The Bishop of Speyer even went so far as to hang the ringleaders. The Archbishop of Mainz also tried to intervene, but he failed and narrowly escaped being slaughtered himself.[11] Then, in the twelfth century, the Cistercian monk Bernard of Clairvaux, though he himself had been instrumental in launching the Second Crusade, helped to head off a new wave of massacres by warning that they would bring Divine retribution.

I can well imagine that these courageous men—and courageous they certainly were—thought they were acting as good Christians. But if so, it was not necessarily in the spirit of Christian love. (Even Bernard, the best of them from the Jewish point of view, referred to Jews with such epithets as "venomous," "coarse," and "wicked.")[12] For around the end of the fourth century, no less an authority than Saint Augustine, the greatest of all the early Christian theologians, had promulgated the doctrine that it was the will of God for the Jews to be dispersed and kept in a state of abject misery. He further decreed, however—and it was out of obedience to this codicil that princes of the Church like the Bishop of Speyer sometimes protected Jews from murderous assaults—that they were not to be killed and that they must also be permitted to practice their religion. In this way the wretched condition they had brought upon themselves by rejecting and crucifying Jesus, and continuing to reject him, would serve as a "witness" to the truth of Christianity.[13]

In a similar vein, the greatest Christian theologian of the High Middle Ages, Saint Thomas Aquinas, declared in the thirteenth century that

> in consequence of their sin Jews were destined to perpetual servitude . . . save for the sole proviso that [sovereigns] do not deprive them of all that is necessary to sustain life.[14]

Adding his own, more detailed, exposition of the same point, Pope Innocent III declared in 1205:

> The Lord made Cain a wanderer and a fugitive over the earth, but set a mark on him, . . . lest any finding him should slay him. Thus the Jews, against whom the blood of Jesus Christ calls out, although they ought not to be killed, lest the Christian people forget the Divine Law, yet as wanderers ought they to remain upon the earth, until their countenance be filled with shame and they seek the name of Jesus Christ, the Lord. That is why blasphemers of the Christian name ought . . . to be forced into the servitude of which they made themselves deserving when they raised sacrilegious hands against Him Who had come to confer true liberty upon them, thus calling down His blood upon themselves and upon their children.[15]

13

In addition to mandating a degree of physical protection against murderous attacks, the "witness" doctrine sometimes compelled efforts by the ecclesiastical authorities to deny the false charges that often triggered such attacks. Thus, Innocent III's successor, Innocent IV, wrote in 1247 that

> Christians charge falsely . . . that [the Jews] hold a communion rite . . . with the heart of a murdered child; and should the cadaver of a dead man happen to be found anywhere they maliciously lay it to [the Jews'] charge.[16]

What the pope was referring to here was the notorious blood libel that had been in circulation since 1144, when the Jews of Norwich were accused by the local authorities of having

> brought a Christian child before Easter and tortured him with all the tortures wherewith our Lord was tortured, and on Long Friday hanged him on a rood in hatred of our Lord.[17]

Another form the blood libel took was the allegation that the reason Christian children were kidnapped and slaughtered every year around Easter was that their blood was a necessary ingredient of the unleavened bread (*matzah*) that Jews ate on Passover. But this was far from the only reason Jews were imagined to need Christian blood. A bizarre list of the others was compiled in 1494 by the citizens of a town who believed that they were in imminent danger of becoming the next victims of Jewish ritual murder:

> Firstly, they [the Jews] were convinced by the judgment of their ancestors, that the blood of a Christian was a good remedy for the alleviation of the wound of circumcision. Secondly, they were of opinion that this blood, put into food, is efficacious for the awakening of mutual love. Thirdly, they had discovered, as men and women among them suffered equally from menstruation, that the blood of a Christian is a specific medicine for it, when drunk. Fourthly, they had an ancient but secret ordinance

by which they are under obligation to shed Christian blood in honor of God, in daily sacrifices, in some spot or other.[18]

Obviously Pope Innocent IV's condemnation of the blood libel had failed to prevent its perpetuation—and the gruesome massacres to which it led—in the two hundred years since he had issued it.

Another of the main medieval libels against the Jews was the accusation that they had caused the Black Death of 1348–50 by poisoning wells all over Europe "so as to kill and destroy the whole of Christianity." Confessions obtained through torture yielded an account according to which a Jew of Savoy had spread the plague on the instructions of a rabbi who said to him:

See, I give you a little package, half a span in size, which contains a preparation of poison and venom in a narrow, stitched leathern bag. This you are to distribute among the wells, the cisterns, and the springs about Venice and the other places where you go, in order to poison the people who drink the water.[19]

For this crime, declared an indictment issued in 1348 by an ecclesiastical tribunal, "all Jews from the age of seven" were to be held responsible, since "all of them in their totality were cognizant and are guilty of the above actions."[20]

Accordingly, about three hundred Jewish communities—extending from Spain to France, Germany, and Poland-Lithuania—were set upon and their inhabitants tortured and killed or expelled. In response to what he himself called this "horrible thing," Pope Clement VI issued a papal bull stating that

certain Christians, seduced by that liar, the devil, are imputing the pestilence to poisoning by Jews. . . . [Yet] since this pestilence is all but universal everywhere, and by a mysterious decree of God has afflicted, and continues to afflict, both Jews and many other nations throughout the diverse regions of the earth to whom a common existence with Jews is unknown, [the

charge] that the Jews have provided the cause or the occasion
for such a crime is without plausibility.[21]

Nevertheless, Clement VI's bull, like Innocent IV's efforts against the
blood libel a century earlier, did not spell the end of the massacres or
halt the monstrous lie that had caused them.

A third medieval libel against which a pope protested to indifferent
effect was the Desecration of the Host. This was the accusation frequently made that Jews would steal or buy the wafers representing the
body of Christ in the Mass so as to crucify him again by sticking pins
into his transubstantiated flesh. In 1338, Pope Benedict XII, disturbed
by certain reports he had heard, ordered the bishop of a town in Austria to protect the Jews there against what he considered false charges.
But both before and after Benedict issued his order, thousands of
equally innocent Jews were burned at the stake in many other cities,
usually on the basis of confessions extorted by torture or the testimony
of witnesses bent for one reason or another on the killing of Jews.

The murders committed under the influence of these phantas-
magoric libels were by no means the sole instances in which the prohibition against murdering Jews was honored in the breach, nor were
the sole perpetrators unlettered peasants who had no idea that they
were doing anything wrong. There were also plenty of clerics who
either turned a blind eye or even instigated persecutions themselves.
This was especially the case with the Dominican and Franciscan
orders—yes, even the Franciscans whose patron saint preached love to
all creatures, including the animals. But to the Franciscan friars of the
later Middle Ages, while Christian love may have extended to the animals, it did not apply to the Jews. "In respect of abstract and general
love," decreed Friar Bernardino of Siena, "we are permitted to love
them [the Jews]. However, there can be no concrete love toward
them."[22] In line with this view, massacres were provoked on more than
one occasion by the preaching of Franciscan agitators like John of
Capistrano ("the scourge of the Jews"), sometimes in collaboration
with Dominicans of like mind.

A different species of massacre was perpetrated by the most notorious of the Dominican enemies of the Jews, the Grand Inquisitor Tomas

de Torquemada. In 1492, all Jews who refused to convert to Christianity were expelled from Spain by King Ferdinand and Queen Isabella. Among those who did convert were some—the *conversos* or Marranos—who continued practicing their religion in secret. An Inquisition was set up to root them out, and in due course Torquemada became the head of it. By the time he was through, many thousands of *conversos* (not all of them guilty of secretly remaining Jews) were burned at the stake.

For a variety of reasons, the expulsion from Spain came to be seen as an exceptionally momentous historical event, but it was neither the first nor the last act of its kind. King Edward I of England had the honor of blazing this particular trail in 1290, a full two centuries before Ferdinand and Isabella. And in the years immediately prior to 1492, there was a veritable epidemic of expulsions, with Jews being forced out of Vienna, Linz, Cologne, Augsberg, Bavaria, Moravia, Perugia, Vicenza, Parma, Milan, and Lucca. Then, shortly after Spain, came Florence and the whole of Tuscany, followed in short order by the kingdom of Navarre. These expulsions gave new life to yet another malignant image that had been around since the thirteenth century— the Wandering Jew. Like the biblical Cain whose punishment for murdering his brother Abel was to become "a fugitive and a vagabond in the earth,"[23] the Jew was being punished for killing Christ, and (in some of the many versions of the myth of the Wandering Jew) was doomed to go on wandering until his Second Coming.

2

GHETTOS

Farther to the east, in Poland, the Church was also steadily engaged in activity against the "perfidious Jews," as they were called in a statute of 1347. Still earlier, in 1266, the Ecumenical Church Council of Wroclaw (Breslau) outlined an anti-Jewish policy that became the model for other such over the next two centuries. The aim of this policy was to force the Jews into what would later be called ghettos:

> The quarter in which the Jews reside shall be divided from the section inhabited by the Christians with a fence, wall, or ditch.[1]

Later, in the fifteenth century, when the Jews petitioned King Casimir IV Jagiellon to ratify certain rights they had been granted under an ancient charter, Cardinal Zbigniew Olesnicki wrote to the king as follows:

> Do not imagine that in matters touching the Christian religion you are at liberty to pass any law you please. . . . I therefore beseech and implore your royal majesty to revoke the aforementioned privileges and liberties. Prove that you are a Catholic sovereign, and remove all occasion for disgracing your name.[2]

The cardinal even imported the "scourge of the Jews" himself, John of Capistrano (now the papal nuncio), to help him persuade the king. Casimir resisted, but not for long. As the historian Herman Rosenthal describes it:

> The repeated appeals of the clergy and the defeat of the Polish troops by the Teutonic knights—which the clergy openly ascribed to the wrath of God at . . . Casimir's friendly attitude toward the Jews—finally induced the king to accede to the demands which had been made.[3]

As might have been expected, monks joined in the mobs that were encouraged by this campaign to attack the Jewish quarters in many Polish cities.

In Poland, then, writes the distinguished Israeli historian Shmuel Ettinger, "the clergy was the driving force behind the persecution of the Jews,"[4] while in general, adds Rosenthal, the "temporal rulers were not inclined to accept the edicts of the Church."[5] In Russia, however, where the Orthodox Church held religious sway, it seems for the most part to have been the other way around. According to some historians, and in contrast to the situation in Poland, if the emperor or empress of Russia was inclined for one reason or another to be relatively lenient toward the Jews, the ecclesiastical authorities were less likely than in Poland to mount an effective resistance. But the dark side of this coin is that the Orthodox prelates did not feel obligated to protect Jews from being set upon by rampaging mobs, as the Catholic Church in theory, and sometimes in practice, did in the West.

But whether or not it is true that the clergy exerted less influence on how the Jews were treated in Russia than its counterparts did in Poland, there can be no disputing that the anti-Semitism of the Russian Orthodox Church had an exceptionally virulent edge of its own. This could be traced back to the fifteenth century, when, in the city of Novgorod, a sect of "Judaizers" came into being whose influence threatened to spread throughout the whole of Russia. Léon Poliakov, the prime authority on these matters, quotes a description by an old Russian chronicler:

A number of priests had friendly commerce with the Jews, and, learning to read in their books, gave themselves up to a life of abjection and became heretics, anti-Christians: thus it was with the priest Alexis, the priest Gavrilo, and many others. And heresy spread everywhere, and numerous, alas, too numerous, were those who thus lost their souls, destined for the flames of hell.[6]

Poliakov tells us that this was not the only case in European history of Jews "influencing newly Christianized people who were in the charge of a half-educated clergy lacking in self-assurance." (One of the examples he cites is the ninth-century statement by Agobard I quoted above.)

It was precisely fear of this kind of thing that also lay behind the policy of segregating the Jews that, as we have already seen, was instituted by an ecumenical council in Poland in 1266:

Since Poland has but lately joined the fold of the Christian Church it may be apprehended that its Christian inhabitants will the more easily yield to the prejudices and evil habits of their Jewish neighbors, the establishment of the Christian faith in the hearts of the believers in these lands having been of such a recent date.[7]

But the threat that the Jews of Poland were feared to pose was as nothing compared to the danger represented by the Judaizers in Russia. For complicated political reasons involving the question of who would succeed him, Grand Duke Ivan III (late fifteenth century) gave the Judaizing heresy his support. As a consequence, says Poliakov, it spread "with lightning-like speed . . . [and] particularly in the circles close to the court."[8] How far it went can be gauged by the lament of another contemporary chronicler:

Never since the day when the Orthodox sun first shone in our land has there been such heresy; in the home, in the streets, at the fair, laymen and priests discuss the faith, basing themselves

no longer on the teaching of the prophets, the Apostles, and of
the Fathers of the Church, but on the ideas of heretics and
renegades from Christianity, with whom they have friendly ties
and who instruct them in Judaism.[9]

Amazingly, it even seemed probable, Poliakov says, that "the
Judaizing heresy would become the official state religion upon Ivan's
death."[10] But after a desperate struggle that went on for a full twenty
years, the Orthodox party finally won out over the Judaizers, who
were then subjected to violent persecutions. Inevitably this spilled over
to the Jews as such, setting a pattern of hate and fear that would
persist for all the centuries to come. Not for nothing did a Russian
word—*pogrom*—become the generic term for murderous attacks on
the Jews wherever they might occur.

As for the Judaizers themselves, they were never completely
uprooted; many of them took refuge in the outer provinces of Russia,
or in the great northern forests, and survived there.*[11] Nor were they
ever completely forgotten. Indeed, it was directly out of the struggle
against them that a policy was instituted of barring the Jews, those
"poisoners of souls," from residence in the Russian heartland.

Pursuing this policy was relatively easy when it was first established
in the sixteenth century, since not all that many Jews lived in the terri-

---

* Poliakov goes on to write that the underground life led by the Judaizers "was
responsible for many of the schisms and dissident movements so characteristic of
Russian religious life." This has led me to wonder about the fact that, in *The
Brothers Karamazov*, Dostoyevsky gives the dissident monk Father Zossima the
same name as the sixteenth-century Metropolitan of Moscow. This historical figure outwardly opposed the Judaizers but was suspected of "devoting himself to
the seduction of the simple, getting them to drink the Jewish poison"—in other
words, of being a Judaizer himself. Since Dostoyevsky surely knew all about his
character's ancient namesake, is it possible that his own reverence for the anti-
ascetic Father Zossima may have signified an attraction to "the Jewish poison"
against which his fierce anti-Semitism served as a protection? That he may have
been attracted is evident from his denial that the survival of the Jewish people
could be attributed "only to persecution and to the instinct for survival. . . . The
primary cause here is not the instinct for survival alone, but a driving and moti-
vating idea, something universal and profound, and it is possible that mankind is
not yet capable of passing final judgment on it" (quoted in Shmuel Ettinger, "*The
Modern Period*," Ben-Sasson, p. 732—see endnote 4). To top it all off, Maxim
Gorky in his *Reminiscences* quotes Tolstoy as saying that "there was something
Jewish in [Dostoyevsky's blood]."

tories then controlled by Russia. But—to get ahead of my story for a minute—it would become much more difficult when, in the second half of the eighteenth century, more than half a million Polish Jews would fall under Russian rule. It was to deal with the problem created by this new situation that a series of laws would be promulgated under which Jews would be permitted to live only in a designated geographical area called the "Pale of Settlement" (about which more later).

Meanwhile, back in the West and around the same time that Orthodoxy was eliminating the main challenge to its dominance in Russia, the Protestant Reformation was presenting a far more serious challenge to the Catholic Church, and one that it proved unable to fend off. "Right at the beginning," Paul Johnson tells us in his *A History of the Jews,* they "welcomed the Reformation, because it divided their enemies." It also seemed a hopeful sign that the Reformation brought with it a new interest in the Old Testament. Yet Johnson—pointing in part to earlier Christian Hebraists like Pico della Mirandola and Johannes Reuchlin, who "were as strongly opposed to Judaism as any Dominican"—also finds little "actual evidence that the interest of the Reformers in the Old Testament made them pro-Jewish as such."[*12]

This is to understate the case greatly where Martin Luther was concerned. At first, Luther, having been an Augustinian monk before breaking with Rome, held on to the view of Saint Augustine himself that the suffering of the Jews was a witness to the truth of Christianity. Later, however, Luther came to believe that present-day Jews could not be held responsible for the sins of the fathers. In his characteristically colorful and pungent style—whatever else Luther may or may not have been, he was without question a great writer—he blamed the pope for the continuing refusal of the Jews to accept Christianity:

> If I were a Jew, I would suffer the rack ten times before I would
> go over to the pope. . . . What good can we do the Jews when
> we constrain them, malign them, and hate them as dogs? When
> we deny them work and force them to usury, how can that help?

---

* As we shall see in chapter 9, however, there is much "actual evidence" of the contrary among the Puritans who came to America.

We should use toward the Jews not the pope's but Christ's law of love. If some are stiff-necked, what does that matter? We are not all good Christians.[13]

Because of this sympathetic attitude, Luther expected that his reforms would bring about the conversion of the Jews to Christianity. But as it became clearer and clearer that they were still as "stiff-necked" as they always had been, his disappointment eventually soured into a hatred that was a match, and more than a match, for that of the Church he had left. (Interestingly, in the seventh century much the same thing, and for exactly the same reason, had transformed the positive attitude toward the Jews originally held by Muhammad.)

The most virulent expression of Luther's feelings in his later years was a pamphlet he wrote in 1543 entitled *Concerning the Jews and Their Lies*. Among the measures he recommended there to the "princes and nobles" of Germany, "so that you and we may all be free of this insufferable devilish burden—the Jews," were these:

First, that we burn their synagogues. . . . Secondly, it is necessary to uproot and destroy their houses in the same way. . . . Thirdly, it is necessary that all their prayer books and their books of the Talmud shall be taken from them. . . . Fourthly, that their Rabbis shall be forbidden on pain of bodily punishment and death to teach henceforward.

And as a last resort,

let us use the simple wisdom of other peoples like those of France, Spain, Bohemia . . . and expel them from the land forever.[14]

Even before writing this execrable pamphlet, Luther had done his best to put at least some of its ideas into practice. The extent to which he succeeded becomes clear from Paul Johnson's succinct summation:

He got the Jews expelled from Saxony in 1537, and in the 1540's he drove them from many German towns. . . . His

followers . . . sacked the Berlin synagogue in 1572, and the
following year finally got their way, the Jews being banned from
the entire country.[15]

On the other hand, Johnson adds—and other authorities concur—
Luther's great Protestant rival, John Calvin, was less hostile to the
Jews and "was even accused by his Lutheran enemies of being a
Judaizer." Which did not prevent Jews from being expelled from terri-
tories controlled by Calvinist rulers.

There was another, more indirect, way in which the Protestant Reformation led to a deterioration in the condition of the Jews living in
those parts of Europe that remained Catholic. It was there that a
Counter-Reformation took hold, and among the other consequences
of this campaign against the spread of Protestantism was a stricter
application of the decrees of the past. One of these was the "witness"
doctrine of Augustine and Thomas Aquinas governing the treatment
of the Jews. Another was the requirement by the Fourth Lateran
Council of 1215 that Jews be made to wear a distinguishing mark,
which usually took the form of a "badge of shame" sewn onto their
clothing. The original intention had been to prevent Jews from min-
gling too closely with Christians (and with Christian women above
all). But beginning with Italy and Austria in the middle of the sixteenth
century, this segregationist purpose was greatly improved upon by the
Counter-Reformation through the herding of Jews into ghettos like the
ones that had earlier been introduced into Poland. (Five hundred years
later, both practices would be resurrected by the Nazis.) The ghetto, by
making life even harder for the Jews than it had been, also greatly
improved upon the "witness" idea. As an eighteenth-century Catholic
apologist would put it,

A Jewish ghetto is a better proof of the truth of the religion of
Jesus Christ than a whole school of theologians.[16]

POETS AND EXEGETES

Before moving on to the next chapter of the story, I want to pause for a minute to dispel the impression that the Ashkenazi Jews* of medieval Europe were nothing but hapless victims of Christian persecution. Still less was this true of the Sephardi Jews† who lived in Spain from the time it was conquered by Muslim armies early in the eighth century up until its final reconquest by Christians in 1492. I have thus far omitted any mention of the Sephardim because only a tiny propor-

---

* "*Ashkenaz* [is the Hebrew] designation of the first relatively compact area of settlement of Jews in N.W. Europe, initially on the banks of the Rhine. The term became identified with, and denotes in its narrower sense, Germany, German Jewry, and German Jews ('*Ashkenazim*'), as well as their descendants in other countries. . . . The Ashkenazi cultural legacy, emanating from the center in northern France and Germany, later spread to Poland-Lithuania, and in modern times embraces Jewish settlements all over the world whose members share and activate it. . . . With the emigration of Ashkenazi Jewry from Western to Eastern Europe in the 15th and 16th centuries, the center of gravity shifted to Bohemia, Moravia, Poland, and Lithuania. . . . In the Slavonic [i.e. Russian] territories their use of the Judeo-German language [i.e., Yiddish] became a prominent distinguishing feature of Ashkenazi Jewry" ("Ashkenaz (reg. Eur.)," *Encyclopaedia Judaica*).

† The descendants of Jews who lived in Spain (*Sepharad* in Hebrew) or Portugal before the expulsion of 1492. After 1492, these Sephardim sought refuge wherever they could find it. Eventually, as conditions permitted, some of their descendants wound up in Italy, Holland, England, and colonial America. But for the most part they settled in North Africa, the Balkans, and the Middle East.

tion of American Jews descend from them, which means that the Jewish experience under Islam plays almost no part in the story I am trying to tell in this book. Even so, their own story is worth at least a brief glance, if only because nothing like it would ever again be seen.

What made these Sephardim unique was that, in the realm of practice, they managed to combine the fullest participation in the world around them with the most rigorous fidelity to Jewish law. They also pulled off an analogous feat in the realm of culture, where for them Jewish learning of the highest caliber coexisted in perfect harmony with equally great secular intellectual and literary achievements of every kind. The most notable among them was Maimonides (Moses ben Maimon). Besides being perhaps the greatest rabbinic scholar ever (it was said that "from [the biblical] Moses to Moses [ben Maimon] there has been none like [either] Moses"), he wrote extremely influential philosophical works in Arabic, as well as learned treatises on medicine (which he also found time to practice).

Then there were the poets: Samuel ha-Nagid, Moses ibn Ezra, Solomon ibn Gabirol, Judah ha-Levi, and many more. All of them composed religious verse but they all also wrote secular poems in Hebrew that, under the influence of the Arabic style, differed in formal terms from older Hebrew religious and liturgical verse. But the difference was not confined to such matters as meter and rhyme. The critic Hillel Halkin, who has translated many of these poems, tells us that, again under Arabic influence, they made

> contact with philosophical thought [which] meant that [their] religious themes . . . were suffused with intellectual concerns, often expressed in wit and paradox, that had been unknown in Hebrew religious poetry until then.

More startling, and more shocking, to many of its contemporary readers, was that the new poetry

> opened its gates, once again under Arabic influence, to a wide variety of non-religious themes that had previously been off-limits to the Hebrew poet.[1]

"Off-limits" is describing it a touch too gently, since through these newly opened gates streamed lusty drinking songs and unabashedly erotic poems involving, in a few cases, lovers of both sexes.

One of these cases was Samuel ha-Nagid. Besides being a great poet, Samuel (who spoke and wrote seven languages) also achieved comparable stature as a statesman and a soldier. But to describe him through such abstractions defeats the purpose of evoking just how extraordinary he was. To get a proper sense of what he was like, we have to imagine—and I do not exaggerate—Henry Kissinger as, all at once, a strictly Orthodox rabbi, a major Talmudic scholar, and the acknowledged head of the Jewish community who could, and did, also lead armies into battle and produce imperishable literary works (in Hebrew).

The conditions that made such a figure possible—and Samuel was extraordinary only in degree; in the breadth of his accomplishments and his interests, he was entirely representative of the Golden Age of Spanish Jewry—were created by the Umayyad caliphs, who were what today would be regarded as moderate Muslims. But before and after them came Muslim rulers who more closely resembled the radical Islamists of our time and under whom Jews were forced to convert to Islam or be put to the sword. So bad were these radical Islamists that many Jews fled to the few cities in northern Spain that had been reconquered by the Christians. Others (including Maimonides himself, who was driven out of his native Cordoba) left Spain altogether and sought refuge in less onerous Muslim lands. By the time the Christian reconquest of Spain was completed in 1492, the Golden Age had become a distant memory. Indeed, even before the Jews of Spain were expelled their condition had long since grown to resemble that of the Ashkenazim—to whom I now return.

In sharp contrast to the Sephardim, the Ashkenazim never enjoyed a period in which they could move freely into and interact with the surrounding Gentile world. Consequently they never produced anything remotely like the cosmopolitan works of the Sephardi Golden Age. Yet suffering from innumerable disabilities and living in constant peril of being set upon by murderers or uprooted and expelled from places into which they had struck roots, they nevertheless managed through their passionate love of the Talmud to develop a religious culture of great depth and richness. More than any other factor, this culture was responsible for the miracle of Jewish survival—then and (I would argue) in all the years to come. Granted, an untold number of Jews submitted to conversion—few seem to have done it voluntarily—but many more, molded by the power of the Talmudic religious culture, held fast to the holy way of life it teased out of the laws that God had commanded them to speak and to think about at all times—and above all to teach their children.[2]

Under the influence of this commandment, literacy became more widespread among them than it was among Christians, and a reverence for learning developed that became a universally recognized hallmark of the Jewish people. These characteristics were already sufficiently salient to inspire the admiration and envy of a twelfth-century monk (who, as a student of the great philosopher Peter Abelard, put so high a value on learning that it could trump any animosity he might otherwise have felt toward the Jews):

> The Jews, out of their zeal for God and their love of the Law,
> put as many sons as they have to letters, that each may under-
> stand God's Law. . . . A Jew, however poor, if he had ten sons,
> would put them all to letters, not for gain, as the Christians do,
> but for the understanding of God's Law; and not only his sons
> but his daughters.[3]

As is evident from another twelfth-century testimony—this one a letter from Rabbi Judah ibn Tibbon to his son—books in themselves were regarded as sacred objects, and even as a source of sensual pleasure:

> My son, make books your companions and make your book-
> cases and shelves your groves and pleasure gardens. Graze in
> their beds and cull their flowers . . . and if your soul grows
> weary and exhausted, move from garden to garden and from
> flower bed to flower bed. . . . For then your will shall be
> restored and your spirit will become beautiful.[4]

Rabbi ibn Tibbon was talking about "books in all the sciences," but it was the holy books, the Hebrew Bible and the Talmud, on which the culture of the Jews under Christian hegemony almost exclusively fed. One product of this intense focus was an exegetical literature of enormous complexity and brilliance; another, running in a very different direction, was a new mystical tradition that took off from and contributed to kabbalistic literature and would in time give birth to the Hasidic movement.

Yet the fact that the Jews of medieval Christendom were able to accomplish all this did not, not even for a moment, dim their awareness of who had imposed upon them the terrible conditions under which they did it. They emerged from the Middle Ages knowing for a certainty that—individual exceptions duly noted—the worst enemy they had in the world was Christianity: the churches in which it was embodied—whether Roman Catholic or Russian Orthodox or Protestant—and the people who prayed in and were shaped by them. It was a knowledge that Jewish experience in the ages to come would do very little, if indeed anything at all, to help future generations to forget.

4

EMANCIPATION: PHASE ONE

If the long story of how and why so many American Jews became liberals begins with the birth of Christianity, it continues with the struggle for Jewish emancipation. And here another great enemy—the kings and nobles who ruled the state—joined forces with the Church to keep the Jews from achieving equal rights before the law.

This part of the story can itself be divided into three parts or phases.[1] The first began in the late seventeenth century, not among the Jews themselves but among Gentile advocates of religious tolerance. One of the earliest was Roger Williams, founder of the colony of Rhode Island. In 1664, while on a trip back to his native England, he published *The Bloody Tenent of Persecution for Cause of Conscience,* a pamphlet dedicated to proving that

> the doctrine of persecution for cause of conscience is . . . guilty of all the blood of the souls crying for vengeance under the altar.

As against this pernicious doctrine, Williams declared that

> true civility and Christianity may both flourish in a state or kingdom, notwithstanding the permission of divers and contrary consciences either of Jew or Gentile.

Therefore, he concluded:

> It is the will and command of God that (since the coming of His
> Son, Lord Jesus), freedom of religion, a permission of the most
> Paganish, Jewish, Turkish, or anti-Christian conscience and
> worship, be granted to all men, in all nations and countries.[2]

Some years later (1689), in *A Letter Concerning Toleration,* the
great English philosopher John Locke also held that

> neither Pagan nor Mahometan, nor Jew, ought to be excluded
> from the civil rights of the commonwealth because of his
> religion. The Gospel commands no such thing.

As to the Jews in particular, Locke had this to say:

> If a Jew do not believe the New Testament to be the Word of
> God, he does not thereby alter anything in men's civil rights.[3]

In Europe it took more than a century before the ideas of these early
harbingers of Jewish emancipation were translated into legislation.
Meanwhile, the argument for toleration kept being pressed. In *The
Spirit of Laws* (1748), for example, Montesquieu quoted a Jew remon-
strating with the Inquisition:

> If heaven has had so great a love for you as to make you see the
> truth, you have received a singular favor; but is it for children
> who have received the inheritance of their father, to hate those
> who have not? . . . If you were wise, you would not put us to
> death for no other reason than because we are unwilling to
> deceive you. If your Christ is the son of God, we hope he will
> reward us for being so unwilling to profane his mysteries; and
> we believe that the God whom both you and we serve will not
> punish us for having suffered death for a religion which He
> formerly gave us, only because we believe that He still continues
> to give it.[4]

In addition to being furthered by such pleas for religious toleration, the cause of emancipation was also helped along by a new idea concerning the economic value of the Jews. In propagating this idea, it was Jews themselves who took the lead.

In the medieval period, one of the main economic functions performed by Jews was money lending. According to Church law, the taking of interest in any amount was considered usury, and from 1179 on, any Christian guilty of this practice was subject to excommunication. Under Jewish law, however, the taking of interest from non-Jews was permitted, but only provided that circumstances made it impossible for Jews to earn their living in any other way. Since such circumstances were created by the restrictions that were placed upon them in most European countries, medieval Jews found ample justification for availing themselves of this permission. If, wrote a rabbinical authority,

> we nowadays allow interest to be taken from non-Jews, it is because there is no end to the yoke and the burden king and ministers impose on us, and everything we take is the minimum for our subsistence, and anyhow we are condemned to live in the midst of the nations and cannot earn our living in any other manner except by money dealings with them; therefore the taking of interest is not to be prohibited.[5]

For this, Jews were popularly reviled and hated, but they were also (more or less secretly) valued by Christian rulers who came to appreciate and profit by the capital they could get from the Jews without violating canon law. These rulers also developed means of taking a cut on all transactions and often they also managed to expropriate the proceedings altogether.

However, a great change in this area began unfolding in the late seventeenth and early eighteenth centuries. For it was then that the Pauline bias against money as "the root of all evil" was gradually being replaced by the new economic theory of mercantilism, which looked favorably upon commerce and stressed the need for states to accumulate as much wealth as possible.

A number of Jewish spokesmen saw in this change of attitude an opportunity to press the case for the full integration of Jews into society. "Wherever the Jews live," wrote Rabbi Simone Luzzatto in 1638 in his *Essay on the Jews of Venice,* "trade and dealings flourish."[6] Menasseh ben Israel, an Amsterdam rabbi, used the same argument (among others) in his *Humble Addresses* appealing to Oliver Cromwell to readmit the Jews to England (from which, we recall, they had been expelled in 1290):

> It is a thing confirmed, that merchandizing is, as it were, the proper profession of the Nation of the Jews. I attribute this in the first place, to the particular Providence and mercy of God towards his people: for having banished them from their own Country, yet not from His Protection, He hath given them, as it were, a natural instinct, by which they might not onely gain what was necessary for their need, but that they should also thrive in Riches and possessions; whereby they should not onely become gracious to their Princes and Lords, but that they should be invited by others to come and dwell in their Lands.[7]

Non-Jews, some of them influenced by these Jewish writings, subsequently took up the cause. In 1693, about twenty years after the Jews had been readmitted to England, Sir Josiah Child, head of the British East India Company, pointed to the economic success Holland had achieved by offering citizenship to the Jews who had settled there, and urged that England follow the Dutch example. The philosopher John Toland pursued the same objective in *Reasons for Naturalizing the Jews of Britain and Ireland* (1714). And still later, in 1748, Montesquieu, in the chapter of his *The Spirit of Laws* titled "How Commerce Broke Through the Barbarism of Europe," even credited the Jews with a significant role in that much to be desired development.[8]

It would be an anachronism to describe these new ideas about the proper treatment of the Jews as "liberal" in the modern political sense. But to the extent that the term connotes tolerance in whatever the context, we are justified in using it of the likes of Roger Williams, John

Locke, and Montesquieu. If, however, these "liberals" *avant la lettre* were friendly as a matter of principle toward the cause of eventual Jewish emancipation, the same cannot be said of the mercantilists. For one thing, as we learn from Shmuel Ettinger:

> Several of the more important proponents of mercantilist theory in Britain and Germany, such as Sir William Petty or Johann Joachim Becher, were among the enemies of the Jews, holding that they brought more harm than advantage.[9]

For another thing, even those mercantilists who supported a Jewish presence in their countries did so not on principle or out of friendliness but rather because there was profit in it. In fact, outright hostility toward the Jews could coexist comfortably with a willingness to keep them around. This comes out clearly from how a leading mercantilist, Louis XIV's finance minister, Jean-Baptiste Colbert, responded to demands by the clergy and competing merchants that the Jews be expelled from France:

> If it were a question of religion, we should be quite ready to expel them [the Jews]; as it is a question of commerce, let them remain so long as they are useful to the country.[10]

Considering that Colbert served an absolute monarch, it was only to be expected that he would take this position. For all the absolute monarchies that, replacing the decentralized feudal order, came into being throughout Europe between the sixteenth and the eighteenth centuries tended to remain faithful to the attitudes toward the Jews of the medieval past. If they wavered, as they sometimes did for Colbert-like reasons, they would immediately be threatened by the clergy with hellfire and would invariably repent and return to the old anti-Jewish path.[11]

Here, then, in the opposition between the advocates of religious toleration and the theorists of absolutism—and making due allowance for anachronistic distortion—we have something that roughly corresponds to the later political divide between liberal and conservative (or, in the label some historians prefer, reactionary), with the former being friendly to Jewish interests and the latter being hostile.

This was even true *within* the world of absolutism. Under the variant that came to be known as "enlightened despotism,"[12] there emerged a willingness to free the Jews of certain disabilities and to extend certain rights to them. One such enlightened despot, Frederick the Great of Prussia, who, like Colbert, valued the Jews only insofar as they were "useful," nevertheless regarded those living in his realm as Prussian subjects. In 1750, he issued a Jewish charter dividing the Jews in his realm into four groups: "generally privileged," "regularly protected," "specially protected," and "tolerated."[13] This was still a long distance from equal treatment, but it was a step forward from where the conservative absolutists were prepared to go.

About thirty years later, in 1782, another enlightened despot, Emperor Joseph II of Austria, took an additional step in the Edict of Toleration (*Toleranzpatent*) that was to govern the Jews of Vienna:

> Since the beginning of our reign we have made it one of our most important aims that all our subjects, whatever their nationality or religion, since they are accepted and tolerated in our states, should share in the public welfare which we are endeavoring to nurture, enjoy liberty in accordance with the law, and encounter no hindrance in obtaining their livelihood and increasing their general industry by all honorable means.[14]

Subsequently Joseph II sent "Letters of Toleration" extending this policy to the Jews living in other parts of his empire as well. Ettinger lists the main provisions:

> Nullification of movement and residence restrictions; concessions as regards occupations (the right to learn crafts, establish factories, and engage in the liberal professions); the right to employ Jewish and gentile domestic servants "according to the needs of their occupation"; the right to send their children to general schools and to establish their own schools; the abolition of several religious restrictions, such as the compulsory wearing

of a beard and the prohibition against going outdoors during Christmas festivals.*[15]

In addition to all this, the universities were for the first time opened to Jews.

Not that flies were entirely absent even from this extraordinarily benevolent ointment. Although Joseph II went very far beyond Colbert and even beyond Frederick the Great, his motive was by his own admission similar to theirs. "This policy paper," he wrote, "aims at making the Jewish population useful to the state," and by useful he meant the degree to which Jews would contribute to the prosperity of the state. As he once said:

> To me, the Jews are human beings, consumers, and tax-payers, and consequently useful, if properly kept in check.[16]

Furthermore, the policy of tolerance was accompanied by new restrictions (such as a ban on the use of Hebrew and Yiddish in certain documents and an intensification of police control over Jewish communities). These restrictions aimed not at forcing Jews to convert to Christianity but rather at forcing them to abandon their more objectionable Jewish ways.

Yet as becomes evident from the sharp contrast between Joseph II and his mother, the Empress Maria Theresa—who so strongly opposed religious toleration that he had to wait until she died before announcing the new policy—the fact remains that even where absolute monarchs were concerned, the more "enlightened" they were, the more tolerant (or "liberal") would be their attitude toward and their treatment of the Jews. They could also be more steadfast. Whereas more conservative absolute monarchs would back away from any Colbert-like softening of the anti-Jewish usages of the past whenever they were hit with clerical pressure, Joseph II did not waver. He even

---

* The one item on this list that may seem strange—the right to hire Gentile domestic servants—had been specifically and unequivocally prohibited by Thomas Aquinas.

held fast when the pope himself, Pius VI (whose own Edict on the Jews reestablished harsh anti-Jewish measures that had been softened by his predecessor, Clement XIV), journeyed from Rome to Vienna to remonstrate with him.

In granting a degree of toleration to the Jews but at the same time attaching conditions that would inevitably lead to a dilution of their Jewishness, the policy of this "enlightened despot" in part foreshadowed and in part reflected the influence of the conceptual framework that was being erected by the major thinkers of the Enlightenment—the *philosophes* in France and their counterparts in Germany and elsewhere. It was this framework that would supply the underlying principle of the laws promulgated in the second phase of Jewish emancipation that began with the French Revolution of 1789 and ended ninety years later with the Congress of Berlin.

THE ENLIGHTENMENT PUZZLE

Above all else, the Enlightenment was anti-Christian,[1] and hence, in line with the adage that the enemy of my enemy is my friend, it could have been expected to be pro-Jewish. And so, in some instances, it was. To an enlightened despot like Joseph II, the Jews were not demonic creatures but "human beings": this was the "enlightened" part of him speaking. But the despotic part added that they had to be "kept in check." The major thinkers of the Enlightenment would have no truck with any such caveat. So far as they were concerned, if anyone had to be kept in check, it was the Christians, who looked upon and treated the Jews as less than human. "Accordingly," says the historian Paul Weissman,

> protests against the persecution of Jews—and especially against the Inquisition, the Enlightenment's *bête noire*—became one of the standard set pieces of eighteenth-century rhetoric.[2]

Here we have one way in which the Enlightenment was pro-Jewish. Another was the more positive insistence that Jews be accorded the same rights as everyone else. And a third was the invidious comparison (most famously advanced by the German dramatist Gotthold Lessing in his play *Nathan the Wise*) between the putative rationality of Judaism and the backwardness of a superstition-laden Christianity.

If this were all, it would add one more powerfully unambiguous reason for the attachment Jews began forming to what would soon be characterized as the Left. But the pro-Jewish aspect of the Enlightenment was very far from all there was to its attitude toward the Jews; it was not even the predominant element in the incoherent Enlightenment mix. Much more typical was the article "Jews (philosophy of)," in the *Encyclopédie,* the bible (so to speak) of the *philosophes.* The author of this article was the editor of the *Encyclopédie,* Diderot himself, who declared that the Jews bore "all the defects characteristic of an ignorant and superstitious nation."[3]

Diderot was not the only *philosophe* who felt this way. Baron d'Holbach, who contributed a number of entries to the *Encyclopédie,* was even more extreme in his contempt and hatred both of Judaism as a religion and the Jews as a people:

> The revolting policy of the Jewish legislator [Moses] has erected a stone wall between his people and all other nations. Since they are submissive only to their priests, the Jews have become the enemies of the human race.

As such, d'Holbach explained,

> the Jews have always displayed contempt for the clearest dictates of morality and the law of nations. . . . They were ordered to be cruel, inhuman, intolerant, thieves, traitors, and betrayers of trust. All these are regarded as deeds pleasing to God. In short, the Jews have become a nation of robbers. . . . They have become notorious for deception and unfairness in trade, and it may be assumed that if they were stronger, they would, in many cases, revive the tragedies which occurred so frequently in their country.

Were, then, all Jews without exception guilty of all these sins? No, d'Holbach generously conceded, it cannot be doubted [that] there are also honest and just people among them, but this is only because they have rejected the principles of that law clearly aimed at creating trouble-makers and evildoers.[4]

In other words, because they have ceased being "Jews."

Above all, there was Voltaire, the most influential of the *philosophes*:

[The Jews] are a totally ignorant nation who, for many years, have combined contemptible miserliness and the most revolting superstition with a violent hatred of all those nations which have tolerated them.

This diatribe might well have been taken as a call for a new Inquisition ("the *bête noire*," remember, of the Enlightenment), but Voltaire was careful to disavow any such intention. In spite of deserving the revulsion they had always inspired, he concluded, "[the Jews] should not be burned at the stake."[5]

No fewer than 30 of the 118 entries in Voltaire's *Philosophical Dictionary* (1764) were devoted by this world-famous enemy of religious bigotry to comparably scurrilous attacks on the Jews. Voltaire apologized for paying so much attention to them:

It is with regret that I discuss the Jews: this nation is, in many ways, the most detestable ever to have sullied the earth.[6]

But he had learned from the English deists of the early eighteenth century that there was good reason to be obsessed with the Jews. It was these English believers in "natural religion"—religion purged of all "superstition" and based entirely on "reason"—who, Ettinger informs us,

were the first to claim, . . . out of their desire to undermine the principles of the Christian churches, that the Jewish Bible was a fabrication, that [the Jews'] forefathers and heroes were immoral scoundrels and their prophets were narrow-minded fanatics who engaged in religious persecution. The Jews, they believed, had always been a barbaric, cruel, and corrupt nation.[7]

It was as though Marcion, to whom, we recall, the Old Testament was the work not of God but of the Devil, had reappeared in secular guise. Ettinger concurs:

> Many of the violently anti-Jewish arguments of the Church Fathers were raised once again in the extensive deistic literature, with the rather transparent aim of attacking Christianity by undermining the foundations of its progenitor, Judaism.[8]

Obviously, this attitude was the polar opposite from Lessing's, and when it was imported from England into France by Voltaire and his fellow *philosophes,* the effect, Paul Johnson observes, was

> to turn on its head the old Augustinian argument that Judaism was a witness to the truth of Christianity. It was, rather, a witness to its inventions, superstitions, and sheer lies. They [the *philosophes*] saw Judaism as Christianity taken to the point of caricature, and it was on this ugly travesty that they concentrated. Here, they insisted, was an ugly example of the distorted effects that the enslavement of religion can produce on a people.[9]

It is at this historical point that we come upon the first of three great and related puzzles in the story of how and why Jews became and have remained so attached to the Left. This one lies in the contrast between how the Jews regarded Christianity and how they felt about the Enlightenment (the progenitor of what, from the French Revolution on, would be called the Left and the writings of whose intellectual exponents were, again in Johnson's words, "the title-deeds, the foundation documents, of the modern European intelligentsia").[10]

Assuming, as I do, that all animals, including humans, are equipped by nature with an instinct for telling the difference between friends and enemies, it can be said that the Jewish fear and distrust of Christianity was both healthy (that is, based on the promptings of instinct) and rational (that is, consistent with a long and bitter accumulation of empirical evidence). On the other hand, the Jewish attitude toward the Enlightenment was neither healthy nor rational. It could even be described as partaking of the pathological.

I know that (as the historian Adam Sutcliffe puts it),

> at several points in his writings Voltaire condemns injustice toward Jews, and . . . on occasion he compares Judaism favorably to Christianity in terms of its toleration of other faiths.[11]

I am also aware that, in spite of the anti-Jewish passions of the *philosophes* and other Enlightenment thinkers, the practical consequence of their writings was to further the cause of Jewish emancipation. This is why the eminent Israeli historian Jacob Katz could say that

> Voltaire did more than any other single man to shape the rationalist trend that moved European society toward improving the status of the Jew.[12]

It is also why some (notably the historian Peter Gay, to whom the Enlightenment thinkers were "the party of humanity") have argued that Voltaire was in the end an ally of the Jews. The same claim was made shortly after his death by a Jewish contemporary:

> The Jews forgive him all the evil he did to them because of all the good he brought them, perhaps unwittingly; for they have enjoyed a little respite for a few years now and this they owe to the progress of the Enlightenment, to which Voltaire surely contributed more than any other writer through his numerous works against fanaticism.[13]

Yet even though Voltaire and his colleagues may have been of benefit to the Jews in the short run, they exacted a wildly extortionate price for their help. For just at the point where anti-Semitism was losing its religious rationale, the thinkers of the Enlightenment stepped in to provide it with a new political justification that, being totally secular, was as well suited to the dawning modern age as Christian anti-Semitism had been to the waning Age of Faith. (A century later, Samuel Cahen, the editor of *Les Archives Israelites de France,* the leading French-Jewish monthly newspaper of the time, would make the same point in more concrete terms: "Evil passions have assumed the mask of republicanism as they had previously covered themselves with the mantle of religion."[14])

Yet radically different as the two rationales for anti-Semitism were, they had one major component in common. In the medieval world, Jews could free themselves from the oppressions of Christian rule by renouncing Judaism and converting to Christianity. Just so, in the Age of Enlightenment, Jews could escape the new species of anti-Semitism by renouncing Judaism and converting to the "Religion of Reason." In the process, they would also be expected to rid themselves of the stigmata of Jewishness. This did not mean only superficial changes like shedding their characteristic way of dressing and beginning to speak German or French instead of Yiddish. More profoundly, it meant giving up their sense of themselves as a people whose members were bound together across national boundaries and wherever they might live.

On the Gentile side, then, the first phase in the struggle for Jewish emancipation, which ended on the eve of the French Revolution, produced a fairly well-established set of conditions that the Jews would be required to meet if they were to be accepted as full-fledged citizens of the modern nation-state and fully integrated into modern society. Taken together, these conditions added up to the demand that the Jews altogether cease being Jews (nothing less would satisfy the *philosophes*), or, at the very least, that they find some way of remaining Jewish without seeming to be so, without persisting in the obnoxious habits, the barbaric customs, and the immoral practices that adherence to so primitive and obscurantist a faith had bred into them, and without continuing to constitute, as they had in the medieval past (as much by choice as by compulsion), what was beginning to be called "a nation within a nation."

But if the Jews never took it as a mark of friendship that under Christian rule they could escape the disabilities and dangers of being Jewish simply by ceasing to be Jewish, why did they fail to recognize that the Enlightenment was offering them the same bargain in modern dress? Why were they unable to see that the French *philosophes* and their counterparts in other countries were in their own way no less an enemy to them as Jews than the early Fathers of the Church?

In search of a solution to this—the first of the three great puzzles in the story I am trying to tell here—I will now take a look at the Jewish side of the struggle for their own emancipation.

6

HASKALAH

The Hebrew word *Haskalah* means "enlightenment," and it was through this movement that, around the last third of the eighteenth century, an ever-growing number of its proponents (the *maskilim* or "enlighteners") began trying to work out a position on the issue of how much Jewishness their people should be willing to surrender in exchange for full emancipation.

The widely accepted view among historians is that the *Haskalah* was only a part or an offshoot of the general European Enlightenment, which is true as far as it goes. But the movement actually had older and deeper and more indigenous roots in Jewish thought. It was Maimonides himself who had originally made the case for two of the main arguments the *maskilim* were bent on advancing. As passionate rationalists who were determined (at least at first) to remain within the Jewish fold, they could take encouragement from the great sage's demonstration that the revealed truths of Judaism were entirely consistent with reason (by which Maimonides meant the philosophy of Aristotle). And they could also lean on the authority of Maimonides in urging that Jewish education should no longer be confined to endless poring over the sacred texts, and that secular subjects should now be accepted as a legitimate and even an essential field of study for Jews.

Both of these positions had generated controversy even when they came from Maimonides himself. Some of his opponents thought that his rationalist defense of Judaism gave primacy to Aristotle over the revealed word of God—that, in other words, it carried the blasphemous implication that the ultimate guarantor of truth was Aristotle, rather than the Torah.* Correlatively, they also thought that in advocating the study of Greek philosophy and science, he was downgrading the importance of the Torah, which to them constituted the only knowledge that mattered. So passionate did these anti-Maimonideans become that they actually tried to excommunicate him, and they even burned his books.

By the time the *maskilim* arrived on the scene, the anti-Maimonidean party had become an embarrassing memory, and Maimonides had triumphed over it to such an extent that he was now universally revered in the Jewish world, with his works standing unchallenged as supremely authoritative guides to the understanding and observance of Jewish law (the *halakhah*). It is therefore not surprising that the "father" of the *Haskalah* movement, a German Jew named Moses Mendelssohn, was not only a student of Maimonides' *Guide for the Perplexed* but also followed his example in producing a rationalist defense of Judaism. In the nineteenth century, with the spread of the *Haskalah* movement from Germany to East Europe, a Galician *maskil*, Nachman Krochmal, would write a *Guide for the Perplexed of Our Time*. But it was Mendelssohn who took the Maimonidean lead. As Maimonides had tried to demonstrate that Judaism was compatible with Greek philosophy, Mendelssohn strove to show that there was no conflict between Judaism and reason as defined by the fashionable philosophical ideas of his own day. (A couplet written in memorial tribute to him summed it up: "There is a God, so Moses taught; / But Mendelssohn the proof has brought."[1])

However, no more than had Maimonides before him did Mendelssohn take this as a warrant for Jews to become less rigorous in their

---

* The word *Torah* in its narrow sense means the first five books of the Hebrew Bible (the Pentateuch). But it has also been used (as it is here) to mean the entire Hebrew Bible (or what Christians call the Old Testament) as interpreted in enormous detail by rabbinical scholars in what was originally an oral tradition. After the fourth century C.E. the oral teachings were set down in writing as well, and became known as the Talmud. Both the Bible ("the written Torah") and the Talmud ("the oral Torah") were believed by the pious to have been given by God to Moses at Mount Sinai.

observance of the commandments. He strongly favored the integration of Jews into the societies around them, and he warmly welcomed the new opportunities that were making this possible to a greater extent than ever before. But, he declared:

> If we can only be united with you Christians on the condition that we deviate from the law which we still consider binding, we sincerely regret the necessity of declaring that we renounce our claim to civil equality.[2]

And here is what he said to his fellow Jews:

> Adopt the mores and constitution of the country in which you find yourself, but be steadfast in upholding the religion of your fathers, too. Bear both burdens as well as you can. True, on the one hand, people make it difficult for you to bear the burden of civil life because of the religion to which you remain faithful; and, on the other hand, the climate of our time makes the observance of your religious laws in some respects more burdensome than it need be. Persevere nevertheless; stand fast in the place which Providence has assigned to you.[3]

To the father of the *Haskalah,* then, it was either emancipation of the Jews as Jews—as what today we would call Orthodox Jews—or no emancipation at all. Mendelssohn managed to pull this off for himself, but not everyone could aspire to being, as he was, one of Frederick the Great's privileged Jews. In any case, there was no chance that the terms he proposed would be accepted by Christians, and still less by the more secularized society envisaged by the Enlightenment. Besides, even if it were accepted, the *maskilim* who were inspired by Mendelssohn in other respects had no intention of "stand[ing] fast in the place which Providence had assigned to them." Mendelssohn said that he could not

> see how those who were born into the household of Jacob [could] in good conscience exempt themselves from the observance of the law.[4]

Yet his very own son Abraham could see it all too well—even to the extent of baptizing his own children (among whom was Felix, the future composer) and then converting to (Protestant) Christianity himself. Mendelssohn's daughter, Dorothea, also converted to Protestantism, which she felt to be a "much purer" form of Christianity than Catholicism. Among its other faults, Catholicism had "too much similarity to the old Judaism, which I greatly despise." (A few years later, however, she changed her mind and, along with her lover and future husband, the philosopher Friedrich von Schlegel, she became "an ostentatious Catholic, and she did not rest until her sons abandoned Judaism and embraced Catholicism."[5])

Many thousands of Jews—and not in Germany alone—would follow suit. But unlike Dorothea von Schlegel, relatively few of them did so because they had come to believe in the truth of Christianity, whether Protestant or Catholic. Most clearly became Christians for the same reason the great German poet Heinrich Heine would later famously give for his own conversion: "to get a passport to European society." (Heine was one of the wittiest men who ever lived, but not even he could match the answer given a century later by a Russian Jewish scholar named Daniel Chwolson. When asked whether he had converted to Russian Orthodoxy out of conviction or expedience, Chwolson replied: "I accepted baptism entirely out of conviction—the conviction that it is better to be a professor in the Academy of St. Petersburg than a *melamed* [a teacher in a Jewish elementary school] in Eisheshok."[6])

To most of the early *maskilim,* however, conversion still seemed too radical, and perhaps too dishonorable, a course. What they were looking for was a way of remaining Jewish that would spare them the need to pay the price of conversion in order to get their own passports to European society.

This is why the formulation coined in the nineteenth century by a Russian *maskil,* the Hebrew poet Judah Leib Gordon—"Be a Jew at home and a man on the street"—would become the lodestar of a future generation of *maskilim.* It was, however, a compromise that turned out to be unworkable. As the great historian of the Jews, Salo W. Baron, tartly observes, Gordon's dictum would soon "wither away under the dictates of full emancipation, which demanded that the Jew be a Western man even at home."[7]

To Gordon's despair, this demand the younger *maskilim* were only too happy to fulfill—and even before full emancipation had been achieved. To "be a Jew at home" did not translate for Gordon into observing the commandments; unlike Mendelssohn, he was not religious. It did, however, entail an immersion in Jewish history and culture, and especially Hebrew, in whose revival as a living language he played an important part. But the younger *maskilim* were not even interested in exploring and preserving the culture out of which they had come: "My enlightened brothers have learned science," Gordon lamented in one of his poems, but "They mock the old mother who holds the distaff."

In this lament over the radical assimilationism to which the *Haskalah* movement was leading, I find a clue to the otherwise inexplicable Jewish willingness, or even eagerness, to explain away the anti-Jewish enmity of so many of the major Enlightenment thinkers. Mendelssohn may have imagined that he was speaking for most of his fellow Jews when he told the Christians of Germany that "we" would rather "renounce our claim to civil equality" than "deviate from the law which we still consider binding," but he was actually speaking only for an ever-diminishing number of them. This group mostly included the leaders of the Jewish communities throughout Europe. Under the old medieval order, the segregation of the Jews and their exclusion from the surrounding societies had resulted in the incidental benefit of communal autonomy, under which the leaders of the community had the power to tax and to enforce Jewish law. Since being, as this system made possible, a "nation within a nation" was incompatible with the integration into society entailed by emancipation, the communal leadership fought bitterly against it. To such Jews as these, the price for emancipation was too high. But to an ever-growing number of other Jews nothing, but nothing, was more important than emancipation; and for many, no price was too high to pay for it.

Insofar, then, as the thinkers of the European Enlightenment paved the way for Jewish emancipation, it was entirely reasonable for Jews to consider them friends and allies. But insofar as the dearest wish of increasing numbers of Jews themselves was to become good modern Europeans who would be indistinguishable from all other good modern Europeans, it even made a perverse kind of sense for them to ignore or explain away the anti-Jewish passion that emerged so blatantly from the writings of Voltaire and the others. Where Voltaire himself was concerned, they did so by shifting the blame to the Christian education he had received in his youth and some of whose baneful effects lingered on. As for the *philosophes* in general, their attacks on Jews and Judaism could be interpreted as (in the historian Arthur Hertzberg's words)

> part of the process by which [Voltaire and his associates] were attempting to dethrone Christianity, and they were not meant to lessen the ultimate claims of Jews upon equal regard in the new world that enlightened men were envisaging.[8]

Yet if truth be told, it was also fairly easy for those Jews who yearned for emancipation to overlook or excuse the anti-Semitic writings of Voltaire and the others. Nor were they in any mood to defend what was under attack, if only because, all on their own, they had come to loathe the way of life into which they had been squeezed by the "yoke of the law." They felt it to be stifling to the spirit, deadening to the mind, and crippling to the character, and the sooner and more completely they could be delivered from it, the better.

Thus did the *Haskalah* movement, whose "father" categorically rejected any deal for emancipation that would involve forsaking the observance of Jewish law to any extent at all, peter out in an enthusiastic acceptance by many of his disciples of the requirement that they give up much more than their religion—that, to state the point bluntly, they "convert" not, as would have been the case in the medieval past, to Christianity but to the new "Religion of Reason" that was fast replacing it in the world of the European intelligentsia.

EMANCIPATION: PHASE TWO

I have said that the first period in the history of Jewish emancipation produced a fairly clear sense of the terms on which it would be achieved, as well as a number of steps toward its implementation. But it was in the second period, which began with the French Revolution, that the process achieved real momentum, becoming a legal and political reality wherever the revolutionary spirit took hold.

In France itself, the basis of the new policy was most famously summed up by Count Clermont-Tonnerre in 1789 during the debates on the "Jewish Question" in the National Assembly: "The Jews should be denied everything as a nation, but granted everything as individuals." He then went on to elaborate:

> It should not be tolerated that the Jews become a separate
> political formation or class in the country. Every one of them
> must individually become a citizen; if they do not want this,
> they must inform us and we shall then be compelled to expel
> them. The existence of a nation within a nation is unacceptable
> to our country.[1]

This was precisely the position that had been developed by the Enlightenment thinkers, and it was also entirely consonant with the stated principles of the Revolution. Of these, the one most relevant to the Jews, as enunciated in the *Declaration of the Rights of Man* of 1789, was that

> no man should be molested for his beliefs, including religious beliefs, provided that their manifestation does not disturb the public order established by law.

Since all that remained was to translate into law what had already been agreed upon in the abstract, smooth sailing might have been expected for the proposed bill granting legal equality to the Jews. Yet it encountered fierce resistance, especially from the Abbé Maury who, before being driven into exile by the revolutionaries, was the leader of the party quixotically trying to defend the interests of both the Church and the King in the National Assembly. Maury's anti-Jewish passions were not tempered by the idea held by some Enlightenment thinkers that the hateful qualities of the Jews were a product of oppression and that full emancipation would soon transform them into good Frenchmen. Just the opposite, he said; and shrewdly basing his case not on any Christian objections but on a point that he knew the revolutionaries themselves were concerned about, he argued that even if the Jews were granted equal rights, they would always constitute a "state within a state," an unassimilable minority.

Even in the second period, then, when the issue of emancipation was already settled in principle, the forces of what was now beginning to be called the Right* went on fighting against equal rights for the Jews. The one great exception was the Abbé Henri Grégoire. Sharing the view that the evils of the Jews stemmed from persecution and could be cured by equality, Grégoire also nourished the "sweet hope"

---

* Wikipedia (for once) provides an accurate account: "The terms *Right* and *Left* refer to political affiliations which originated early in the French Revolutionary era, and referred originally to the seating arrangements in the various legislative bodies of France. The aristocracy sat on the right of the Speaker (traditionally the seat of honor) and the commoners sat on the left. . . . the defining point on the ideological spectrum was the *ancien régime* ('old order'). 'The Right' thus implied support for aristocratic or royal interests, and the Church, while 'The Left' implied opposition to the same."

of the Catholic Church "that the Jews will enter its bosom." Thus, he argued,

> the granting of religious liberty to the Jews would be a great step forward in reforming and, I even dare say, in converting them, for truth is most persuasive when it is gentle.[2]

Conversely, what was now also beginning to be described as the Left continued pushing for full emancipation, although here, too, there was one great exception. This was a radical deputy named Jean-François Reubell, who represented the peasantry of Alsace, where there was a deeply rooted hatred of the Jews as, in Reubell's words, "moneylenders and bloodsuckers."[3] Accordingly—in an ominous foretaste of how the radical Left would deal with the Jewish Question in the century ahead—Reubell emphasized economic factors in arguing against equal rights for the Jews. Speaking, he said, on behalf of "a numerous, industrious and honest class of my unfortunate compatriots" who were being "oppressed and ground down by these cruel hordes of Africans[!] who have infested my region,"[4] he contended that the proposed legislation would only make it easier for Jewish usurers and exploiters to heap more suffering upon the heads of the farmers they had already beaten down with their cunning practices.[5]

These arguments had enough force behind them to delay the full enfranchisement of the Jews for two years. But neither the one coming from the Left nor still less the one coming from the Right could prevail against the overwhelming sentiment among the revolutionaries for the enfranchisement of the Jews. So powerful was this sentiment that later, during the Reign of Terror, opposition to egalitarianism was treated as a counterrevolutionary crime and hence punishable by the guillotine. On this point more moderate Girondists like Clermont-Tonnerre were in accord with such radical Jacobins as the fearsome Robespierre. And the two parties were also in accord on the limits to Jewish emancipation as formulated by Clermont-Tonnerre.

Limits or no, to the Jews themselves, the law of September 1791 was a great and happy turning point and they credited it to the victory of revolutionary principles. As such, it served to cement their conviction that—no matter how anti-Jewish the Enlightenment progenitors of the Left might have been in theory—when push came to shove, it was on the Left that the only reliable friends of the Jews could be found. And since it was no secret that, the Abbé Grégoire notwithstanding, the supporters of the old order considered the new law an insult both to the Church and to the traditions of France itself, the Jews had all the evidence they needed that their enemies were still located where they had always been found—on the Right.

It was the same everywhere in Europe as the French revolutionary armies led by Napoleon went forth to spread the new Gospel of the Rights of Man. But following Napoleon's overthrow a so-called Conservative Order was put in place by the Congress of Vienna (1814–15), which brought with it a restoration throughout Central Europe of the conditions under which the Jews had lived before the French invasion.

It was not, however, only in their legal and political status that the position of the Jews deteriorated under the restoration of the new Conservative Order. What was perhaps even more consequential was the great wave of anti-Jewish polemics that followed in the wake of the Congress of Vienna. As it would be in the future, so in the years between 1815 and the revolutions of 1848, the worst of these polemics were written by Germans—and highly educated Germans at that. There was, for instance, Friedrich Rühs, professor of history at the University of Berlin, who gave vitriolic new life to the old idea that the Jews constituted a "nation within a nation" and were therefore incapable of being loyal citizens of the countries in which they lived. Moreover, he said, Judaism was "a proliferating sickness of peoples, whose force increases through the power of money."

Chiming in to agree with this assessment was Jakob Fries, professor of philosophy at the University of Heidelberg (who would be described by Goethe as "the most savage enemy of the Jews" in his day[6]):

If the Jews do not leave Judaism, they will be obliged to remain irrevocably in their miserable condition. It would be an immeasurably important deed to liberate our people from this plague.[7]

Otherwise, Fries recommended that the Jews be destroyed "root and branch."[8]

Hartwig von Hundt-Radowsky, in a pamphlet titled *The Mirror of the Jews,* was even more vitriolic:

> No people in the world has so excelled in evil and lust for
> revenge, in cowardice, arrogance, and superstition, as the Jews.
> All Jews—whether rich or poor, educated or ignorant—are
> members of a united gang of criminals.[9]

It was all reminiscent of the *philosophes* at the height of their anti-Jewish fevers, and a reaction against it was triggered in 1830, when yet another French revolution erupted. This one ended after three bloodless days with the overthrow of the Bourbon dynasty that had been restored to the country by the Congress of Vienna. In its place came a constitutional monarchy under Louis-Philippe that eschewed the absolutist principle of hereditary right and accepted the principle of popular sovereignty.

The liberals in Germany (and elsewhere in Europe) were greatly encouraged by this victory over the Conservative Order, and among the causes for which some of them now spoke out was the extension of equal rights to the Jews. I say "some" because there were also liberals who opposed equal rights and who wanted to make it a condition of full emancipation that the Jews give up observing the dietary and other religious laws that kept them apart from the rest of society.

But these liberals were a small minority within their own political circles. In any case, they were far less influential than the much more numerous and more vehement conservative opponents of equal rights, who were provoked by the new climate of opinion into still another round of diatribes. One post-1830 line of conservative attack revived the argument first advanced in the eighteenth century by Colbert and picked up by other absolutists to the effect that the Jews should be tolerated only so long as they were "useful." Another, reversing the terms of the debate, contended that the real problem to be solved was not the emancipation of the Jews but rather "the emancipation of Christians from Jewry."[10]

In medieval times, in what was taken to be the fulfillment of a much quoted prophecy of Isaiah ("Thy destroyers and they that made thee waste shall go forth of thee"*[11]), converted Jews often became the most dangerous enemies of the people from whom they stemmed. Among these was Johannes Pfefferkorn, who in the early sixteenth century produced one ferociously anti-Jewish tract after another[†] and who became especially notorious for advocating that the Talmud and other Jewish books be confiscated and burned. Now, in the 1840s, a similar phenomenon began to emerge, as exemplified early on by one Friedrich Julius Stahl, professor of law at the University of Berlin.

Stahl, like so many Jews both before and after him, seems to have converted to Christianity to advance his career, but if so, what began as opportunism developed into fiery conviction. In his lectures and his writings, where he called for the mobilization of the Christian state against liberalism and democracy, he sounded a theme that was becoming a staple of the romantic nationalism sweeping the German Right: the idea that the Jews posed a threat to the "German essence."[12] The composer Richard Wagner would pick up the same idea a few years later in his *Jewishness in Music,* and—with the wells that the Jews had been accused of poisoning in the Middle Ages transmuted into the wellsprings of German culture that the Jews would literally be accused of polluting—it would eventually make its way into the arsenal of Nazi propaganda.[‡]

Despite the best efforts of the conservatives, however, the post-1830 period saw a steadily rising tide of liberal democratic sentiment that finally crested in 1848, when a series of republican revolts broke out against the monarchical regimes all over Central Europe. This time Jews themselves entered the fray ("They were," Ettinger tells us,

---

* The "destroyers" in this verse are actually conquering armies who will be driven out, but it was interpreted to mean that the Children of Israel would be laid waste by their own progeny.

† It is interesting to note that one of these had the same title—*The Mirror of the Jews*— as the pamphlet by Hundt-Radowsky mentioned above.

‡ Yet in a twist that makes one's head spin, "Stahl's philosophy was later repudiated by the Nazis as an expression of Jewish theocracy" (Ed. Staff, "Stahl, Friedrich Julius," EJ).

"among the first victims in battle and were buried in mass graves together with other revolutionaries").[13] Nevertheless anti-Jewish riots broke out everywhere among the revolutionary mobs. In some cases they accused the Jews of siding with the hated governments. In others they were driven by the opposite fear that the Jews would co-opt the revolution as a vehicle for emancipation: what these mobs wanted, as Ettinger puts it, was "freedom *from* rather than *for* the Jews."[14] But they were not to get their wish. In the wake of the revolutions of 1848, equal rights for the Jews—along with such liberal democratic reforms as universal manhood suffrage and freedom of the press and of assembly—were forced through in many countries, even in Prussia, Austria, and Germany, homes to the greatest degree of absolutist rule still extant in Western Europe.

The roller coaster, however, had yet another downward plunge to make. Once the previously supine monarchical armies roused themselves, the revolutionaries were brutally suppressed, and the liberal reforms they had sponsored were abrogated. In the process the Jews were hit hard. As in the years following the Congress of Vienna, this new conservative restoration resulted in a large step back from the progress the Jews had already made, though it was worse in some places than in others. In Rome, Pope Pius IX, no doubt inspired by the example set by his predecessor Pius VI after the fall of Napoleon, herded the Jews back into the ghettos once again. Elsewhere various forms of anti-Jewish discrimination of differing degrees of severity were instituted or reinstituted.

As it would turn out, the new restoration was unable fully to suppress the liberal tendencies that had been leading to Jewish emancipation. In fact, in the thirty years before the second period ended, the roller coaster shot up again, with these tendencies picking up a new head of steam. And in combination with developments having little or nothing to do with the Jews as such (the unification of Germany and of Italy and nationalist movements in other countries), they made emancipation a political and legal fact throughout Central Europe. But whatever the particular circumstances in this country or that, writes the historian Benzion Dinur, "the relation between the new liberal political climate and the emancipation of the Jews was decisive"[15] as, on the other side, was the relation between the upholders of the old order and opposition to Jewish emancipation.

I noted a minute ago that Jews fought and died on the barricades of 1848, but taking up arms was not the only thing they began doing in the second phase of their struggle for emancipation. Even more consequential was their entry into the political arena—what Baron calls their "political debut." Before 1848, very few Jews had been active players in the debates over their own emancipation. But, Baron adds, 1848 marked a major transformation in "the newly acquired active participation of Jews—both professing and converted—in domestic and international politics."[16] Everywhere, Baron goes on—in France, Austria, Prussia, Italy, and Romania—

> Jews played from the outset a most active political role. They belonged, often in leading positions, to various political parties and were influential in the general press. Their youth actively participated in the uprisings and mass demonstrations.[17]

Very few of these new Jewish leaders spoke as representatives of Jewish interests in fighting for emancipation. For the most part, they appealed to the general principle of equality. For example, Rabbi Isaac Noah Mannheimer, who was elected to the Reichstag in Vienna, issued a warning to his fellow Jews:

> What shall be done for us now? Nothing! Everything for the people and the Fatherland, as you have done it in the last few days. . . . No word about Jewish emancipation unless others speak up for us. . . . No petitions, no requests, implorations or complaints in behalf of our rights. . . . First the right to live as men, to breathe, think, speak, first the right of a citizen, of a noble, free citizen in his legitimate aspirations in his dignified position—afterward comes the Jew. They should not reproach us that we always think first about ourselves![18]

Most other Jewish deputies throughout Europe took the same position, and most of them also (to quote Baron again) "belonged to the moderates in the Center or Left Center."[19] Which is to say that, like the great majority of their fellow Jews in Western and Central Europe, they were liberals. A favorite explanation for this political preference was the influence of the prophets of the Hebrew Bible. A prominent Jewish leader in France, expressing a widely shared view, wrote around this time:

> The two principles which the [Second French Republic] had
> inscribed on its flag, equality and fraternity of all men, have
> emerged from our Holy Scriptures. It was the voice of our
> prophets which proclaimed them for the first time. Transferred
> by our immortal Revolution from the religious to the political
> sphere, they have lent strength to liberty.[20]

But even if this and similar rationalizations were solidly grounded (which, as I will be arguing later on, is not at all self-evident), they were surely supererogatory. For considering the history I have been tracing, it would have been astonishing if Jews, once having made their "political debut," were to have joined the political Right. (One Jewish deputy, asked why he was seating himself on the left in the Reichstag chamber, replied with a witty pun on the term *Right: "Wir haben nicht keine Recht"*—"We have no right[s]," and less cleverly but more straightforwardly, an editorialist in *Orient,* a German-Jewish weekly, declared: "The Jew stands or falls with democracy."[21])

What does, on the other hand, demand explanation is the movement of an increasing number of Jews to the left of liberalism. To the extent that they still cared about Jewish emancipation—and many, having repudiated both Judaism and their own Jewishness, no longer did—these Jews took the view that emancipation could be achieved only through the overthrow of capitalism and its replacement by a socialist society. Which brings me to the second of the three related puzzles in the story I am trying to tell.

THE SECOND GREAT PUZZLE

In the years immediately preceding the revolutions of 1848, the members of a group known as the "Young Hegelians" were working to push the master's philosophy in a leftward direction, and this necessarily involved mounting an attack on Christianity as a retrograde force. As the *philosophes* had done before them, the Young Hegelians also directed their fire against Judaism as the root of all Christian evil. Before long, however, Bruno Bauer, one of the leading Young Hegelians, was extending this animus against Judaism as a religion to the Jewish people themselves. On the Right, the charge was commonly made that Jews were revolutionaries bent on overthrowing the social order. But in *On the Jewish Question* (1843), Bauer launched the opposite charge—that they were bulwarks of the old order and hence great obstacles to liberal and democratic reform.

Another Young Hegelian by the name of Karl Marx immediately fired off a response to Bauer—most emphatically not because he wanted to defend the Jews but because he thought he could make a better case against them than Bauer (who was not Jewish) had done. Marx, the scion of a long line of rabbis and Jewish scholars, was baptized at age six by his father and never for the rest of his life bothered to learn anything about Judaism. Even so, I think he can still be grouped with the "destroyers" like Pfefferkorn and Stahl, who, as we have seen, were raised and educated as Jews and then converted to Christianity in adulthood. It appears that Marx did become an ardent Christian in his early teens, but this was only a phase through which he passed on the road to the materialistic philosophy that would make him into one of the most influential thinkers in European history. Yet even as a young man, and long before becoming famous, he wrote about Judaism and the Jews in secular terms that were at least as vitriolic as the religious variety preached by the likes of Pfefferkorn and Stahl.

Bauer's mistake, said Marx, was to treat the Jewish Question as a "theological" issue. Instead, Marx proposed:

> Let us consider the actual, worldly Jew—not the *Sabbath Jew,* as Bauer does, but the *everyday Jew.*
> Let us not look for the secret of the Jew in his religion, but let us look for the secret of his religion in the real Jew.
> What is the secular basis of Judaism? *Practical* need, *self-interest.* What is the worldly religion of the Jew? *Huckstering.* What is his worldly God? *Money.*

Marx then goes on to explain that this "worldly God" has corrupted not only the Jews themselves but everyone else as well: "The god of the Jews has become secularized and has become the god of the world." In the process, all of Christendom has been infected with the

> contempt for theory, art, history, and for man as an end in himself, which is contained in an abstract form in the Jewish religion. . . . Christianity sprang from Judaism. It has merged again in Judaism.[1]

By this secular route Marx arrived at exactly the same conclusion that was being reached in almost the same words by Christian extremists of the Right like Julius Stahl: "The *social* emancipation of the Jew is the *emancipation of society from Judaism.*"[2] The only difference was that the emphasis on the Right was nationalistic and religious, whereas on the Left it was social and economic.

In Marx and Stahl we see—neither for the first nor for the last time in the history of anti-Semitism, and not only among Jewish apostates like them—the extremes brought together into a de facto alliance by hatred of the Jews. Yet while scarcely a Jew anywhere was attracted to the likes of Stahl, innumerable Jews were mesmerized by Marx, and as time went on they either joined or sympathized with one or another of the various socialist movements he spawned. The question thus arises of why the Jews who joined the radical camp were not put off by the egregious anti-Semitism of Marx or that of several other major figures of the socialist movement, including Charles Fourier (to whom the Jews were "the leprosy and the ruin of the body politic") and Pierre-Joseph Proudhon (to whom the Jews were "the race which poisons everything [and] the enemy of the human race").[3]

The answer, I believe, is that, like the more radically assimilationist *maskilim* before them, whose loathing for Judaism and for the Jewish world into which they had been born was hardly less intense than Voltaire's, the Jewish socialists of the nineteenth century and after for the most part shared in Marx's hatred and contempt for, or willful indifference to, the people from whom they stemmed and on whom he—and they—had angrily turned their backs.

My own favorite example of this cast of mind is Rosa Luxemburg (1871–1919), one of the founders of the German Communist Party. Like Marx, she was descended from a long line of rabbis, and her maternal grandfather and uncle were also rabbis. But unlike Marx, she never converted to Christianity; and unlike him, too, she was not so much anti-Semitic as totally indifferent to the fate of the Jewish people. When a friend wrote to her bemoaning the condition of the Jews, she replied:

> Why do you come with your special Jewish sorrows? I feel just
> as sorry for the wretched Indian victims in Putamayo, the
> Negroes in Africa. . . . The "lofty silence of the eternal" in
> which so many cries have echoed away unheard resounds so
> strongly within me that I cannot find a special corner in my
> heart for the ghetto.[4]

As for the Jewish socialists who were neither so violently anti-Jewish nor so indifferent to "special Jewish sorrows," they either ignored Marx's anti-Semitism or explained it away as (in Arthur Hertzberg's paraphrase) "an unfortunate personal idiosyncrasy" that had no real bearing on his main ideas.[5]

But what was it about Marx's ideas that proved so seductive to so many emancipated Jews? Paul Johnson shrewdly remarks that to them Marx's *Capital* "became a new kind of Torah,"[6] and so it did, in the sense that (contrary to what they themselves imagined) their embrace of Marxism had the feel and the force not of an abandonment of Judaism in favor of a wholly secular philosophy, but rather of a conversion from Judaism to another religion.

The Yiddish novelist I. J. Singer, in *The Brothers Ashkenazi,* captures this well in the character of Nissan, the scholarly son of a pious rabbi who becomes a disciple of "the prophet Marx," after which he

never let his copy of *Das Kapital* out of his sight and carried it everywhere, as his father had carried his prayer shawl and phylacteries. And just like his father, who held that the Torah wasn't to be studied just for one's own edification, he felt it his mission to spread the new Torah. . . .[7]

Furthermore, "just as his father had admonished those who dared stray even a hair from the Torah," Nissan warned against "anyone who dared question the absolutism of Marxist dogma."[8]

The central premise of the Torah itself was that the Jewish people were the vehicle chosen by God to make His will manifest to the whole world, and that they were therefore forbidden to shed their distinctive identity and character. But the promise held out by this new religion looked in exactly the opposite direction: toward a world in which the distinction between Jew and Gentile would become irrelevant and therefore erased—a world in which, as Saint Paul had put it of the new religion that *he* was preaching eighteen hundred years earlier, there would be "neither Jew nor Greek."[9]

Marxism has often been interpreted as a translation into secular terms of Jewish messianism, with History replacing God and with the proletariat substituted for the Children of Israel as the vehicle through which deliverance from all evils will ultimately come to everyone. The same interpretation has been used to explain the appeal of Marxism to so many "enlightened" Jews for whom it supposedly played on, and subliminally served to satisfy, an atavistic messianic yearning. Thus, of the same Nissan whose Marxism unknowingly aped his father's Judaism, Singer writes:

> Just as his father, the rabbi, had spent his whole life awaiting the Messiah and his redemption, his son had spent his whole life awaiting the revolution and its redemption. He hadn't been able to estimate its exact arrival, but he had never doubted that it would come—it was one of the inexorable laws of Marxism.[10]

And yet, with all due respect to the role played by messianic fantasies in the attraction of Marxism to many young Jews, it seems to me that the classless egalitarian utopia of Marxist eschatology is much closer to the Christian—that is, Saint Paul's—vision of a world where all the stubborn particularities of the Torah will be abrogated. In that new world, the Torah's relentless insistence that everything is what it is and not something else will also be left behind, and especially the distinction between Jew and Gentile.* It was, in my view, this promise of liberation from the burdens of Jewishness without being forced to undergo the painful dishonor of conversion to Christianity that exerted the deepest appeal of Marxism to the Jews who were seduced by it. Indeed, the vision of a world in which there would be "neither Jew nor Greek" was already being fulfilled for converts to the faith of "the prophet Marx": as Singer's Nissan says of himself and his comrades, "We know nothing of gentiles and Jews."[11]

To be sure, there was both more and less to it than that for many of these Jews, especially the ones who lived in Eastern Europe. After the

---

* But also the distinction between slave and free and, most radically, between male and female. The verse from Paul's Letter to the Galatians (3:28) reads in full (in the King James translation): "There is neither Jew nor Greek, there is neither bond nor free, there is neither male nor female."

quashing of the revolutions of 1848, a certain number of Jews from Central Europe lost faith in the possibility of full emancipation and, says Ettinger, "the emigration of many of them to the United States was the natural consequence of their disillusion."[12] No one knows exactly how large this emigration was (one estimate has it at about 250,000), but there is no doubt that it was dwarfed by the great mass of Jews from Eastern Europe who would flee to the United States between 1881 and 1924 (after which the gates were closed).

Most of these later Jewish immigrants to America came from Russia, where by 1880 (thanks to the successive annexations of large swatches of Poland) they numbered about four million—a population twice the size of the total Jewish population in the rest of Europe. By this time—the end of the second period in the history of emancipation—equal rights had been granted to the Jews throughout Western and Central Europe. In Russia, however, the very last bastion of monarchical absolutism, not even the first phase of emancipation had been reached. True, there had been enlightened Russian despots like Catherine the Great in the late eighteenth century and the relatively benign Alexander II (reigned 1855–81) who had extended greater toleration to the Jews than the likes of Ivan the Terrible (reigned 1533–84), but not a step toward legal emancipation had yet been taken.

Since 1791, the Jews, with very few privileged exceptions, had been forbidden to live anywhere on Russian-controlled land but the Pale of Settlement. This was a kind of geographical ghetto made up of twenty-five provinces (including Ukraine, Lithuania, Belorussia, Crimea, and what had formerly been eastern Poland). Since physical segregation was accompanied by onerous exclusions and other forces that confined them to a very narrow range of economic activities, the overwhelming majority of the Jews living under the rule of the czars were dirt poor.

Things had certainly been bad for them before, but after the assassination of Alexander II in 1881, they grew even worse. Although the assassination had been carried out by a non-Jewish anarchist, it was used as an excuse for a yearlong series of pogroms that were not merely tolerated by the police and the army but organized and incited by the Ministry of the Interior. Under these auspices, it was not the rampaging mobs who were blamed but their Jewish victims for having incited the attacks by being so hateful. Later, when groups of young Jews organized to defend themselves, it was they who were arrested and jailed so that the murderers could continue their bloody work without any Jewish hindrance.

As if this were not enough, the pogroms also became the excuse for a new package of anti-Semitic legislation, the May Laws, and these were then followed by the relentless imposition of more and more disabilities (in all, over six hundred such measures were promulgated), followed by more and more pogroms. In one four-year period alone (1903–7), there were 284 mob assaults. The most notorious of all was the one in Kishinev in 1903, the horrors of which finally captured the attention of the outside world. Even the *New York Times,* whose German-Jewish owners usually tended to bend over backward to avoid the appearance of partiality to their own people, was shaken:

> It is impossible to account the amounts of goods destroyed in a few hours. The hurrahs of the rioting. The pitiful cries of the victims filled the air. Wherever a Jew was met he was savagely beaten into insensibility. One Jew was dragged from a streetcar and beaten until the mob thought he was dead. The air was filled with feathers and torn bedding. Every Jewish household was broken into and the unfortunate Jews in their terror endeavored to hide in cellars and under roofs. The mob entered the synagogue, desecrated the biggest house of worship and defiled the Scrolls of the Law. The conduct of the intelligent Christians was disgraceful. They made no attempt to check the rioting. They simply walked around enjoying the frightful sport.[13]

Among those who enjoyed the frightful sport were twelve thousand soldiers, who stood by for three days and did nothing until—the government having decided that enough was by now enough—they were ordered to put an end to the slaughters by threatening to shoot, not for a change at the Jews, but actually at the rioters.

What one historian writes of the reign of Alexander III (1881–94), then, applies even more fully to the situation under his successor, Nicholas II:

> Expulsions, deportations, arrests, and beatings became the daily lot of the Jews, not only of their lower class, but even of the middle class and the Jewish intelligentsia. The government . . . waged a campaign of war against its Jewish inhabitants. . . . The Jews were driven and hounded, and emigration appeared to be the only escape from the terrible tyranny of the Romanovs.[14]

Some years after Alexander III's death, his finance minister, Count Sergei Witte, was interviewed by Theodor Herzl, the father of political Zionism. In response to Witte's complaint that a large number of Jews were involved in the revolutionary movement, Herzl asked him "to what circumstances do you attribute that?" Witte's answer was surprising:

> *Witte*: I believe it is the fault of our government. The Jews are too oppressed. I used to say to the late Czar Alexander III, "Majesty, if it were possible to drown the six or seven million Jews in the Black Sea, I would be absolutely in favor of that. But if it is not possible, one must let them live." What, then, do you want from the Russian government?
> *Herzl*: Certain encouragements.
> *Witte*: But the Jews *are* given encouragements—to emigrate. Kicks in the behind, for example.[15]

Another prominent Russian statesman, Konstantin Pobedonostsev, went further than Witte. The goal of Russian policy, he said, was to get a third of the Jews to emigrate, to convert another third to Christianity, and to kill off the rest. Then there was the minister of the interior, Wenzel von Plehve, who thought that the Jews were even more prominent in the revolutionary movements than Witte did. In his estimate, Jews made up no less than 90 percent of the revolutionaries in the south of Russia and 40 percent in the interior. It was on this basis that he told a Jewish delegation, "We shall make your situation so untenable that Jews will be forced to leave . . . to the very last man."[16]

The "kicks in the behind" did not suffice to achieve von Plehve's goal, but they did the trick well enough to drive more than two million Russian Jews to America between 1881 and 1924. These were joined by some 350,000 of their coreligionists from Galicia and other former provinces of Poland that were now part of the Austro-Hungarian empire of the Hapsburgs. Conditions under the Hapsburgs were far better for the Jews than in Russia, but the yen to run off in search of a better life in the "Golden Land" of America nevertheless took hold. Smaller contingents from Romania and Hungary also caught the contagion.

Unlike their coreligionists to the West, the Jews of Russia had no reason to place their hopes for emancipation, or even for an easing of oppression, in what the Marxists were now calling "bourgeois liberalism." For one thing, only minuscule numbers of Russian Jews were even remotely bourgeois in terms of income and still less in terms of acculturation. Cecil Roth gives us a vivid description:

> Culturally they were hardly what an English or French Jew . . . would have considered enlightened, notwithstanding their passionate devotion to an older wisdom. Their intellectual interests were confined to the Talmud and allied literature; or, in the case of the Hasidim, to the prodigious attributes of one *Zadik** or another. They universally spoke Judeo-German, or Yiddish, which they wrote in Hebrew characters. In dress, they clung with unnecessary conservatism to the fashions of a century or more earlier. Except for a very small minority of well-to-do merchants, their usual occupations were petty trading, innkeeping, and farming the various government monopolies; but a large proportion lived on the edge of destitution, with no means of sustenance whatsoever.[17]

* Literally, a righteous man, but used here to mean the spiritual leader of any of the many Hasidic sects.

From this portrait—marred though it is by an unfortunate touch of condescension—we can easily understand why most Russian Jews did not look to politics at all for any improvement in their condition, let alone for their deliverance from all evil. Strictly Orthodox in their piety and their observance of the commandments, they were quietists in politics who placed their trust and their hopes not in any worldly movement (emphatically including the recently nascent Zionism) but in the Messiah who would be sent by God in His own good time to end their exile and return them to the Holy Land.

There was, however, another group of Russian Jews who were anything but quietists. The members of this group were intellectuals who, like so many Jews in the West before them going back to the early days of the Enlightenment and to the *maskilim,* had rebelled against the religious culture in which they had been reared and who were now swallowing Russian literature as hungrily and as avidly as they had once memorized huge tracts of the Talmud. It was they to whom Count Witte was referring when he complained to Herzl about the large number of Jews involved in the revolutionary movement.

No more than a handful of these intellectuals were attracted to the liberal reformers, if only because Russian liberals were proving to be too weak and ineffectual to make a serious dent in the autocracy. Moreover, the interest of the liberals in ameliorating the Jewish condition was halfhearted at best.

Again like their predecessors in the West, some of these Russian Jewish radicals were mesmerized by the Marxist promise of a world in which there would be "neither Jew nor Greek." Indeed, this applied even to those who for one reason or another were reluctant to shed every last trace of Jewishness. A striking example was one Aaron Lieberman. When he began publishing a socialist paper in Hebrew, he insisted that he was using the language not to propagate anything Jewish (asked to state his religion, he answered, "I am a socialist"), but only as a way of spreading the socialist gospel to Jewish workers.[18] The same justification was offered for the publication of papers in Yiddish by the Jewish Socialist Party, popularly known as the Bund.[19]

Although the Jewish radicals added up to only a tiny segment of the Jewish population as a whole, they do seem to have formed a disproportionately large percentage of the various factions on the Left working to overthrow the Czarist regime, particularly the Bolsheviks, who would eventually succeed in seizing control of the government. Many of these radicals stayed in Russia to carry on the fight, but others (among them members of the Menshevik faction that would lose out to Lenin's victorious Bolsheviks) eventually fled to America. Along with the two million more or less traditionalist Jews who were also making their way to the Golden Land in those years, they would become the immediate ancestors of the great majority of the Jews living in America today. As such, they all played a crucial role in the formation of the political culture of their American descendants—even unto the fourth generation.

But a crucial role would also be played by another tiny minority who fled not to America but to Palestine in the hope of building a new Jewish state in the ancient Land of Israel. Strange as it may seem in retrospect, these Zionists, as they were just beginning to be called, were opposed by most of their fellow Jews, both in Europe and America. The reasons (about which more later) were various, but all the early opponents would have been astonished if they had lived to see the day when the dream of a Jewish state would be realized and would then enlist the passionate political support of all but a very few members of the American Jewish community.

THE GOLDEN LAND

America was, of course, different. For a start, by the time the East European Jews arrived, legal emancipation had long since been achieved. Already in colonial times under the English, the tiny number of Jews in America—they amounted only to about twenty-five hundred in 1776—enjoyed a range of liberties that went far beyond even the fondest dreams of their coreligionists on the European continent. These Jews—a mixture of Sephardim and, after 1720, a larger contingent of Ashkenazim from Central and Eastern Europe—could live anywhere they wished, they could pursue any economic activities they chose, and they could practice their religion without let or hindrance. The one legal disability from which they suffered was strictly political. This generally assumed the form of an oath that had to be sworn as a requirement of holding public office, but whose Christian (or, to be more precise, Protestant) wording made it impossible for Jews to take. Yet not even this exclusionary practice was aimed specifically at the Jews. Its main target was Catholics (a minority in every colony) and members of a different Protestant denomination from the one that dominated a particular colony.

In the mother country of England, the Jews were in a similar condition. They enjoyed much the same range of liberties as in America, and there, too, the prerequisite of an oath (in this case of loyalty to the established Anglican church) prevented them, as well as Catholics, from holding public office. But whereas the oath was amended in 1828 to read "on the true faith of a Christian," so that it would no longer be an obstacle to Catholics, it took a much harder struggle, lasting until 1866, to permit an alternative formula to which Jews could in all good conscience swear.*

On this, America had led the way, almost a century earlier, and only a (relatively) short time after it became independent. In 1786, the state of Virginia, inspired by Thomas Jefferson, adopted an Act to Disestablish the Anglican Church as well as a Statute of Religious Liberty, which provided that "religious opinions and beliefs shall in no wise diminish, enlarge, or affect civil capacities." Georgia, Pennsylvania, and South Carolina soon followed suit. Making these words even more explicit with regard to the exclusionary oath, Article VI, Section 3 of the Federal Constitution (ratified a year later, in 1787) laid it down that "no religious test shall ever be required as a qualification for any office of public trust under the United States."

Finally, with the adoption of the First Amendment in 1791 ("Congress shall make no law respecting an establishment of religion, or prohibiting the free exercise thereof"), the federal government was deprived of the power to favor any religion over another. Even though this did not automatically apply to the individual states, seven of the thirteen shortly followed suit. The six holdouts took longer. In Maryland, for instance, the Christian oath was not abolished until 1824; in North Carolina, it remained on the books until 1868; and in New Hampshire, it was not repealed until 1876. Yet even in these states, the

---

* This was also the case at Oxford and Cambridge, as I would discover at first hand. In 1952, shortly before I was about to graduate from Cambridge, the Senior Tutor of my college informed me that—in accordance with a tradition going back to the time when the colleges of Oxford and Cambridge were monasteries (mine, Clare, had been founded in 1326)—degrees were granted "in the name of the Father, the Son, and the Holy Ghost." Did I—being a Jew—have any objection to this procedure? Taken by surprise, and fearing that I might be causing myself unnecessary trouble, I hesitated before answering yes, but to my great relief he assured me that it was no problem. "We can arrange to have your degree granted 'in the name of the God of all,' which is the formula we also use for our Hindu students."

oath itself had in practice become a dead letter long before being formally made illegal.

In short, in America there was no trace, or any remotely functional equivalent, of the kind of autocratic power that had been one of the two great enemies of the Jews of Europe from time immemorial. In Europe, autocratic governments fought against emancipation and at best extended at their own convenience a degree of toleration that could be, and often was, withdrawn at a moment's notice. But in the democratic republic set up in America, government acted as a bulwark against, and not an enforcer of, any form of legal discrimination against its Jewish citizens.

It was the same with the other and even greater enemy of the Jews of Europe—the Christian churches. In Europe the churches—whether Catholic, Orthodox, or Protestant—could and did institute and enforce anti-Jewish measures. But in America, they had no such power. Even if they had wanted to harm the Jews, their hands would have been tied by the disestablishment clause of the First Amendment, not to mention the facts that Jews were in the country by right rather than on sufferance and that their legal and political status was equal to that of any other American citizen.

But with respect to the Jews, there was another, and in some ways more significant, difference between the Christianity of the European churches and the Christianity of the English Puritans who in the early decades of the seventeenth century settled what later became known as New England.* To put it simply: the Puritans did not share in the relentless and remorseless hostility to the Jews that prevailed in the churches of Europe.

This difference has often been noted, and it has sometimes also been overstated to the point where the Puritans begin to look like the Judaizers of tenth-century Russia who were secretly attracted to

---

* There was a split, going back to the beginnings of the movement, between the Pilgrims, who landed at Plymouth in 1620, and their fellow Puritans, who arrived ten years later. But in spite of the issue that divided the "Separatists," as the later arrivals called the Pilgrims, they did not differ at all in how they interpreted the journey to America and what they had been sent here by God to do. I have therefore made no effort to distinguish between them in the following account.

Judaism. Actually, back in England, before the Puritans were driven out, there were a few who did hold what Cecil Roth tells us were termed "Judaistic opinions." As we learn from Roth, they, too,

> regarded the "old" dispensation as binding, and even reverted
> to its practices of circumcision and the observance of the
> seventh-day Sabbath.

Among them were the

> followers of the Puritan extremist, John Traske, . . . [who] were
> imprisoned in 1618–20 on a charge of Judaizing. In this case, the
> accusation was so far from being exaggerated that a number of
> them settled in Amsterdam and formally joined the synagogue.[1]

Yet unlike these English Judaizers and their precursors in old Russia, the Puritans who came to America were fanatically devout Calvinists to whom conversion to Judaism would have been inconceivable. Still less were they liberals or carriers *avant la lettre* of the modern interreligious spirit.

On the other hand, it is true beyond question that, in sharp contrast to the Christians of Europe, who downplayed the Old Testament and concentrated mainly on the New, the Puritans tended to be more attracted to—and even fixated on—the Old rather than the New. A good measure of this is that, according to the calculation of the historians Paul Masserman and Max Baker,

> fully half of the statutes in the Code of 1655 for the New Haven
> colony contained references to or citations from the Old Testa-
> ment, while only approximately three percent refer to the New
> Testament.[2]

In choosing names for their children, the Puritans also invariably went not to the New Testament but to the Old (Ezra, Enoch, Rachel, and Jonathan were all popular) and they did the same in hitting upon place names: Rehoboth, Goshen, Sharon, Shiloh, Bethesda, Bethany, Zion.

The reason for this special interest in the Old Testament is that the Puritans felt a great affinity with the ancient Children of Israel. What Pharaoh was to the Children of Israel, the English king was to the Puritans; as the Children of Israel had crossed the Red Sea, the Puritans had crossed the Atlantic Ocean; as Canaan was the Promised Land to the Children of Israel, to the Puritans it was America (which they even called New Canaan). As *A Life of Roger Williams,* written in verse by one Romeo Elton, would later have it:

Like Israel's host, to exile driven,
Across the flood the Pilgrims fled;
Their hands bore up the ark of Heaven,
And Heaven their trusting footsteps led,
Till on these savage shores they trod,
And won the wilderness for God.[3]

Finally, like the ancient Israelites, the Puritans made a covenant with God. "If we keep this covenant," said John Winthrop, the first governor of Massachusetts, "we shall find that the God of Israel is among us."[4]

Then there was a memorial prayer that (as the noted scholar Abraham I. Katsh rightly observes) bore an uncanny resemblance to the Haggadah, the book that Jews recite from every year at the festive Passover banquet (the *seder*):

Ought not, and may not the children of these fathers rightly say, our fathers were Englishmen, which came over this great ocean, and were ready to perish in this wilderness; but they cried unto the Lord; and he heard their voice, and looked on their adversity; Let them therefore praise the Lord, because he is good and his mercy endureth for ever; yea, let them who have been redeemed of the Lord, shew how he hath delivered them from the hand of the oppressor, when they wandered in the desert wilderness out of the way, and found no city to dwell in; both hungry and thirsty, their soul was overwhelmed in them. Let them there[fore] confess before the Lord his lovingkindness, and his wonderful works before the children of men.[5]

There was more, much more, of this kind of thing. Thus a Puritan synod declared that "the ways of God towards this His people are in many respects like unto His dealings with Israel of old."[6] Thus, too, in his *History of Plymouth Plantation,* William Bradford, its first governor, likened the migration of the Pilgrims from England to "Moses and the Israelites when they went out of Egypt." The book itself was described as "the Genesis, Exodus, and Joshua of the Colony," and Thomas Prince, Bradford's successor as governor of New Plymouth, compared him to Joshua, who took over leadership upon the death of Moses:

> At such a time and when the condition of this colony was such
> as hath been declared, God was pleased to mind it, even in its
> low estate, and when he had taken unto himself not only our
> Moses, but many of the elders and worthies of our Israel, he
> hath not hitherto left us without a Joshua, to lead us in the
> remaining of our Pilgrimage.[7]

The enormously influential Puritan divine Cotton Mather went Prince one better in identifying John Winthrop with Moses himself:

> Accordingly when the noble design of carrying a colony of
> chosen people into an American wilderness, was by some
> eminent persons undertaken, this eminent person was, by the
> consent of all, chosen for the Moses, who must be the leader of
> so great an undertaking.[8]

This passionate identification with the ancient Israelites colored the Puritans' attitude to the Jews of their own time. It would be a gross exaggeration to say that they became philo-Semitic, but it would not be going too far to say that they helped to create a climate in which it was possible for Jews to feel that they had found a home in America.

Nor did this end with the colonial era. Perry Miller, the great authority on American Puritanism, argues that it came to be

> one of the continuous factors in American life and thought . . .
> because descendants of the Puritans have carried traits of the

Puritan mind into a variety of pursuits and all the way across the continent. Many of these qualities have persisted even though the original creed is lost.[9]

One of these "traits of the Puritan mind" that outlasted the death of the original creed and that influenced "American life and thought" in general was a far more positive attitude toward the Jews than existed anywhere in Christian Europe. For example, Harriet Beecher Stowe (who, by virtue of being the author of *Uncle Tom's Cabin,* was greeted by Abraham Lincoln as the "little woman who wrote the book that started the [Civil] war") once said:

> I think no New Englander, brought up under the regime estab-
> lished by the Puritans, could really estimate how much of
> himself had actually been formed by [his] constant face-to-face
> intimacy with Hebrew literature.[10]

Her own husband, Calvin, was one case in point. A scholar not only of the Hebrew Bible but even of the Talmud (which is written in Aramaic), he habitually wore a skullcap and was referred to by his wife as "my old rabbi."[11] Her grandfather was another such case:

> My grandfather [at family prayers] always prayed standing, and
> the image of his mild, silvery head, leaning over the top of the
> high-backed chair, always rises before me as I think of early
> days. There was no great warmth or fervor in those daily
> exercises, but rather a serious and decorous propriety. They
> were Hebraistic in their form; they spoke of Zion and
> Jerusalem, of the God of Israel, the God of Jacob, as much as if
> my grandfather had been a veritable Jew; and except for the
> closing phrase, "for the sake of Thy Son, our Savior," might all
> have been uttered in Palestine by a well-trained Jew in the time
> of David.[12]

But ideas were not the only thing Harriet Beecher Stowe traced to Jewish influence:

New England, in her earlier days, founding her institutions on the Hebrew Scriptures, bred better Jews than Moses could, because she read Moses with the amendments of Christ. The state of society in some of the districts of Maine, in these days, much resembled in its spirit that which Moses labored to produce in ruder ages. It was entirely democratic, simple, grave, hearty and sincere—solemn and religious in its daily tone, and yet, as to all material good, full of wholesome thrift and prosperity.[13]

Stowe's account finds scholarly confirmation in the work of Katsh:

Most of the official acts of the colonies were determined by the [Hebrew] Scriptures. One of these, the Connecticut Code of 1650, adopted a near Mosaic form of government. Its fifteen Capital Laws, Pentateuchal citations and phraseology are later found in the Massachusetts Code of 1660. The guide of early Connecticut was Thomas Hooker, a man deeply touched by the Bible and its spirit, and called by some "the founder of American democracy." The influence of the [Hebrew] Bible on Hooker is obvious in nearly everything he said or wrote.[14]

Another telling example is the Harvard literary scholar Barrett Wendell, whom the critic Edmund Wilson describes as "the perfect type of old-fashioned snob in regard to every kind of American not of strictly Anglo-Saxon origin." Snob or not, Wendell could write:

I had a queer theory the other day about the Yankee Puritans, whose religious views were so strongly Hebraic. They came chiefly, it seems, from Norfolk and Lincolnshire. These counties, some two or three centuries before the Reformation, had been the chief strongholds of the English Jews, who were finally expelled from the kingdom by one of the Plantagenet kings. At the time of the expulsion, many changed their faith and remained to be absorbed in the native population. It is wholly possible, then, that the Yankee Puritan, with all his Old Testament feeling, was really, without knowing it, largely Jewish in blood. There is in the Yankee nature much that would give color to the theory.[15]

Another New Englander, James Russell Lowell—who is almost entirely forgotten today, but who as a poet, literary critic, and editor was perhaps the leading man of letters during his own lifetime (1819–91)—independently arrived at much the same theory and spelled it out in obsessive detail. Here is how his English friend Leslie Stephen—another great literary figure of the Victorian age who has faded into obscurity—described it:

> [Lowell] was so delighted with his ingenuity in discovering that everybody was in some way descended from the Jews . . . that it was scarcely possible to mention any distinguished man who could not be conclusively proved to be connected with the chosen race.[16]

From an unsigned article that appeared in the *Atlantic Monthly* titled "Conversations with Mr. Lowell," we also get this:

> At the mention of some medieval Jew, Lowell at once began to talk of the Jews, a subject which turned out to be almost a monomania with him. . . . He spoke of their talent and versatility, and of the numbers who had been illustrious in literature, the learned professions, art, science, and even war, until by degrees, from being shut out of society and every honorable and desirable pursuit, they had gained the prominent positions everywhere.[17]

Yet another almost entirely forgotten writer who was well-known in his own day was the poet, playwright, and critic John Jay Chapman. At one point in his life he waxed even more rhapsodic about the Jews than Lowell:

> There is a depth of human feeling in the Jew that no other race ever possessed. We do no more than imitate and follow it. . . .

Compare the Greek—the Chinese, the Roman. These Jews are more human than any other men. It is the cause of the spread of their religion—for we are all adopted into Judah. The heart of the world is Jewish. . . . Their sacred books and chronicles and traditions and history make the annals of every other nation mere rubbish—and I feel this same power in the Jews I know. They are the most humane and the strongest people, mentally and physically. They persist.[18]

JEWS FROM GERMANY

During the years in which Stowe, Wendell, Lowell, and Chapman were forming such attitudes, the Jewish population was growing apace. Up until 1830 it is estimated to have been a paltry 6,000, many of whom were recent immigrants from Germany. But beginning around 1830 and accelerating after 1848, a much larger contingent of Jews from Germany began pouring in. Thanks to this second great wave of immigration to America (and to high birthrates), the Jewish population of America reached some 15,000 by 1840, grew to 150,000 by 1860, and peaked at about 280,000 by 1880 (just on the eve of the third great wave from Eastern Europe that would increase this number by tenfold and more). Meanwhile, says the historian Lloyd Gartner, "U.S. Jewry . . . spoke English with a German accent when it was not speaking its native German."[1]

What drove the German Jews to America? The answer given for the Bavarian Jews by a Leipzig newspaper in 1839 undoubtedly applied to their coreligionists in all other parts of Germany (as well as to the Germanized Jews from Hungary and Bohemia who joined them):

> [In America] one becomes a merchant; i.e., carries on trade in
> the ever-roaming wagons and steamboats, . . . or one carries on
> one, two, three trades. . . . A German is gladly accepted as a

workingman in America; the German Jew is preferred to any other. Thus, hopelessness at home, a secure future overseas, no pressure or persecution of one or another sort lead the Bavarian Israelite to take up the wanderer's staff.[2]

More concrete confirmation was provided by success stories sent back home in letters to relatives and then published in the local papers:

A Jewish journey-man from Bavaria who was ready and willing to work, who traveled through Germany and the neighboring countries for ten years and obtained work only rarely, so that he could not even earn his bread in this way, migrated to North America last summer. Now he has written home to his parents that he has found a place as a journey-man in the house of a baker at Petersburg immediately after his arrival and that he receives 40 florins of wages a month in addition to free board, laundry, and room. Blessed land of freedom and prosperity![3]

A great many of these German Jews did indeed "carry on trade in the ever-roaming wagons" as well as on foot (though only a few, if any, in the steamboats). In thus becoming itinerant peddlers, they were following a trail that had been blazed in colonial times, when Jews set out in covered wagons to sell furs, dry goods, and household items to pioneers living wherever the frontier happened to be at any given moment, and to the Indians as well.

To take the full measure of the courage and grit of these people, one has to bear in mind that most of them were, when they started out, religiously observant (or what we today call Orthodox). This meant not only that they had to carry their phylacteries and prayer shawls and prayer books with them for daily use, but that they had to find ways of adhering to the dietary laws under conditions that made this enormously difficult, kosher butchers not exactly having been a standard feature of the American frontier.

After a while, most gave up trying to observe the dietary laws, but not all. Among the more obdurate was a fur trader in colonial

Philadelphia named Bernard Gratz. As a close student of the subject, the writer Louis Berg, tells us, Gratz

> learned in the absence of a ritual slaughterer to butcher his own meat in the prescribed traditional manner. . . . His brother Michael, on one of many excursions into Indian territory, carried kosher meat (salted) in his pack train.[4]

It was even harder during the Gold Rush of 1848. Berg again:

> Jewish peddlers in the West who tried to keep the faith found the way of the Torah rockier and more thorny than the trail from Sacramento to Carson City. Isadore Schnayder, when long-awaited pictures of his family arrived on the Sabbath, would not cut the string until nightfall. Abraham Rackovsky sent to Denver for kosher meat, but it spoiled in transit: he turned vegetarian.

But the vast majority of even these hardy souls, adds Berg, found

> strict Orthodoxy too much to carry on backs already overburdened. Some . . . were lucky enough, in time, to find Christian girls to marry—to which circumstance we owe Barry Goldwater, grandson of Big Mike Goldwasser, peddler and saloon-keeper.[5]

When, as would inevitably happen, these peddlers (among them an 1848 immigrant named Levi Strauss, the inventor of jeans) decided to stop traveling and settle down in a particular place, great retail establishments and factories would soon be built by and around them. This was how so many department stores all over America acquired identifiably Jewish names, even if most later came to be owned by descendants who converted to Christianity or were absorbed into larger conglomerates.

More astonishing yet, a number of American cities originated as trading posts set up by such peddlers. One of these, Abraham Mordecai—

who, believing that the Indians were descended from the Ten Lost Tribes of Israel, threw off the "yoke" of Jewish law, went native, and married an Indian girl—was actually the founding father of Montgomery, Alabama, cradle city of the Southern Confederacy.[6]

Like the Jews who preceded them as far back as colonial times, the new arrivals from Germany soon came to feel that they had found a home in America. And why not? According to Gartner, in addition to the complete absence of political disabilities,

> the decades between 1820 and 1860 were a period of broad freedom and social acceptance in America. . . . Of actual anti-Semitism there was very little.[7]

But of economic opportunity there was a very great deal. Many, if not most, of the peddlers and storekeepers who started with next to nothing became more and more prosperous, to the point where some amassed enough capital to become bankers, and very rich ones at that.

A good example of the process was the Seligman brothers. The oldest, Joseph (1819–80), emigrated from Bavaria in 1837 at the age of eighteen. After working for a while in a small mining town in Pennsylvania, he sent for his brothers and together they went peddling dry goods, first in Pennsylvania, then in Alabama and Missouri. By 1846 they had settled down in New York, where they went into business as wholesale clothiers. Two years later, with the Gold Rush in full swing, they presciently set up shop in San Francisco, where they had no competition in the sale of clothing and were paid in gold. From there it was a short step into banking and in the fullness of time to the financing of railroad construction, the Panama Canal, and many industrial firms like General Motors and Republic Iron and Steel.

Marcus Goldman, who left Bavaria for America in 1848 at the age of twenty-seven, and who later founded the investment banking firm of Goldman Sachs, also started as a peddler. So did Meyer Guggenheim, who arrived in the same year at the age of twenty. In his case the route out of peddling led not to Wall Street but first to a business dealing in stuff he had previously peddled from a wagon and then ultimately to the purchase of silver, lead, and copper mines, leaving the Guggenheim family wealthy beyond the dreams of avarice.

As the name of Andrew Carnegie reminds us, it was not only Jewish immigrants who made such rags-to-riches journeys. Nor, as the name of Rothschild reminds us, were Jewish bankers unknown to Europe (indeed, some—including Warburg and also Kuhn, Loeb—now set up shop in New York), and there were rich Jewish merchants as well. But in Europe these were all special cases attributable to special circumstances. Nowhere was there anything remotely approaching the range and availability of opportunities that were open to Jews in America; and nowhere in Europe were so many Jews able to take advantage of them.

The Civil War also played a part. An estimated ten thousand Jews served—seven thousand in the North and three thousand in the South—and more than five hundred of them lost their lives. At the same time, others were able to share in the prosperity the war brought to the North. Given the heavy representation of Jews in the clothing business, they were perfectly positioned to supply the huge demand for army uniforms (which is how the ready-made clothing industry was born). Jewish banking firms also did well both for themselves and for the Union in helping to finance its wartime needs. The Seligmans in particular made an even greater contribution through their success in selling Union bonds on the European market.[8]

After the war, Jews at the bottom rung of the economic ladder, retracing the early steps of their now-wealthy coreligionists, went south to try their luck as peddlers and as often as not wound up as storekeepers. Gartner:

> One contemporary attributed part of their success to the habit
> they had of addressing Black customers as "Mister" rather than
> by given name.[9]

For the Jews, then, America was beyond all doubt a "blessed land of liberty and prosperity." They were free and equal in the political realm, and no less free to take as much advantage of the economic system as their energies and talents allowed. But where the other more elusive goal of emancipation was concerned—social acceptance and complete integration into the surrounding world—the German Jews were discovering that America was not so different from Europe as they had imagined. It was a discovery that would have important implications for the story I am trying to tell in this book.

11

ANTI-SEMITISM, PATRICIAN STYLE

For the most part, the uglier passions of Protestant America had always fed not on the Jews but on the Catholics. In fact, hatred and fear of Catholics went all the way back to the same Puritans whose attitude toward them was the polar antithesis of their feelings about the Jews. Thus a ditty children were taught to sing by the *New England Primer* of 1688 instructed them to

> *Abhor that arrant Whore of Rome,*
> *And all her blasphemies;*
> *And drink not of her cursed cup,*
> *Obey not her decrees.*[1]

This current of anti-Catholicism remained ever present in American culture, but it did not burst into flame until masses of immigrants from Ireland began pouring into the country—especially after 1845, when a terrible famine hit Ireland that ended by killing about a million people and by driving nearly two million of the survivors to America.* At

---

* As it happens, the single largest national group of immigrants in the nineteenth century was not the Irish (or the Jews) but the Italians, all of whom were Catholics. Yet for some reason, anti-Catholic sentiment seems to have been focused mainly on the Irish.

that time, the anti-Catholic case was based not, as with the Puritans, on theological differences but on the conviction that their loyalty to the pope and the authoritarianism of their Church made it impossible for them ever to develop into good democratic American citizens. Catholicism, declared the American Protestant Association, was "subversive of civil and religious liberty," and George Bancroft, the preeminent American historian of the day, was certain that "the one will of the Pope rules the creed, the politics, the conduct of all [Catholics]" and that this "malign influence" extended to the United States.[2]

Still, enough room was left in nativist hearts for anti-Jewish sentiment as well. It all started during the Civil War, when there was an eruption of the kind of anti-Semitism that had hardly existed in America before. At first it took the form of accusations of war profiteering, and from there it progressed to the rediscovery and revival of the old familiar canard that the loyalty of the Jews was to one another and not to the United States—or as it was generally put in Europe, that they were "a nation within a nation."

The irony was that the German Jews, as though launching a series of preemptive strikes against this very charge, had been doing their best to show that they were Americans first and Jewish (if at all) only second. The first generation may have spoken English with a German accent, but their native-born children emerged from the free public schools with the accents and manners of old-stock American Protestants. (Not for nothing were these supposedly neutral public schools accused of actually being Protestant parochial schools by the Catholics, who refused to send their children to them.)

All of which is to say that, like their forebears of the *Haskalah* in Europe, many German Jews were willing, and even eager, to purchase social acceptance at the price of erasing obvious signs of Jewishness from the way they lived—and the way they worshipped as well. Hence the German Jews of that period went to extraordinary lengths to make their religion look and sound as much like Protestantism as it possibly could without actually crossing the line into Christianity.

Back in Germany itself, a Reform movement had recently arisen to modernize Judaism, which entailed radical changes both in doctrine and in practice. Transplanted to America, this movement was even more extreme than the prevailing German version. In Germany an effort (admittedly not a very vigorous one) was made to retain certain traditions of practice and liturgy while introducing "Western standards of aesthetics and decorum" into the synagogue. But in the Reform "temples" of America—often designed to resemble Protestant churches—Hebrew was almost entirely replaced by English, organs were introduced, women were seated with men, and heads were not only permitted but required to be uncovered. The leading such temple was Emanu-El in New York, whose assistant rabbi, Judah L. Magnes, once reported:

> A prominent Christian lawyer of another city has told me that
> he entered this building at the beginning of a service on Sunday
> morning and did not discover that he was in a synagogue until a
> chance remark of the preacher betrayed it.*[3]

As for doctrine, the authoritative Declaration of Principles formulated by the Pittsburgh Platform of 1885 included the following points:[4]

> We hold that all such Mosaic and rabbinical laws as regu-
> late diet, priestly purity, and dress, originated in ages and
> under the influence of ideas altogether foreign to our present
> mental and spiritual state. They fail to impress the modern Jew
> with a spirit of priestly holiness; their observance in our days
> is apt rather to obstruct than to further modern spiritual
> elevation.
>
> We recognize, in the modern era of universal culture of heart
> and intellect, the approaching of the realization of Israel's great
> messianic hope for the establishment of the kingdom of truth,
> justice, and peace among all men. We consider ourselves no
> longer a nation, but a religious community, and therefore expect
> neither a return to Palestine, nor a sacrificial worship under the

---

* Magnes did not last long at Emanu-El, since he shifted toward a more traditionalist Judaism and was a Zionist to boot. Eventually he moved to Palestine,
where he was mainly responsible for the establishment of the Hebrew University,
of which he became the first chancellor and later president.

sons of Aaron, nor the restoration of any of the laws concerning the Jewish state.[5]

Translated into less exalted terms, the Pittsburgh Platform decreed that all traditionally binding beliefs and practices that separated or distinguished Jews from the surrounding society were to be abandoned, along with any trace of the idea that the Jews were a nation. To be retained by them as a strictly "religious community" were a number of customs and ceremonies but especially moral laws that might have originated with Judaism but that were now so universally accepted as no longer to be identifiably Jewish.

What more, they might reasonably have asked, could anyone want of us by way of proof that we were more American than Jewish? Yet as they were soon to discover, in America no more than in Europe would a very high degree of assimilation necessarily guarantee full social acceptance. This became clear when, in 1876, the banker Joseph Seligman—who a few years earlier had been offered (and had declined) the post of secretary of the Treasury by President Ulysses S. Grant—was turned away from a hotel in the resort town of Saratoga. Other hotels also adopted an open "no Jews allowed" policy, as did many private clubs and country clubs. It was around this time, too, that elite schools and colleges began to institute quotas limiting the number of Jews who could be admitted.

Again as in Europe, where the aristocracy was the major secular force blocking the full acceptance of the Jews into society, so it was turning out to be in America. Here, of course, there was no aristocracy in the strict sense of the term, but there was a functional equivalent in the upper echelons of the Wasp patriciate. Within those precincts, anti-Semitic ideas—including the one that portrayed the Jews as engaged in a conspiracy to take over the whole world—had begun to circulate in the years after the Civil War, and they fed and justified the exclusionary practices that were becoming more and more common.

Since philo-Semitism has often turned into its opposite, it is less curious than it may seem that the anti-Semitic pack was joined even by a few members of the American patriciate who had originally been, or even still professed to be, great admirers of the Jews. For example, after giving vent to his veritable awe of the Jews in his interview with the anonymous reporter from the *Atlantic Monthly,* James Russell Lowell was unable to leave it at that:

> Finally [Lowell] came to a stop, but not to a conclusion, and as no one else spoke, I said, "And when the Jews have got absolute control of finance, the army and navy, the press, diplomacy, society, titles, the government, and the earth's surface, what do you suppose they will do with them and with us?" "That," he answered, turning toward me . . . "that is the question which will eventually drive me mad."[6]

"Though Lowell admired the Jews," the critic Edmund Wilson rightly observes in commenting on this passage,

> he conceived them as a power so formidable that they seemed on the verge of becoming a menace. In this vision of a world run entirely by Jews there is something of morbid suspicion, something of the state of mind that leads people to believe in the *Protocols of Zion,* in a Jewish international conspiracy to dominate the civilized world.[7]

As for John Jay Chapman, the near-worshipful philo-Semitism of his younger days gave way in later years to its exact opposite. As though in response to Lowell's fear of Jewish domination, he wrote:

> Life is a simple matter to [the Jews]: a bank account and the larder. No, they will never rule the world. . . . They strike me as an inferior race, in spite of their great advantages. . . . These people don't know anything. They have no religion, no customs except eating and drinking.[8]

On this passage, too, Wilson gets it right:

> Note here again the specter of Jewish power. As Chapman watches a crowd of Jews behaving in a perfectly natural way, he

concludes that they will not "rule the world." Why should he have expected them to?—and why should he be surprised that these citizens from Philadelphia show an interest in their larders and their bank accounts? Do Americans of other stocks not give evidence of similar interests?[9]

Perceptive as Wilson's analysis is, however, it falls short by failing to recognize that in general, and not just in an individual case like Chapman's, attributing common human vices or unattractive qualities exclusively to Jews alone has always been a key anti-Semitic tactic.

But the most anti-Semitic of them all was also the most aristocratic of them all: Henry Adams. The direct descendant of two American presidents (John Adams was his great-grandfather and John Quincy Adams his grandfather), this brilliant and bitter writer, historian, and intellectual was given to anti-Semitic outbursts so frenzied and obsessive that even some of his friends, though not exactly philo-Semites themselves, were taken aback. One of them was John Hay, who had been Abraham Lincoln's private secretary and ultimately became secretary of state in the McKinley administration. Adams, he once said, was "clean daft" on the subject of the Jews:

> [He] believes the earthquake at Krakatoa was the work of Zola
> and when he saw Vesuvius reddening the midnight air he
> searched the horizon to find a Jew stoking the fire.*[10]

Henry Adams's brother, Brooks Adams, shared the same paranoid fantasy of Jewish power, extending even to the totally unfounded notion that the great financier J. Pierpont Morgan was Jewish:

> I tell you Rome was a blessed garden of paradise beside the
> rotten, unsexed, swindling, lying Jews, represented by Pierpont
> Morgan and the gang who have been manipulating the country
> for the last few years.[11]

---

* Hay did not mean that *he* thought Zola was a Jew, though to Adams the role played by the French novelist in the Dreyfus case (see chapter 13) evidently was enough to make him Jewish (so to speak) by association.

Henry Adams himself was no less violent in his hatred of the Jews than his brother:

> I detest [the Jews], and everything connected with them, and I live only and solely with the hope of seeing their demise, with all their accursed Judaism. I want to see all the lenders at interest taken out and executed.[12]

Or again:

> I am myself more than ever at odds with my time. I detest it and everything that belongs to it, and live only in the wish to see the end of it, with all its infernal Jewry.[13]

And yet again:

> The Jew has got into the soul. I see him—or her—now everywhere, and wherever he—or she—goes, there must remain a taint in the blood forever.[14]

Adams, as will soon become clear, had plenty of company among the patrician intellectuals of the period in believing that the Jews represented a veritably diabolical threat to the purity of the American bloodstream. But it was yet another gauge of how different America truly was that only in Europe could and would this kind of obsessive malevolence ultimately be acted upon.

JEWS WITHOUT MONEY

From reading the outbursts of Lowell and Adams, one might have thought that all Jews everywhere in the world were either bankers or industrialists. But the truth was that the vast majority were poor and powerless. And it was precisely Jews like these from Eastern Europe who were already on the way to swamping their more prosperous German coreligionists. Between 1881 and 1892, 190,000 arrived; between 1892 and 1903, another 370,000; and between 1903 and 1914 (when the outbreak of World War I enforced a temporary halt), about 900,000. Immigration resumed after the war, and from then until the gates were closed in 1924, the total rose to more than two million.

Confronted with this development, the American counterpart of the anti-Jewish aristocratic European could now add, to the social and political menace represented by rich Jews, the cultural threat posed by poor ones. Chapman:

> A New York boy who goes away to boarding school returns to
> a new world at each vacation. He finds perhaps on his return
> from boarding school, that the streets where he and his compan-
> ions used to play ball is given over to a migration of Teutons.
> When he turns from college, the Teutons have vanished and

given place to Italians. When he reaches the Law school, behold, no more Italians—Polish Jews to the horizon's verge.[1]

When he wrote these words, Chapman was not yet as virulently hostile as he would later become to the foreigners who had been taking over his hometown. Like many opponents of immigration then and now, however, he did believe that only a homogeneous society could produce a truly high level of civilization. Perhaps the most forceful statement of the case for this belief was made in 1906 by Prescott F. Hall, founder of the Immigration Restriction League:

> It must be remembered . . . that . . . our institutions were
> established by a relatively homogeneous community, consisting
> of the best elements of population selected by the circumstances
> under which they came to the new world. Today, much of our
> immigration is an artificial selection by the transportation of the
> worst elements of European and Asiatic peoples. If the founders
> of the nation had been of recent types, can we suppose for a
> moment that this country would enjoy its present civilization?[2]

Hall was not speaking here only of the Jews, but he surely would have agreed with Chapman, who also feared that American culture would be debased by the new immigrants, that the greatest danger came from the Yiddish-speaking "Polish" (i.e., East European) Jews among them.

The same worry afflicted even so large-minded and cosmopolitan a product of the American patriciate as the novelist Henry James. In 1905, James, who had long been living abroad, returned for his first visit in more than twenty years. While in New York, he was taken on a tour of the Lower East Side of Manhattan. As he crossed into the Jewish section—the "New Jerusalem"—he became aware of "the extent of the Hebrew conquest of New York," which struck him as "a great swarming":

> There is no swarming like that of Israel when once Israel has got
> a start, and the scene here bristled, at every step, with the signs

and sounds, immitigable, unmistakable, of a Jewry that had
burst all bounds.[3]

Then, sitting in the Café Royale, which was a gathering place of
Yiddish-speaking writers and actors, he fancied that in these "torture
rooms of the living idiom" he could hear the "Accent of the Future,"
and he was certain that, by the time these people got through with the
English language, "whatever we shall know it for, . . . we shall not
know it for English."[4] This did not elicit any serious anti-Semitic
reflections in James, as it would in Chapman. The worst James could
manage was expressed through a slightly sinister question he asked
himself: "Who can ever tell . . . in any conditions, . . . what the genius
of Israel may, or may not, really be 'up to'?"[5] Little did he suspect that
what the genius of Israel had in store for the English language and its
literature was, among other things, the production of a goodly number
of offspring who within a mere fifty years would be busy writing doc-
toral dissertations on, precisely, the novels of Henry James.

Like their European counterparts who dreamed of restoring the
ancien régime, all these American aristocrats were upholders of an old
order of their own. Speaking of his father's generation, Edmund Wilson writes:

> The period after the Civil War—both banal in a bourgeois way
> and fantastic with gigantic fortunes—was a difficult one for
> Americans brought up in the old tradition. . . . They had been
> educated at Exeter and Andover and at eighteenth-century
> Princeton, and had afterwards been trained, like their fathers,
> for what had once been called the learned professions, but they
> had then had to deal with a world in which this kind of educa-
> tion and the kind of ideals it served no longer really counted
> for much.[6]

To the European aristocracy, one of the sorrier consequences of the
overthrow of the ancien régime was the emancipation and empower-
ment of the Jews; and to the American patriciate of the Gilded Age it
seemed that the Jews were also the prime beneficiaries of the woeful

changes that were ruining America. At one end of the scale, the rich among them, with their "fantastic fortunes," were "the gang that was manipulating America" (never mind that most members of this "gang" were no more Jewish than Pierpont Morgan); at the other end, the newly arrived immigrants were serving as a base for the political machines in the big cities that were corrupting American political life (never mind that it was the Irish and not the Jews who controlled these machines and that the East European immigrants did not even get involved in local politics until much later).*

The upshot is that in America, as in Europe, it was the conservative upholders of the old order who were hostile to the Jews, whether they were rich or poor and whether they had immigrated from Germany or from Eastern Europe.

Like the German Jews before them, the East Europeans came to America not only to escape persecution but also (and, in the case of those who lived under the Hapsburgs rather than the Romanovs, mainly) to find their way out of poverty. It has sometimes been said that they thought there was "gold in the streets" in America, but what they really meant when they called America the "golden land" was that opportunities existed there that were entirely beyond their reach in Russia and the like of which were scarce even under the Hapsburgs.

This did indeed turn out to be true in the relatively short run for those who—following in the footsteps of the German-Jewish peddlers we have already looked at—had the grit and the energy to get out of New York and venture into the American hinterland. But the single largest group of the new immigrants were in some crude Darwinian sense less fit for survival in America. It was as though all the venturesomeness they had in them had been used up in mobilizing the nerve to leave home, often in defiance of their fathers (who rightly feared that they would cease being religiously observant once they got the chance);

---

* "Immigrant Jews," writes the literary and social critic Irving Howe in *World of Our Fathers* ([New York: New York University Press, 2004], p. 368), "having an elaborate network of social services of their own, were [not] as dependent as other immigrant groups on the ministrations of Tammany . . . Only when immigrant Jews started moving outward in large numbers, toward the business and professional centers of the city, could Tammany be of crucial help as a link to agencies of power."

then making their arduous way to the port of Hamburg or Bremen in Germany, or Rotterdam or Amsterdam in Holland, or Antwerp in Belgium; and then enduring the trip over the ocean in steerage. The experience of steerage alone left them, said the historian Oscar Handlin,

> exhausted—worn out physically by lack of rest, by poor food, by the constant strain of close, cramped quarters, worn out emotionally by the succession of new situations that had crowded upon them.[7]

And so they stayed put where they landed, huddling together in a latter-day ghetto on the Lower East Side of Manhattan and clinging to one another for dear life. Their children and grandchildren would in time prove that the "golden land" was no myth, but they themselves remained stuck in the working class, where in their material circumstances they fared little better, and sometimes worse, than they had in Europe.

The Jews who left New York, on the other hand, were rewarded for the chance they had been brave enough to take. Most of them settled in cities like Chicago, Philadelphia, Rochester, Baltimore, and Cleveland, where they also lived in ghettolike slum neighborhoods, but—thanks to the enterprise that went with their energy—many even of the first generation managed to open stores and start other small businesses. They thus succeeded in climbing out of poverty more quickly and in greater numbers than the relatives and fellow townspeople they had left behind on the Lower East Side of New York.

There, in an area of less than two square miles, lived several hundred thousand of these relatives and townspeople. A typical example of the filthy tenements into which they were crammed "like sardines in a box," with no hot water and inadequate toilet and bathing facilities, was described by an investigator from the New York Association for Improving the Conditions of the Poor:

> In [room] No. 76 a peddler lives, with his wife and four small children. The rooms, like the rest of this floor, are very dirty. In a corner next to these rooms a pile of garbage about two feet

high lies, right at the head of the stairs as you go up. The
children on this floor are very poorly clad . . . nothing but a
loose gown and no underclothing at all.[8]

Most of the Jewish inhabitants of such rooms emerged every morning to work as cutters and pressers in the "needle trades" in which
ready-made clothes were produced. The hours were long (sixty or even
seventy a week), the pay was low, and conditions were perhaps even
fouler than the rooms in which the workers lived. The reformer Jacob
Riis rode the Second Avenue Elevated "through the sweaters' district"
and reported that

every open window of the big tenements that stand like a
continuous brick wall on both sides of the way, give . . . a
glimpse of one of these shops. . . . Men and women bending
over their machines or ironing clothes at the window, half-
naked. . . . Morning, noon, or night, it makes no difference.[9]

"Was this sweated labor?" asks Paul Johnson, in his history of the
Jews, and his answer is that of course it was. But, he goes on,

it was also the great engine of social mobility. . . . By their
needles, too, the eastern Jews pushed their way into independence and respect.[10]

This was undoubtedly true of a substantial minority. Irving Howe, in
his World of Our Fathers, cites two examples:

Samuel Silverman, beginning as a sweatshop worker, became a
cloak manufacturer with a fortune estimated at $500,000. . . .
Israel Lebowitz moved from peddling to a modest "gents
furnishing shop" on Orchard Street and by 1907 was one of the
largest shirt manufacturers in New York.

Tracing a rather different path of upward mobility was Joseph Barondess.

Beginning as a cloakmaker in 1888, when he earned five dollars a week for thirteen hours a day, six days a week, Barondess catapulted himself into union leadership.[11]

But the best the great majority of the Jews working in the needle trades could hope for was much more modest improvements in their condition, and it was only through the revival of a previously moribund Jewish labor movement—and the International Ladies Garment Workers Union (ILGWU) in particular—that this was achieved.

The early history of the Jewish labor movement was marked by complicated factional fights. But for the purposes of the story I am trying to tell, the point to bear in mind is that all the early leaders of this movement were Marxists who had brought their ideological convictions from Russia to America. Some were more orthodox in their Marxism and more radical in their commitment to socialism than others, but to every one of them, labor unions were a weapon in a war whose ultimate objective was the overthrow of capitalism.

In this they were at odds with Samuel Gompers, the founder and president of the American Federation of Labor (AFL) from 1886 until his death in 1924. Gompers was Jewish, and though he had no great love for capitalism, he was no socialist. On the contrary: he passionately opposed the socialist idea that it was impossible to improve the condition of the working class under capitalism, and he was equally passionate in rejecting the contention of the socialists that the workers in whose name they presumed to speak shared their ideological objectives. What the workers wanted, he famously said, was "More," and so far as he was concerned, the job of the labor movement was to get it for them. This meant building strong unions, not as a first step in the overthrow of capitalism, but in order to force employers to bargain with them and thus to compromise with the demand of their employees for higher wages, shorter hours, and better working conditions.

The socialist leaders of the Jewish labor movement regarded collective bargaining as a form of collaboration with the enemy. Yet in the first decade of the twentieth century, they themselves, under the irresistible pressure of certain events, began engaging in it, and it was only then that their movement rose from its deathbed and sprang to life.

But far from acknowledging that this meant that Gompers was right and that they had been wrong, they continued preaching the socialist gospel with scarcely diminished fervor. Hence they looked for and found ways to persuade themselves that abandoning class warfare for collective bargaining did not mean that they were being untrue to socialism.

This explains why in 1917 they greeted the overthrow of the czar and the seizure of power in Russia by the Bolsheviks with wild enthusiasm. For the doubts that some of them had secretly been entertaining about the chances for a socialist future in America were now, Irving Howe tells us, swept away by the sight of

> a working-class state [being] proclaimed in the most backward country of Europe. . . . This seemed radiant evidence that the victory of socialism was at hand.[12]

Thus it was a that a new faction now arose within the socialist movement in America—the Communists. According to Howe,

> the number of card-carrying Jewish Communists in the early twenties was small, [but] their influence in the Jewish labor movement was large. A militant segment of needle-trade workers responded with enthusiasm to the call of Lenin; the majority of left-wing Jewish writers, intellectuals, and speakers faced left.[13]

Within a few short years, however, and largely as the result of a bitter and utterly ruthless fight waged by the Communists for control of the garment unions, they lost the sympathy and the sense of comradeship originally felt for them by old-line socialist leaders of the Jewish labor movement like David Dubinsky (president of the International Ladies Garment Workers Union from 1932 until his death in 1982). From then on and forever after, the likes of Dubinsky would become the most fervent anti-Communists in America. To this the Communists would reciprocate with an undying hatred of the socialists.

In the context of our story, nothing is more suggestive than the fact that in the wake of the split with the Communists, the socialists—the socialists!—were generally described on the Left (even by analysts who sided with them) as "right wing." For anything to their right was simply off the radar. Soon the Communists were going even further. A song composed in the early thirties by an anonymous wit (with instructions that it be sung with a Yiddish accent) parodied the line the Communists took in the ultra-Left days of the "Third Period" (1929–34) when all non-Communist socialists were "social fascists":

> Oh, the cloakmakers' union is a no-good union,
> It's a company union of the bosses.
> The right-wing cloakmakers and the Socialist fakers
> Are making by the workers double crosses.
> And the Hillquits and Dubinskys and the Thomases
> Are making by the workers false promises,
> They preach Socialism, but they practice Fascism
> To preserve Capitalism by the bosses.
> Hoo Ha!

Well, they were certainly not practicing fascism, but neither were they practicing the socialism they preached. It was even true that what they were actually doing in the thirties was helping to preserve capitalism while still harboring the Marxist idea that it was doomed to collapse of its own "internal contradictions" or by being forcibly overthrown.

To be more precise, it was Dubinsky and the other "old guard" unionists who helped "preserve capitalism" by joining Franklin D. Roosevelt's New Deal coalition. Abraham Cahan, the enormously influential editor of the largest Yiddish-language daily, the *Forward*, and a supporter of Dubinsky's position, quipped that (as Irving Howe paraphrases it),

> Roosevelt ought to take out a card in the Socialist Party, so strongly was he carrying through proposals that Socialists had always favored; while the [Norman] Thomas wing [of the Socialist Party] . . . saw the New Deal as a patchwork meant to save a sick and unjust social system.[14]

So far as the workers themselves were concerned, it was Dubinsky all the way. Most of them cared less, if at all, about ideology than about improving their lot. They might nod piously at the socialist rhetoric that the leadership kept spouting, and they might even vote for a socialist candidate in a local election, but it was higher wages, shorter hours, and better working conditions they were after, not the overthrow of capitalism. So long as the union was able to produce such improvements, their loyalty to it made perfect sense, as did their opposition to the antilabor forces of the Right—both of which sentiments went deep enough to last them for the rest of their lives.

But let me return now to Europe, where developments were unfolding that would do infinitely more than the antilabor forces of the Right—more, indeed, than anything since the Middle Ages—to confirm Jews in the belief that the entire right side of the political spectrum was enemy territory.

EMANCIPATION: THE BACKLASH

By far the most important of these developments, of course, took place in 1932, when the Nazis behind Adolf Hitler came to power in Germany. For here, in the country that had given birth to the Jewish Enlightenment; the country so many Jews, and not Jews alone, regarded as the most civilized and the most highly cultured in the world; the country whose Jewish population had not only been fully emancipated in the legal and political sense but had attained to greater prominence in every field of endeavor than anywhere else in Europe: here, in Germany of all places, an openly and poisonous anti-Semitic party had taken over the government and had, moreover, done so not by a coup or a *putsch* but through a democratic election.

True, Hitler had won only about a third of the vote, but that was cold comfort when set against the horrifying fact that a large enough number of Germans had backed him to make the Nazis the largest party in the Reichstag and thereby to force his appointment as the head of a coalition government. And to make the situation even more horrifying, when, shortly after becoming chancellor, he seized on a staged pretext to demand that the Reichstag allow him to suspend the constitution, two-thirds of the deputies acceded, enabling him to turn what had been an exemplary democracy into a dictatorship in which he soon enjoyed absolute power.

Jews everywhere were amazed by this succession of events. But in retrospect, we can see that Nazi triumph did not come out of the blue. On the contrary: the takeover of a major European country by a party whose platform called for the revocation of the civil rights of Jews, and by a leader whose speeches and writings promised even worse to follow, signified not the beginning of a new era but rather the culmination of the third period in the history of Jewish emancipation.

To recapitulate: the first period covered the 150 years leading up to the French Revolution (1640–1789), and the second, lasting about ninety years (1789–1878), was marked by the achievement through fits and starts of emancipation throughout Western and Central Europe. In the third period, which got under way in 1878, further progress was made in the extension of emancipation to Eastern Europe.

In each of these periods the opposition to granting legal equality to the Jews was based on a different rationale. Life being messier than analytic divisions, there was considerable overlapping, with the rationale of one period spilling over into and coexisting with the next. Nevertheless, it remains the case that each period came up with a prevailing justification suitable to the temper of its time until the climate of opinion began to change, at which point there was a gradual shift into a more relevant rationale.

At the start of the first period, the prevailing justification, left over from the Middle Ages, was religious: the Jew was debarred from equal treatment simply by virtue of the fact that he was not a Christian. But as creeping secularization began undermining the religious rationale, a new one, political in nature, was developed that would ultimately take precedence (without, however, entirely dislodging the religious objection). Now Jews were to be denied equal treatment because they were an unassimilable minority—"a nation within a nation." But by the time the second period ended, the political objection—even in de facto collaboration with the religious one in those circles where "nation" meant "Christian nation"—had proved itself unable to prevent full legal emancipation from being enacted everywhere in Western and Central Europe. In spite of this failure, the political rationale remained very much alive even while pride of place was being given to yet a third rationale that was more suited to the times: that the Jews were neither a religious community nor a nation but a race.

In the late nineteenth century (as witness the claims of the Marxists, the Freudians, and the social Darwinians), a theory needed to be deemed scientific before it could win widespread acceptance—and so it was with the racism that became the latest and most up-to-date basis for opposition to, or rather rollback of, Jewish emancipation. According to this new theory (bolstered by such putatively scientific techniques as phrenology), race trumped all other factors in determining the characteristics of a people, and these characteristics were unalterable. There was also a hierarchy of races, and the Semitic one to which the Jews belonged was vastly inferior to the "Aryan" or "Indo-European" race to which the nations of northern Europe belonged.

Even before the unfolding of the horrendous consequences that this theory would generate under the Nazis, it spelled more trouble for the Jews than the religious or political justifications for opposing emancipation. Under the religious dispensation, Jews could at least free themselves from their miserable condition by converting to Christianity; and under the political dispensation they could try to assimilate to the point where they became indistinguishable from everyone else. But under the new racist dispensation, permanently locked as the Jews were into the genetic prison of the Semitic race, there was literally nothing they could do to make themselves acceptable to the Aryan world. (Being Jewish, said the great French novelist Marcel Proust, himself the son of a Jewish mother, was "an incurable disease."*)

In 1879, at the very onset of the third period, a journalist named Wilhelm Marr, the author of an influential pamphlet entitled *The Victory of Judaism over Germandom, Considered from a Non-Religious Point of View*, founded the first popular political organization devoted entirely to defending "Germandom" from the Jewish threat. He called it "The League of Anti-Semites." Because this previously unknown term jibed so well with the new racism, it immediately caught on and became the name of choice for the many anti-Jewish organizations and

---

* The same remark has been attributed to Heinrich Heine.

political parties that followed, as well as for the movement of which they were the constituent parts.

No less a personage than the most eminent historian of the day, Heinrich Treitschke, lent himself to this movement. "The Jews," he said in a phrase that became one of its main slogans, "are our misfortune." Merging the older political rationale with the new racism, Treitschke charged that the Jews refused to assimilate into German society and that this was leading to the creation of a "mongrel" German-Jewish culture. An even greater emphasis on the racial factor was placed by the German philosopher and economist Karl Eugen Dühring, who did not shrink from drawing the conclusion to which the idea of the Jews as an incorrigibly inferior race logically led (and to which Adolf Hitler would carry it in practice): the only way to solve the "Jewish question," he wrote, was "by killing and extirpation."[1]

Still, not even many of the new racist anti-Semites were yet ready to go that far. Around this time, the first International Congress of Anti-Semites was convened in Dresden, and the most it could do was call on "the governments and peoples of the Christian countries which are in danger because of Jewry" to unite in one "international Christian alliance" to fight off the Semitic menace. Then, at the second meeting of the Congress, there was a move to make Dühring its patron saint ("the racial theory of the greatest thinker in the world is the rock on which Jewry will be dashed to pieces"), but it ran into the opposition of retrograde anti-Semites who were still stuck in the old dispensations and who were unwilling to give them up in favor of an exclusive reliance on the new racist ideology.[2]

Hence most of them devoted themselves to trying to undo what they had failed to prevent before. One such effort was a petition, mounted in 1881, that demanded

> the closing of Germany to Jewish immigration, the dismissal of Jews from posts involving administrative authority, and the separate registration of Jews in all statistical surveys.[3]

It garnered a quarter of a million signatures. Some years later, a call for war "on the destructive Jewish influence over our national life" issued from the ruling Conservative Party, which reluctantly took this position in order to fend off political competition from the increasingly popular anti-Semitic parties. And when, still later, the Anglo-German racist Houston Stewart Chamberlain (son-in-law of the rabidly anti-Semitic composer Richard Wagner) published a book purporting to prove that the Jews were a "mongrel race" whose very existence constituted a crime against humanity, it sold several hundred thousand copies. We learn from Ettinger that even the kaiser (who had at one time deplored the excesses of anti-Semitic propaganda)

> read it aloud to his children and proposed that it be included in the program of studies in officer cadet schools.[4]

Because the new anti-Semitic movement originated in enlightened Germany, it lent legitimacy to opponents of Jewish emancipation everywhere who had been derided as backward by liberal opinion. This was the argument made in 1881 by Ivan Aksakov, a leader of the Slavophiles in Russia (who, like Treitschke, melded the new racist rationale with an older justification—in his case the religious rather than the political):

> The anti-Semitic movement, this anti-Semitic alliance created recently in Germany, in the country which leads European culture, is not the outcome of religious intolerance, crude ignorance, reaction, etc., as our naive "liberals" think. It is a characteristic feature of the times, attesting to the awakening of public awareness, which may have come too late. In any case, the Western European Christian world will be faced in the future, in one form or another, with a life-and-death struggle with Jewry, which is striving to replace the universal Christian ideal by another, Semitic ideal, also universal, but negative and anti-Christian.[5]

Aksakov was right about "the awakening of public awareness." In the late 1870s, the renewed effort to undo Jewish emancipation had already spread from Germany to the Hapsburg empire. In Austria, the cry went forth for an offensive against "Semitic control of money and words" (that is, finance and the press). Then, in Hungary, a leading member of Parliament demanded the expulsion of all Jews from the country (and he even advocated the establishment of a Jewish state in Palestine to which they could be sent). By the 1890s things had grown even worse. In 1895, an avowedly anti-Semitic campaign made the "Catholic Christian Socialist" Karl Leuger the mayor of Vienna.[6] But it was in France that the most notorious episode in the early phase of third-period anti-Semitism took place.

It began in 1894, when Captain Alfred Dreyfus, the only Jew ever to have served on the French General Staff, was suddenly charged with and, on the basis of what would prove to be forged evidence, convicted of treason for having passed military secrets to the Germans. The anti-Semitic passions unleashed by the Dreyfus Affair, epitomized by the cry "Death to the Jews," came as a great shock to the Jews of France. They were, after all, the first beneficiaries of emancipation, and in the century since it had been won, they had done their utmost to keep their part of the bargain by turning themselves into exemplary Frenchmen. The secularized among them—like Dreyfus himself—had assimilated to the point where they were indistinguishable to all appearances from their non-Jewish fellow citizens. "Frenchmen by country and institutions," wrote a member of the prominent Halévy family.

> it is necessary that all]French Jews] become so by customs and language . . . that for them the name of Jew become accessory, and the name of Frenchman principal.

Said another: "Let there be neither Jews nor Christians, except at the hour of prayer for those who pray!"[7]

As for those who still prayed, many of them made sure that the hour of prayer would look more Catholic than Jewish. Paul Johnson describes the scene:

> Rabbis dressed almost like Catholic priests. They even considered holding the Sabbath services on Sunday. They had ceremonies for

children very similar to baptisms and First Communions. Flowers on coffins, collection plates, visits to the bedsides of the dying, singing, organs, sermons—all were modeled on Christian practice.[8]

In addition to all this, French rabbis never ceased identifying (in the words of the Grand Rabbi of Paris) "the French genius [with] the fundamental spirit of Judaism" and even in ceding the title of chosen people to the French "of modern times." Another rabbi called the French Revolution "our flight from Egypt, . . . our modern Passover." And yet another declared that France was

> designated by Him to direct the destinies of humanity . . . to spread throughout the world the great and beautiful ideas of justice, equality, and fraternity which had formerly been the exclusive patrimony of Israel.[9]

To top it all off, the prayer book contained a "Prayer for France" that read as follows:

> Almighty protector of Israel and humanity, if of all religions ours is the most dear to You, because it is Your own handiwork, France is of all countries the one which You seem to prefer, because it is the most worthy of You. . . . Let [France] not keep this monopoly of tolerance and justice for all, a monopoly as humiliating for other states as it is glorious for her. Let her find many imitators, and as she imposes on the world her tastes and her language, the products of her literature and her arts, let her also impose her principles, which it goes without saying are more important and more necessary.[10]

Yet if the assimilated Jews of France had been paying attention to what had been going on in the world of ideas, the Dreyfus Affair would not have come as so great a shock. Although they would blame it all on the influence of German anti-Semitism, it was a Frenchman, the Comte de Gobineau, a man of letters turned ethnologist and demographer, who in his *Essay on the Inequality of Human Races* (1853–55) did more than anyone else in the world to build a putatively scientific foundation for the idea that there was a hierarchy of racial groups and that the Jews were at the bottom of the heap. Ten years later, in the even more influential *Life of Jesus,* the historian and philosopher Ernest Renan argued that "the Semitic race, compared to the Indo-European race, represents an inferior level of human nature" (Jesus, however, though a Jew, was "immune to almost all the defects of his race").[11]

But what has been described as the most successful anti-Semitic book ever published[12]—Edouard Drumont's *Jewish France* (1886)— did even more to pave the ideological way for what happened in the wake of the conviction of Dreyfus. Here again the new racist rationale manifested itself in the portrayal of a war between Aryans and Semites as the central drama of history, only for Drumont the struggle was mainly for control of France. He then went on to found the Anti-Semitic League and to edit *La Libre Parole,* a daily newspaper that contributed mightily to inflaming the anti-Semitic passions unleashed by the Dreyfus Affair.

Working in de facto collaboration with the new racists were the Assumptionists, a Catholic order founded in 1847 and chosen by Rome to "re-Christianize France." Three enemies stood in the way of accomplishing this mission: Protestants, Jews, and Freemasons. But since the Freemasons were regarded as an outgrowth of the Kabbalah, and since the Assumptionists also (in Paul Johnson's words) "believed that many Protestants had been secret Jews and marranos ever since the sixteenth century,"[13] the other two members of this "trio of hate" could easily be incorporated into the Jews. *La Croix,* the mass-circulation daily the Assumptionists started putting out in 1883, thus backed up the new racist rationale with a revived and refurbished religious justification for going after the Jews. Indeed, just when Drumont's *La Libre Parole* began asserting that the "whole of Jewry" was behind the "traitor" Dreyfus, *La Croix* joined in by throwing its own brand of fuel onto the fire.

From the moment he had been charged to the day he was sentenced to Devil's Island for life, Dreyfus never ceased protesting his innocence

("Soldiers! An innocent man is being degraded! Soldiers! An innocent is dishonored! Long live France—long live the Army!").[14] At first, however, except for his family, no one in an embarrassed Jewish community came to his defense. This disgusted a young Jewish writer named Bernard Lazare who, having looked into the case, concluded that Dreyfus had been framed.

In *A Judicial Error—The Truth About the Dreyfus Affair,* a pamphlet he wrote in 1896, Lazare was the first to charge that Dreyfus was a victim of anti-Semitism:

> Because [Dreyfus] was a Jew he was arrested, because he was a Jew he was convicted, because he was a Jew the voices of justice and of truth could not be heard in his favor.[15]

Lazare was instrumental in helping to mobilize the Dreyfusard party, which was composed mainly of leftist intellectuals and which proceeded to engage in a decade-long struggle to prove Dreyfus's innocence. The opposition was led by Charles Maurras (the future leader of the pro-fascist and virulently anti-Semitic movement *Action Française*), who now organized the League of the French Fatherland to "defend the honor of the army and France." The struggle between the Dreyfusards and the anti-Dreyfusards grew so passionate that it led to more than thirty duels (one of them between Lazare and Maurras from which both men escaped unharmed). It was also so all-consuming that Paul Johnson, in his brilliant account of the affair, could say that "for the educated classes it became the only thing that mattered in life."[16] In the end, the Dreyfusard cause—to which Emile Zola's article *"J'Accuse"* furnished perhaps the most potent and effective weapon—won out. Dreyfus, aged beyond his years and broken in spirit, was freed, and, after a certain amount of stalling by the army, was completely exonerated. For Dreyfus himself, this was the end of the affair, but for the Jewish people its consequences were destined to linger on for a very long time to come.

"DEFILERS" OF THE CULTURE

Perhaps the most important of these lingering consequences of the Dreyfus Affair was that it persuaded many Jews how mistaken they had been in believing that assimilation was a sure way to eliminate resistance to their complete emancipation. Among those on whom the affair had this disillusioning effect was Theodor Herzl, the Paris correspondent of a Viennese paper who, like Bernard Lazare, had always been a great proponent of assimilationism. Having been present at the public degradation of Dreyfus and having heard the shouts of "Death to the Jews" that accompanied it, Herzl now decided that, if this could happen in the very birthplace of emancipation, only one possibility remained for the achievement by the Jews of freedom and equality, and that was to build a state of their own.

Within the larger context of Jewish history in general, its effect on Herzl was the most far-reaching consequence of the Dreyfus Affair. But in the context of the story I am trying to tell in this book, the main result of the affair was to refresh the age-old awareness of the Jews that, even in the age of emancipation, their enemies were still full of fight, that they were still where they had always been—on the political Right and in the Church—and that the only friends the Jews had were still to be found on the Left.

On the other hand, from a strictly political point of view, the Dreyfus Affair could have been seen by the Jews of France as reassuring. The anti-Semitic campaign mounted by the forces of the Right, which had at first looked unstoppable, were in the end beaten back, and decisively, by the forces of light. Moreover, in addition to emerging victorious in the struggle to rehabilitate Dreyfus, the Left won big in the election of 1906, the Assumptionists were banished, and a law was passed separating church and state. At the same time, Ettinger points out, "as a comprehensive political force, the *specifically* anti-Semitic political parties in Germany and Austria," which had been doing well, "began to decline both in Germany and Austria."[1]

The trouble was that the situation in the cultural realm, which would prove to be more decisive than the political, was anything but reassuring. In the years leading up to the Dreyfus Affair, assimilated Jews, along with Christians of Jewish origin (who in spite of having been baptized continued generally to be regarded as Jews), had been growing more and more prominent in every area of European culture. They were journalists, they were writers, they were musicians, they were painters and sculptors. Many of them had imagined that so thorough an immersion in and so deep a devotion to the languages and the traditions of the surrounding societies would be welcomed as a mark of how faithfully they were keeping their part of the bargain under which emancipation had been granted. Yet it was becoming increasingly clear that the opposite was the case—that the more complete the integration, the more resentment it was engendering.

In its early stages, this manifested itself in a nationalist unease over the "takeover" of the culture by people who, however much they might pretend otherwise, were not really flesh of our flesh and bone of our bone and therefore had no right to speak in "our" name:

> There is today in France a Jewish literature that is not French literature. . . . For what does it matter to me that the literature of my country should be enriched if it is so at the expense of its significance? It would be far better, whenever the Frenchman comes to lack sufficient strength, for him to disappear rather than to let an uncouth person play his part in his stead and in his name.[2]

This was written by the novelist André Gide in 1914, but the sentiment it expressed harked back to the days when the political ground for opposing emancipation—that the Jews, being a "nation within a nation," were unassimilable—still held sway. Once the new racism took hold, such feelings were provided with a much more powerful rationale in the idea that Jews were not merely foreign but mortally dangerous, and all the *more* so when they strove to assimilate. Richard Wagner, who argued that Jews were incapable of artistic creativity because they were by nature rootless cosmopolitans, did not stop with this essentially nationalist (or *"Völkisch"**) argument; reinforcing it with the new racism, he went on to denounce "the Jewish race as the born enemy of pure humanity and everything that is noble in it."[3]

A great boost was given to this deadly marriage of *Volk* ideology and racism in the years leading up to World War I. For example, when, in 1897, the composer and conductor Gustav Mahler was appointed to head the court opera in Vienna, a storm of protest erupted against giving so important a musical post to a Jew. Under the older anti-Jewish dispensations, the fact that Mahler had converted to Catholicism would have deflected or at least lowered the temperature of any such protest. But in the eyes of the new *Völkisch*-racist anti-Semitism, Mahler was, and would always remain, a Jew, and therefore incapable of understanding and conveying the true spirit of German music.†

In the Weimar Republic that was established in the wake of the German defeat in World War I, the new *Völkisch*-racist anti-Semitism came into its own. Indeed, Jews had become so visibly prominent in all areas of the culture that talk of a "takeover" could no longer be dismissed as wholly the product of the anti-Semitic imagination. Several influential liberal newspapers, highly regarded publishing houses, and

---

* An untranslatable German word that was used of a movement which, as Paul Johnson (*A History of the Jews* [New York: Harper & Row, 1987], p. 392) describes it, held that "German culture (benign, organic, natural) . . . was in perpetual enmity" with the "cosmopolitan and alien" Jews, "the one race which had no country, no landscape, no culture of their own."

† Yet Wagner himself chose Hermann Levi, a Jew, to conduct the premiere of his (heterodox) Christian opera, *Parsifal*. Evidently, Wagner did not let his anti-Semitic theories stand in the way of getting the best possible performance of his own music.

art galleries were owned by Jews, and a disproportionate number of literary, art, and music critics were Jewish. As Paul Johnson says, "They appeared to be in charge, to set the trends and make the reputations."[4] At the same time, Johnson makes a strong case against the notion—as widespread now as it was then—that this amounted to a Jewish takeover of German culture during Weimar. And he goes on to make the same point, though a bit less persuasively, about the German cinema and the theater.

In any event, the fantasy of a Jewish conspiracy to kidnap German culture, dangerous though it was, would prove to be less consequential than the idea stemming from the new *Völkisch*-racist anti-Semitism that the Jews were defiling German culture by intermingling with it. The same maniacal idea would soon be applied by the Nazis to sexual relations between Jews and Aryans or, even more dementedly, to Jewish mother's milk. Thus Otto Georg Thierack, the Reich minister of justice, reported on a case to Hitler in April 1943:

> A full Jewess, after the birth of her child, sold her mother's milk to a woman doctor and concealed the fact that she was a Jewess. With this milk, infants of German blood were fed in a clinic. . . . The purchasers of the milk have suffered damage, because the milk of a Jewess cannot be considered food for German children.[5]

It would be a mistake to think—as did many German-Jewish intellectuals who, even after the Holocaust, were unable to rid themselves of the conviction that German culture was superior to all others (especially American)—that only semiliterate thugs fell for the *Völkisch*-racist view of the Jews. Here, to cite only one prominent intellectual who shared this view, was the psychoanalyst Carl Jung, who, in the very act of applying it to "medical psychology," denied that he was being anti-Semitic:

> The Jew as a relative nomad had never created, and presumably will never create, a cultural form of his own, for all his instincts and talents are dependent on a more or less civilized host

people. . . . In my view it has been a great mistake of medical psychology to apply Jewish categories . . . to Christian Germans and Slavs. In this way the most precious secret of Teutonic man, the deep-rooted creative awareness of his soul, has been explained away as a banal, infantile sump, while my warning voice, over the decades, was suspected of anti-Semitism.[6]

It seems probable that only a very few American Jews in 1933 fully understood that the aim of the party that had just come to power in Germany was not to launch a new anti-Semitic movement but rather to restart the counterattack against Jewish emancipation that had begun about fifty years earlier and had failed to achieve its objectives. But it also seems probable that even fewer American Jews were *un*aware of the fact that this party, even though it called itself National Socialist, had come not from the Left but from the Right—precisely where their worst enemies had always been located.

ENTER FDR

s it happened, *Völkisch*-racist thinking was by no means alto-gether foreign to America. In the early years of the twentieth century, David Starr Jordan, a biologist and the first president of Stanford University, said that "the blood of a nation determines its history and the history of a nation determines its blood."[1] With immigration already reaching into the millions, there seemed a growing possibility that the American character might be corrupted by an infusion of "bad blood."

This dread of "mongrelization" had been given extensive expression in a popular book by Alfred P. Schultz called *Race or Mongrel: A Theory That the Fall of Nations Is Due to Intermarriage with Alien Stocks . . . A Prophecy That America Will Sink to Early Decay Unless Immigration Is Rigorously Restricted* (1908). As is clear from the title, Schultz (and not Schultz alone) had been influenced by the racism pervading German thought, with the concept of a superior Aryan race stretched to include America as one of its members. And "of all the white races threatening 'Aryan' America with mongrelization," notes the historian Howard M. Sachar, "none was regarded with greater trepidation, even alarm, than the Jews."[2] Thus in *The Passing of the Great Race* (1916), a book that became even more popular than Schultz's, no less authoritative a figure than Madison Grant, resident anthropologist at the American Museum of Natural History, lamented that

> the Jew['s] dwarf stature, peculiar mentality, and ruthless concentration on self-interest are being engrafted onto the stock of the nation.[3]

Thus too, the Reverend A. E. Patton, a prominent Protestant minister, warned that "a filthy, greedy, never patriotic stream" of Jews was "flowing in to pollute all that has made America as good as she is."[4] And along with the racist theme of pollution, Patton, in what could have been a translation of *Völkisch* thinking into American terms, insisted that the very nature of the Jew clashed with the salubrious qualities involved in closeness to the soil. The Jew was

> too lazy to enter into real labor, to cowardly to face frontier life, too lazy to work as every American farmer has to work.[5]

The familiar tactic of accusing the Jews of simultaneously being one thing and its opposite (revolutionaries and counterrevolutionaries, for example) was also brought into play with an entirely original set of charges. On the one hand, according to Professor Edward A. Ross of Stanford, Jews were "too cowardly to engage in violent crimes," but according to Theodore Bingham, the New York police commissioner, criminality was rampant among them.[6]

The clear political objective of the American exponents of *Völkisch*-racist ideas was to put a stop to immigration, especially (as the anthropologist William Z. Ripley explicitly said) of

> the great [Polish Jewish] swamp of miserable human beings [that] threatens to drain itself off into this country as well, unless we restrict its ingress.[7]

But *Völkisch* racists and their allies ran into enough resistance to delay their victory until 1924. In the winter of that year—after earlier bills had been vetoed for political reasons of their own by Presidents

Cleveland, Taft, and Wilson—Calvin Coolidge (who had once written an article invoking "biological laws" to prove "that Nordics deteriorate when mixed with other races"[8]) signed the Johnson-Reed Act drastically reducing further immigration from Asia and Southern Europe into law. Even under this "second Declaration of Independence," as one of its authors modestly described it, more than a million and a half immigrants were admitted, but the geographical quota system it set up ensured that only a very small number of them were Jews. Whatever else it accomplished, then, the Johnson-Reed Act most definitely did succeed in preventing the "swamp" of East European Jews from "drain[ing] itself off into this country."

It would be an oversimplification to identify the opponents of immigration entirely with the forces of the Right or of conservatism alone. The American Federation of Labor (AFL) under Samuel Gompers, fearing that the immigrants would take jobs away from its members, was as restrictionist as the professors who worried about the mongrelization of the American race. And in their own way the radical Populists in rural and small-town America were at least as nativist, and at least as anti-Semitic, as the conservative patricians on the East Coast who never ceased blaming the Jews for the degenerate state into which a previously pristine America had fallen after the Civil War.

It was, however, above all at the hands of the old Wasp establishment to which the patricians belonged that the Jews of America—both those who had immigrated earlier from Germany and the latecomers from Eastern Europe—were subjected to various forms of discrimination. They were quietly turned away from fields like engineering and from industries like banking, transportation, and insurance. They were kept out of many residential areas. They were barred from the most prestigious private clubs, hotels, and resorts. Quotas strictly limiting the number of Jews were adopted at all the Ivy League colleges, and it became extremely difficult for a Jew to win appointment to their faculties. Medical schools also adopted quotas. So did law schools, and not even the few Jews who managed to get accepted and to do well in their studies would be hired by the leading corporate firms. This did not prevent large numbers of young Jews from earning law degrees from less prestigious institutions or from night school, but once they graduated, bar associations did their best to place obstacles in the way of their entry into the profession.

Thanks to this kind of thing, Hitler's accession to power in the early years of the Great Depression of the 1930s led a good many Jews to wonder anxiously whether "fascism"—the term that was generally preferred at that point over Nazism—could break out in America as well. Jews were not the only such worriers, as witness Sinclair Lewis's dystopian novel of 1935, *It Can't Happen Here,* written to show that it *could* happen here, and in fact had already begun to do so. But Jews had special cause for concern.

"There is no way of calculating the effects of anti-Jewish agitation during the past two years," the *American Jewish Yearbook* declared in 1936. "[This] is the first time in American history that it has been carried on by so many agencies and on so wide a scale."[9]

According to the Anti-Defamation League of B'nai Brith, there had been only five significant anti-Semitic organizations before 1932, but between 1933 and 1940, no fewer than twelve hundred (!) had sprung up. Among them were fundamentalist Protestant groups in which no trace remained of the philo-Semitic attitude of their Puritan forebears—groups like the American Christian Defenders and the Silver Shirts, whose leader, William Dudley Pelley, described himself as the "American Hitler" and who ran for president in 1936 on the "Christian Party" ticket.

Commanding relatively small constituencies, these groups had more bark than political bite. But the same could not be said of the "radio priest" Father Charles E. Coughlin, who added a Catholic voice to the anti-Semitic Protestant din. Coughlin's weekly hour-long program attracted a very large audience, mostly made up of low-income Irish Catholics; his weekly newspaper, *Social Justice,* reached a circulation of two hundred thousand; and the organization he founded, originally called the National Union for Social Justice and then renamed the Christian Front, had branches all over the country. Coughlin lashed out at Roosevelt as a tool of the Jews ("the Kuhn-Loebs, the Rothschilds . . . the scribes and Pharisees, the Baruchs"[10]), he took to praising Mussolini's fascist regime, and he did not shy away from expressing support for Hitler's war against "world Jewish domination."

What else were Jews to conclude from all this than that their most rabid enemies were still, and as always, to be found among Christians— Protestant and Catholic alike—and that the religious anti-Semites were, moreover, still in at least a de facto alliance with the anti-Semites on the secular political Right? Conversely, how could Jews fail to conclude that casting their lot with Roosevelt was in their best interests, when the "Jew Deal" had become the prime target of anti-Semitic agitation?

As we have seen, when the leaders of the Jewish labor movement came to this same conclusion in 1932, it was not out of any specifically Jewish concern but rather because Roosevelt's program included legislation that would—and did—strengthen the hand of the unions; and to make the pot even sweeter, the New Deal also included a number of welfare measures that they, as socialists, had long been advocating. As we have also seen, for throwing their support to Roosevelt, they were attacked by the Communists. But then in 1935, and literally overnight, the Communist line executed a 180-degree turn.

In the five years leading up to 1935 (the "Third Period"), the theory of "Social Fascism" had formed the basis of Communist thinking and action. According to this theory, socialists were a greater "class enemy" than the fascists themselves—which was why, incredible as it seems in retrospect, the Communists in Germany had refused to join with the socialists to block the appointment of Hitler as chancellor. But by 1935, Stalin had finally come to the conclusion that he had been mistaken in thinking that the Nazis would soon give way to the Communists (*Nach Hitler uns*—"After Hitler Us"—had been the Communist justification for helping him come to power). Clearly Hitler was there to stay, and fanatical anti-Communist that he was, he just as clearly posed a threat to the Soviet Union.

Hence Stalin now decided that it would be the better part of prudence to forge an alliance with the "bourgeois democracies." Fascist under the skin no more, they were from now on—or at any rate for the time being—to be treated as allies of the Communists *against* fascism. In implementing this new "Popular Front" strategy, Communists everywhere were instructed to stop acting and talking like revolutionaries. Instead they were to portray themselves as no different from the formerly despised liberals except in their impatience to bring about the same reforms: they were "liberals in a hurry." And far from representing a threat to the country, or from being the instrument of a foreign power, Communism itself was—in the words of Earl Browder, then the leader of the Communist Party USA (CPUSA)—a wholly indigenous product of America: "twentieth-century Americanism," to use the slogan he and his comrades and their fellow travelers now adopted.

Under the new imperative, the Communists went to almost comical lengths in dressing themselves up to look like "one-hundred-percent Americans." Everything they did was made to seem as American as possible. What had been the Young Communist League one day became on (literally) the very next American Youth for Democracy, whose local chapters now named themselves after legendary figures from American history like Molly Pitcher and Paul Revere. The "educational" institution the party set up in New York was named after Thomas Jefferson. When men were recruited by the Communist Party to fight against Hitler's ally Franco in the Spanish Civil War, it was the Lincoln Brigade they were asked to join. When party literary hacks like Howard Fast wrote novels, they were now likely to be about heroes of the American Revolution, albeit—like *Citizen Tom Paine*—the more radical ones.

Within the context of our story, the most important consequence of the Popular Front was its creation of an ecumenical Left in which all the old distinctions and conflicts among the various factions of the socialist movement, and between them and "bourgeois liberalism," were set aside so that they could all be comfortably subsumed under the newly honorific rubric of liberalism (minus any qualifier). Thus the Jews, for the majority of whom socialism had been the default political position, were now almost compelled to regard themselves as liberals. This was not true of the dedicated Communists, who were only pretending to be liberals, but it was certainly true of their many sympathizers.

In practical political terms, the great merger removed whatever lingering Jewish doubts remained about Franklin Delano Roosevelt. In 1932, with the help of Dubinsky and Sidney Hillman of the Amalgamated Clothing Workers of America, Roosevelt had already received

83 percent of the Jewish vote. In 1936, it went up to 85 percent, plus the nearly 250,000 votes he got from old-line socialists on the newly created American Labor Party (ALP) ticket,* and in 1940, it reached an astonishing 90 percent.

But if it was Roosevelt's friendliness toward the labor movement and his quasi-socialist domestic program that won him the large Jewish votes he garnered in his first two campaigns for president, it was mainly his foreign policy that accounted for the record jump to 90 percent in the third.

By 1936, it was becoming clear to all with eyes to see—and who were willing to believe the evidence of those eyes—that the Nazi regime was intent on rearming in defiance of the restrictions that had been placed on Germany at the end of World War I by the Treaty of Versailles. Furthermore, that Hitler had territorial ambitions was, or should have been, clear when, also in defiance of the Versailles and Locarno treaties, he sent German troops into the demilitarized Rhineland. Roosevelt was evidently disheartened by the failure of the British and the French to stop Hitler at that point (which, as we now know, they could easily have done). But there was little he himself could do beyond making sure it became known that he favored taking action against what he called the "aggressors." Historians disagree as to how serious he was about this, but even assuming that he would really have wished to follow through on a private proposal he made to blockade Germany, his hands were tied by the strength of isolationist sentiment in the country. And very strong it was: shortly before he began his second term, Congress passed the first of a series of Neutrality Acts, and shortly after he was inaugurated, a Gallup poll revealed that 94 percent of Americans wanted to keep the United States out of all foreign wars.

By 1936, too, Hitler had demonstrated that the threats he had long

---

* Dubinsky was convinced that "nothing facing labor [in 1936] was more important than insuring Roosevelt's return for another four years," and together with Sidney Hillman and others, he set out "to develop an instrument that would persuade other lifelong socialists to cast their votes for him." The ALP turned out to be that instrument. (Quoted in Howard M. Sachar, *A History of the Jews in America* [New York: Vintage Books, 1993], pp. 462–63.)

been making against the Jews were not mere bluster (or "rodomon-tade," to borrow the term the philosopher Hannah Arendt would apply many years later to Adolf Eichmann in dismissing his boast that he would die happy because he had sent five million Jews to their graves). In 1935, at a Nazi convention in Nuremberg, the first in a long parade of laws was passed depriving the Jews of Germany of their rights as citizens, and forbidding them to marry or to have sexual rela-tions with Aryans.

We now also know that Roosevelt made little effort, either then or even while the Holocaust was in full swing, to help Hitler's Jewish vic-tims. He did not push for changes in the immigration laws that would have lifted the barriers against Jewish refugees and thereby saved innu-merable lives, and he also stood by while the State Department took measures of its own to raise these barriers even higher. Most of the new restrictions were the brainchild of Breckinridge Long, an old acquain-tance of Roosevelt's who headed the State Department's Visa Division and who scarcely bothered to conceal his hostility to Jews. Thanks to Long's machinations, many more thousands of Jewish refugees were turned away and left to perish when they could have been saved under the existing law. During the war itself, another official, John J. McCloy, assistant secretary of war, denied one request after another to bomb the Auschwitz death camp, but every one of the reasons he gave (including, incredibly, that it "might provoke even more vindictive action by the Germans") would be devastatingly refuted in 1978 by the historian David Wyman.[11] Questioned about this long after the war, McCloy would pin the responsibility on Roosevelt.

Roosevelt's defenders argue that, like the isolationists with whom they overlapped, the opponents of a liberalized immigration policy, many of them Democrats, were very determined and, moreover, had public opinion behind them. If, then, he had tried to buck them, he would probably have failed while risking the breakup of his political coalition to no practical end. The defenders also argue that Roosevelt feared feeding more grist to the isolationist mill. Since the isolationists were already charging that the Jews were trying to drag us into a war we had no business entering, any "favoritism" shown to Jewish refugees would strengthen their hand.

If Roosevelt truly did harbor this fear, it would become increasingly evident that he had good cause, as witness a notorious speech delivered to the America First Committee, the flagship of isolationism, by the great national hero Charles Lindbergh:

> The three most important groups who have been pressing this country toward war are the British, the Jews, and the Roosevelt administration. . . . Instead of agitating for war, the Jewish groups in this country should be opposing it in every possible way, for they will be among the first to feel its consequences. . . . The greatest danger to this country lies in [the Jews'] large ownership and influence in our motion pictures, our press, our radio, and our government.[12]

But whatever may have been going on in Roosevelt's dizzyingly complicated mind, what the Jews of America knew about him as of the mid-'30s was that he opposed the isolationists who were bent on preventing the United States from taking sides against Hitler. About this, at least, the Jews were right, and to that extent their passionate support for Roosevelt was entirely consonant both with their interests and their political sympathies.

What the Jews also knew and were right about was that, although there was no lack of isolationist and even pro-German sentiment among the Democrats (the patriarch of the Kennedy family, Joseph Kennedy, then the U.S. ambassador to England, being a prime example), its main bastion was the Republican Party. And since the Republicans were also unambiguously and unreservedly against the labor movement and the social-welfare programs of the New Deal, it made perfect sense to regard them as opposed to Jewish interests and concerns all across the board.

IN ROOSEVELT'S WAKE: TRUMAN

By 1940, and in spite of his persistent denials, Roosevelt was pretty clearly trying to maneuver the country inch by inch into the war. Because of this, the Jews of America now more than ever saw him as their champion in the struggle to defeat Hitler, and once again they gave him 90 percent of their vote in his unprecedented run for a third term. Four years later when, with victory in sight, he ran for a fourth term, the 90 percent held.

But the statistics alone, astonishing though they assuredly are, do not capture the color and flavor of (in Irving Howe's words)

> the massive enthusiasm for Roosevelt within the Jewish community: the whole of it, from working class to bourgeois, from east European to German, from Right to Left.[1]

To which may be added: from religious to atheist, and from affiliated to assimilated. Roosevelt had become far more than a popular politician or even a great leader to the Jews of America. To say that he was the Messiah would be going too far, but not by all that much. Herbert London of the Hudson Institute recalls how his father felt:

> To say anything negative about Roosevelt was a blasphemy that rarely went unpunished. . . . For my father, God was a

Democrat, and one didn't frivolously disagree with God's party.[2]

No wonder that, in his classic study, *The Political Behavior of American Jews,* Lawrence H. Fuchs writes:

> The synagogues were more crowded after Franklin Roosevelt's death than they had been for a long time. . . . The *Hartford Jewish Ledger* recorded, "We loved him. He has found a place in the annals of Jewish history even as his name will go ringing down the ages as one of the prophets of a new day." A well-known rabbi exclaimed, ". . . for the people of Israel he was the luminous center about which gathered all yearning for justice, our hope for a better world, all aspirations of good and just men everywhere."[3]

Fuchs also tells us that many rabbis took to their pulpits to compare Roosevelt to the greatest of all the Hebrew prophets—Moses himself. (And not only rabbis: at age fifteen, in a grandiloquent poem written for my high school paper on the day of Roosevelt's death, I drew a parallel between Moses, who led the Children of Israel to the Promised Land but was forbidden to cross over into it, and Roosevelt, who had led us to the brink of victory in the war but would now never live to see it actually happen.)

In some ways even more evocative than Fuchs's account is a wonderful quip made around the same time by a New York City politician named Jonah J. Goldstein. To understand it, however, a little background is necessary.

In 1945, the Republicans, no doubt calculating that it was Roosevelt and not his party to which the Jews of New York had become loyal, and that, like all other ethnic groups, they would vote for one of their own, offered Goldstein their nomination for mayor. Although Goldstein was "a popular cigar-chewing" Democrat who had come up through the Tammany machine,[4] he accepted the Republican nomination. To increase his chances, he also secured the endorsement of the

Liberal Party, which would give those Jews who were still reluctant to vote Republican a chance to register their support for him.*

Goldstein's Democratic opponent in the race for mayor was the Irish Catholic William O'Dwyer, who countered the Liberal Party's endorsement of Goldstein by getting the nomination of the American Labor Party. This conversely gave those Jews for whom the Tammany Democrats were too far to the Right a chance to vote for O'Dwyer.

For their part, the Tammany bosses were neither on the Right nor on the Left: all they cared about was winning. This simple truth would be most memorably expressed many years later by Daniel P. Moynihan (still a young professor of political science) in talking about the then leader of Tammany, Carmine De Sapio:

> The extent of his *ideological* commitment may be measured by his pronouncement to the Holy Name Communion Breakfast of the New York Sanitation Department that "there is no Mother's day behind the Iron Curtain."[5]

But if Tammany was not ideological, it was without a doubt corrupt, and this brought a third candidate into the race—Newbold Morris, a Wasp patrician running on the good-government anti-Tammany platform of the No Deal Party (which had only just been born and which would die with this campaign).

Goldstein, then, was the only Jew in the field. But neither this, nor the additional fact that he had been active in Jewish affairs, cut any ice with his fellow Jews. Not only did O'Dwyer do better with them on the Democratic line than Goldstein did on the Republican line; O'Dwyer even got more Jewish votes on the ALP line than Goldstein received as the Liberal Party candidate. More humiliating still, Morris attracted more Jewish votes to the evanescent No Deal ticket than Goldstein managed to pile up as a Republican and Liberal combined.

---

* It will be recalled that the American Labor Party had been established for the very same purpose, but the Communists subsequently infiltrated and managed to take it over, at which point Dubinsky and his colleagues created the Liberal Party as an anti-Communist third-party alternative.

It was these results that elicited Goldstein's wonderful quip. To the Jews, he said in Yiddish, there were three *velt'n* (worlds): *die velt* (this world), *yenner velt* (the world to come), *un* Roosevelt.[6]

But this was a local election in New York, which left room for doubt as to whether the Jewish devotion to Roosevelt would generate a commensurate degree of loyalty to his party in a national election. The test came in 1948. The Republicans, who nominated Governor Thomas E. Dewey of New York, were confident that with Roosevelt gone, his great popularity would not spill over and stick to the seemingly lackluster Harry Truman, who as vice president had ascended to the Oval Office upon Roosevelt's death. To make Republican prospects even brighter, two groups of disaffected Democrats had split off to form new parties and were fielding presidential candidates of their own. On the Left, Henry A. Wallace was running on the Progressive Party ticket, and on the Right, there was the "Dixiecrat" candidate Strom Thurmond. Yet in spite of how weak the Democrats looked, the long Republican nightmare was not quite ready to end. In what was probably the greatest upset in the history of American presidential elections, Truman emerged the victor, snagging almost half of the popular vote (49.9 percent) as against 45.07 percent for Dewey.

Jewish voters, however, were an entirely different matter. A much higher percentage of them (75 percent, to be exact) than of the electorate as a whole went for Truman, with only a minuscule 10 percent going for Dewey. Clearly, then, while the Jewish commitment to the Democratic Party was less intense than it had been under Roosevelt, it was still very strong, whereas the revulsion against the Republicans remained as great as it had been before.

The intensity of this revulsion can be gauged by a humorous remark that Martin Peretz, then editor of the *New Republic,* would make many years later. Playing off a famous verse about Jerusalem in the book of Psalms, Peretz said he believed that if he were ever to pull the Republic lever, his right arm would wither.[7] So, too, the novelist David Evanier, writing about his childhood in the 1940s:

> I came from a . . . lower-middle-class Queens world in
> which . . . voting Republican was seen as the ultimate act of

treife—unkosher food, unkosher thought—really unthinkable in the environment in which I . . . grew up.[8]

I myself, born in 1930 and bred in the heavily Jewish Brownsville section of Brooklyn, never even laid eyes on a Republican until I reached high school, where I was amazed to discover that one of my English teachers was actually a member of that exotic species. (As faculty adviser to the school paper, she dutifully steeled herself to swallow her disgust at my eulogy for Roosevelt and approved its publication.)

The essayist Joseph Epstein had much the same experience. As a boy growing up in Chicago in a Jewish "house that was Democratic and devoted to Franklin Delano Roosevelt," he knew only one Jewish Republican, and he did not meet another until he was in his twenties.[9]

It might seem from this that the Jewish vote in 1948 was more anti-Republican than pro-Truman, but that was not in fact the case. For in the three and a half years since assuming the presidency, Truman had done four big things to earn the support of the Jews. One was his veto of the antiunion Taft-Hartley Bill (overridden, however, by Congress). By 1948, Jews were no longer predominantly in the working class, not even in the needle trades in New York. Nevertheless, most of them still regarded the unions as a noble cause, so that Truman's effort to kill Taft-Hartley sat very well with them.

The second of Truman's acts that sat well with the Jews was the support he gave to the Negroes (as they were then called) in their fight for civil rights. He desegregated the armed forces, he pushed for a permanent Federal Employment Practices Commission (FEPC), and he tried (unsuccessfully) to get Congress to pass antilynching legislation and to abolish the poll tax. In backing such measures, Jews believed that they were not only being altruistic but—on the dubious theory that "bigotry is indivisible"—that they were serving their own interests as well.

The third reason Truman had given the Jews to vote for him was the strong stand he took against what came to be called "McCarthyism": congressional investigations into the extent of Communist influence in various sectors of American life. On this issue, all the surveys showed that the Jews were far more hostile than any other

131

segment of the population to McCarthyism. They were especially angered by the charge that the federal government under Roosevelt was riddled with Communists and that some of these Communists had been spying for the Soviet Union. That there was a good deal of truth in this accusation can no longer be doubted, but doubt it at the time most Jews did.

However, the most important of the four things Truman did that earned him Jewish backing was his recognition of the state of Israel only eleven minutes after its establishment was proclaimed on May 14, 1948. In the years to come, as we shall see, virtually the entire American Jewish community would be "Zionized"—at least in the minimal sense of believing in the need for a sovereign Jewish state and caring deeply about its security and survival—but in 1948, there were still important groups who had their doubts about its advisability. Nevertheless the establishment of Israel aroused such great enthusiasm within the community that it has often been alleged that Truman, foreseeing this, did what he did on May 14 mainly because he was trying to collar the Jewish vote in the coming election. But according to Clark Clifford, one of the few of Truman's advisers who urged him to go ahead with recognition, the Jewish vote was very far from the most important factor driving Truman. In fact, as we learn from Howard Sachar:

> By early 1948, Truman had brushed aside the whole matter of the Jewish vote. "I don't know about the Jewish vote," he complained in a testy private conversation. "I think a candidate on an anti-Semitic platform might sweep the country."[10]

It is also hard to believe that concern for the Jewish vote would have been enough to give Truman the spiritual wherewithal to resist the enormous pressures coming at him from within his own administration. As he would later write:

> The Department of State's specialists on the Near East were, almost without exception, unfriendly to the idea of a Jewish state. . . . Like most of the British diplomats, some of our

diplomats also thought that the Arabs, on account of their numbers . . . and . . . oil resources, should be appeased. I am sorry to say that there were some among them who were inclined to be anti-Semitic.[11]

Nor was this attitude confined to third- and fourth-level officials. It was also held by the secretary of state himself, who at that moment happened to be none other than George Marshall, the chief of staff in World War II, and revered by Truman as "the greatest living American." After a meeting on the issue in the Oval Office, Marshall recorded the words he had spoken to Truman:

I said bluntly that if the President were to follow Mr. Clifford's advice and if in the elections I were to vote, I would vote against the President.[12]

Truman's secretary of defense, James V. Forrestal, felt much the same way and made no secret of it. "There are thirty million Arabs on one side and about 600,000 Jews on the other," he told Clifford. "Why don't you face up to the realities?"[13]

But saying that Truman was not courting the Jewish vote in recognizing Israel is not the same thing as saying that it had no effect on the Jewish vote. Although Sachar disagrees ("By Election Day, Truman's earlier recognition of Israel had done little one way or the other to enhance his political prospects"[14]), it seems highly unlikely that the wild enthusiasm with which Jews all over the country greeted Truman's announcement could have faded in so short a time and to such a degree as to have played no part in their vote for him. I also differ with Sachar when he argues that Truman "was given too much credit in future years as the 'father of the Jewish state.'" He did not deserve that credit, Sachar contends, because

from beginning to end, he had regarded the issue of Palestine as a matter of sanctuary for a miserable people ravaged by war, and in no sense as an act of statecraft following two thousand years of Jewish exile.[15]

As against this, we have the further testimony of Clark Clifford that Truman's repeated readings of the Old Testament left him feeling that "Jews derived a legitimate historical right to Palestine."[16] Equally telling is that Truman once identified himself with Cyrus, the Persian emperor who, after conquering Babylonia in the sixth century B.C.E., sent the exiled Jews back to Jerusalem to rebuild their Temple, thereby leading the prophet Isaiah to praise this pagan king as anointed of God.

Richard Holbrooke, who helped Clifford write his memoirs, sums it all up:

> Israel was going to come into existence whether or not Washington recognized it. But without American support from the very beginning, Israel's survival would have been at even greater risk. Even if European Jewry had not just emerged from the horrors of World War II, it would have been an unthinkable act of abandonment by the United States. Truman's decision, although opposed by almost the entire foreign policy establishment, was the right one.[17]

The heavy Jewish vote for Truman, then, exactly like the even heavier votes for Roosevelt, made perfect sense in terms both of Jewish interests and Jewish aspirations. And so—in spite of the fact that the Jews had by now become relatively prosperous—they did not, writes Fuchs, "vote as other well-to-do Americans did. They held fast to the Democrats."[18]

FROM 1952 TO 1968

It was almost the same in 1952, when Truman's handpicked successor, Adlai E. Stevenson, ran against Dwight D. Eisenhower. Fuchs lists all the reasons why Eisenhower might have been expected to do well among Jews. He had been the commander in chief of the victorious war against Nazism. Unlike his main rival for the Republican nomination, the isolationist Robert Taft, but like Roosevelt, he was a strongly committed internationalist, and he also promised to maintain Roosevelt's welfare state while running it more efficiently. Finally, there was no apparent difference between his stated position on Israel and Stevenson's. Nevertheless, while Eisenhower won by a landslide (55.2 percent to 44.3 percent), he attracted only 36 percent of the Jewish vote, with 64 percent going to Stevenson.*

One of those Jewish votes for Stevenson was mine. In 1948, I was eighteen years old and too young to vote, but the admiration I had felt for our heroic Soviet ally during the war was still strong enough to make me root for the pro-Soviet Henry Wallace. (My eulogy for Roosevelt was not the only grandiloquent poem I wrote in my early teens: there was also a long celebration in blank verse of the Soviet victory at

---

* Fuchs, writing in 1956, gives the Jewish vote for Stevenson as 75 percent, but more extensive studies done later put it at 64 percent.

Stalingrad in 1943, when I was thirteen.) Yet the war had also made me into a fervent American patriot, so that as the campaign wore on—and in a portent of my future political development—I was more and more put off by Wallace's exclusive attachment of blame to the United States for our deteriorating relations with the Soviet Union. The result was that I found myself delighted by Truman's surprise victory and relieved at how much worse Wallace's showing of under a million votes was than the ten million that had been expected.

Voting for the first time in 1952, when I was doing graduate work at Cambridge University in preparation (as I then thought) for an academic career, I enthusiastically filled out an absentee ballot for Stevenson. Like just about everyone in the academic world, I was entranced by Stevenson's cultivated rhetoric and misled by it into taking him for an intellectual (only to learn with amazement after his death that he hardly ever read a book). My guess is that, given the reverence for learning that was practically built into the Jewish DNA, a fair number of Jews outside the academic world who might otherwise have been tempted by Eisenhower were also excited by the prospect of so seemingly cultured a president (in much the same way as their offspring would be by Barack Obama more than fifty years later).

In 1956, Stevenson, again pitted against Eisenhower, carried the Jewish vote, but by 4 points less than he had in 1952, giving Eisenhower 40 percent. At first sight, this result is puzzling. Both Eisenhower himself and his secretary of state, John Foster Dulles, had been noticeably cool toward Israel, and they had also been tilting toward the Arab states in the supply of arms. To make matters worse, even as the 1956 campaign was in full swing, Eisenhower forced the Israelis to withdraw from the Sinai after they had invaded it as part of a joint operation with the British and the French to take over the Suez Canal from Egypt.

Eisenhower was furious with the Israelis because he suspected that they had timed the Sinai campaign to coincide with the election, calculating that fear of losing the Jewish vote would prevent him from taking action against them. "If the Israelis keep going," he confided to his son,

I may have to use force to stop them. . . . Then I'd lose the
election. There would go New York, New Jersey, Pennsylvania
at the least.

But unlike "so many politicians of the past," who had bowed to what
in future years would be stigmatized as "the Jewish lobby," he would,
he boasted, "handle our affairs exactly as though we didn't have a Jew
in America."[1]

Eisenhower was wrong about the timing of the Israeli action, which
had been planned in coordination with the British and the French. But
he was also wrong about the Jewish vote, since on this particular issue
Jewish support for Israel was by no means universal. Indeed, many
Jews agreed with Eisenhower about the Suez campaign. Their numbers included former "non-Zionists" who were still nervous about
charges of "dual loyalty"; doctrinaire liberals who shared Eisenhower's animus against "imperialism" and "colonialism"; and old
anti-Zionists of the Left who had grudgingly abandoned their longtime opposition to Jewish statehood as a form of "reactionary bourgeois nationalism" but who were by now only too ready to criticize
Israel when it failed to live up to their exalted standards. Even one of
the leading American Zionists, Rabbi Abba Hillel Silver, thought that
Israel had made a mistake in invading the Sinai and he assured Eisenhower that he could win the election without a single Jewish vote.

Eisenhower did win the election—and with the largest share of the
Jewish vote that any Republican presidential candidate would get
from then on. But the key point to bear in mind about the election of
1956 is that not even the immensely popular Eisenhower was able to
break up the Jewish love affair with the party of Roosevelt. It went on,
albeit (the bloom having faded somewhat from the Stevenson rose
since 1952) with a slightly lesser degree of passion than before. Still, to
judge by the next three presidential elections, the old passion was
capable of being rekindled and set once more aflame. All it would take
was Democratic candidates running against Republicans who, unlike
Eisenhower, were (or at least seemed to be) in thrall to the right wing
of their party.

The first such Republican to follow Eisenhower was his own vice president, Richard Nixon. In retrospect we can see that Nixon was closer to the Center-Right than to the Far Right, but that was not how he looked at the time to Jewish eyes. To them he was a McCarthyite *avant la lettre,* having earned that reputation even before Senator Joseph McCarthy himself had appeared on the scene.

In 1948, Nixon, then a congressman from California, had become a member of the notorious House Committee on un-American Activities. (So notorious was it for what Nixon himself called its "frequently irresponsible conduct" that he had only agreed to join it with "considerable reluctance."[2]) It was in that capacity that Nixon took the lead in pursuing a sensational accusation made by Whittaker Chambers, an ex-Communist now working for *Time* magazine. In sworn testimony to the committee, Chambers said that he had been part of a cell of Communist spies and that one of his colleagues had been Alger Hiss. At that moment Hiss was president of the Carnegie Endowment for International Peace, but he had previously held a number of important posts in the State Department. In his own sworn testimony to the committee, Hiss vehemently denied Chamber's charge, and eminent personages from all sides (including Dean Acheson, then secretary of state under Truman, and John Foster Dulles, who would become secretary of state under Eisenhower) rushed to his defense. To no avail: after a long and complicated series of hearings and trials, Hiss was convicted of perjury and sent to prison.*

Scarcely anyone today still believes that Hiss was innocent, but at the time, and for years thereafter, many (most?) liberals certainly did. And so far as they were concerned, the villain of the piece was not Hiss or even Chambers, but Nixon. Not only had he ruined the life of an innocent man, but he had used the case as a way of creating the false impression that the Roosevelt administration had been filled with Communist spies and even of casting doubt on the loyalty of the liberals who had so passionately supported it.

Such blasphemies—not to mention the undercurrent of anti-

---

* Since the statute of limitations had run on the charge of espionage, Hiss could only be tried for perjury in denying that he had been a Soviet espionage agent.

Semitism many Jews thought they could hear in Nixon's insinuations—were bound to drive most Jews, even those who had voted for Eisenhower, into the arms of Nixon's Democratic opponent. And if they needed any additional impetus, there were dark suspicions concerning Nixon's attitude toward Israel. In his memoirs, Nixon would acknowledge that the anti-Israel policy pursued by "Eisenhower and Dulles" (i.e., not Nixon) in the Suez crisis had been "a serious mistake" that planted "the seeds of another Mideast war."*[3] But as of 1960, no one doubted that Nixon had stood solidly behind the threat "Eisenhower and Dulles" had made to cut off all aid to Israel and even to deny tax-exempt status to private contributions. True, as I noted earlier, several Jewish groups supported this policy, but since they constituted only a minority of the Jewish community as a whole, they were unable to do Nixon much good at the ballot box. Kennedy defeated Nixon by a hair, but among Jewish voters he won by a landslide: 82 percent (as compared with Stevenson's 60 percent four years earlier) to 18 percent for Nixon (as compared with Eisenhower's 40 percent in 1956).

It is a reasonable inference that there was more anti-Nixon sentiment here than pro-Kennedy enthusiasm. This had nothing to do with Kennedy's being a Catholic: in 1928, Jews had given 78 percent of their vote to Al Smith, the first Catholic ever to run for president. The trouble, rather, was that Kennedy showed no sign of being a liberal cut from the Rooseveltian cloth or—apart from the usual campaign pandering—of being a great friend of the Jews. He was the son of Joseph P. Kennedy, who had come to hate Roosevelt, who had opposed American entry into the war against Hitler, and who was suspected, not without reason, of being anti-Semitic. JFK's younger brother Robert had worked for Joe McCarthy; JFK himself had conveniently been absent from the Senate when the motion to censure McCarthy came up for a vote; and so "hard" an anti-Communist was he that he attacked Nixon—Nixon!—for being soft on the Soviet Union and China.

---

* Eisenhower evidently felt the same way. According to Max Fisher, one of the few Jewish leaders who belonged to the Republican Party, Eisenhower told him in 1965 that he regretted having pressured Israel to evacuate the Sinai.

In all probability, then, it was fear of the Republican Party in general and Richard Nixon in particular that largely accounted for the overwhelming Jewish vote for Kennedy in 1960. (At least one of those Jewish votes for Kennedy—mine—was cast reluctantly. As I will recount in detail later on in this book, I had been moving leftward since 1956, and by 1960, I had become a fairly visible exponent of the nascent radicalism that would soon be called the New Left. From that vantage point, I regarded "establishment" liberals like Kennedy and his entourage of "the best and the brightest" as the main obstacle to the sweeping changes I favored both in domestic and foreign policy. Even so, he was, as I then saw it, infinitely better than Nixon.)

When in 1964 the Republicans nominated Barry Goldwater to run against Lyndon Johnson (who had risen from vice president to president a year earlier upon the assassination of Kennedy), the same fear of the Republicans came into play where the Jewish vote was concerned, only far more heavily than before. Goldwater's paternal grandfather (the "Big Mike" Goldwasser we have already encountered) had been Jewish, but this did nothing to soften the attitude of Jewish voters toward him. What the vast majority of them undoubtedly felt about the Goldwater candidacy was given its most sophisticated expression by Hans J. Morgenthau of the University of Chicago. Writing not as a Jew but as a political theorist (though he could hardly help being influenced by having grown up Jewish in Nazi Germany), Morgenthau saw in Goldwater himself an "innate democratic decency," but he feared that

> it [was] exactly this unwitting decency which [made] him the
> natural prey of people less decent than himself. . . . There
> looms, then, the specter of a victorious Republican Party . . .
> pulled by its own dynamics toward a fascist position.[4]

Given an assessment like this, it is understandable that the Jewish vote for Johnson reached the Rooseveltian height of 90 percent, nearly 30 points higher than the 61 percent he received from the electorate as a whole. But it seems fairly certain that there was a larger pro-Johnson component in this vote than there had been for Kennedy's in 1960.

This was even true of me and many of my political friends on the Left. The issue of Vietnam would shortly turn us all into ferocious opponents of Johnson, but it had not yet heated up. On the other hand, in the few months since moving into the White House, Johnson had already launched a "War on Poverty" as a first step in what he himself characterized as "a revolutionary new program" that went far beyond anything Kennedy had tried to do and was in some respects surprisingly close to what we radicals of the Left were advocating. As Johnson would write in his memoirs:

> The pattern of social reform in America has been like a vast pendulum, swinging over the years from creative activity to almost total inaction, and then back to action again. . . . We rested while the disasters of the late 1920s accumulated and brought about new demands for urgent change—demands met by Franklin Roosevelt's New Deal. After the upheaval of World War II, the desire to relax grew strong once more. President Truman, who perceived the need for social change in the United States as clearly as any leader in our history, had to fight this apathy throughout his administration.[5]

Now, Johnson continued, conditions were ripe for action, and he believed that he could provide the necessary leadership to do what Truman had been unable to accomplish—that is, complete the unfinished business of the New Deal. It was, I believe, also because he thus took up the mantle of Roosevelt that Jewish voters in 1964 gave Johnson the same level of support they had given to Roosevelt himself in 1940 and 1944.

In 1968 it was Nixon again for the Republicans, and Hubert Humphrey for the Democrats. Nixon won, but he did just as poorly with Jewish voters as he had in 1960 (18 percent then, 17 percent now), while Humphrey did about as well as Kennedy had (81 percent to Kennedy's 82 percent). Since no greater champion of Rooseveltian liberalism, and no greater friend of the Jews, could be found than Hubert Humphrey, he might have been expected to reach the 90 percent mark. But as Johnson's vice president he had been obliged to support continuation of the war in Vietnam—the very policy that had just driven Johnson himself out of the race—and this probably cost him enough Jewish votes to depress the total. Still, even with the Vietnam albatross hanging on his neck, and even with the young antiwar activists—many of them Jewish—screaming "Dump the Hump" at him wherever he went, he managed to garner 81 percent of the Jewish vote. (As for me, I had campaigned for Eugene McCarthy, who was running on an antiwar platform in the Democratic primaries, but after he dropped out, the soft spot I had always had for Humphrey rose to the surface. Talking myself into the admittedly faint hope that, if elected, he would change his position on Vietnam and get us out, I wound up casting a sheepish vote for him.)

What I have been trying to show is that the attachment of most American Jews to the liberal tradition stemming from Roosevelt, and their concomitant loyalty to the Democratic Party, was up to this point in harmony with their interests as Jews. But then, as we learn from Greenberg and Wald,[6] in the decades following the end of World War II they found themselves getting more and more out of political step with the other white members of the Roosevelt coalition. The attachment of these non-Jewish ethno-religious groups to the Democrats was steadily declining in direct proportion to the improvement in their economic and social condition, so that by 1990, fewer than half of the ethnic Catholics and only a third of the white Southerners, who (along with the Jews) had been at the heart of the New Deal coalition, still called themselves Democrats. But increasing prosperity was having no such effect on the Jews, 75 percent of whom on average kept voting for the Democratic candidate in presidential elections.

The reason Jews had been attracted to the Democratic Party in the first place was that it represented the closest American counterpart to the forces on the Left that had favored Jewish emancipation in Europe—just as the Republicans seemed to represent an American version of the conservative forces that had opposed equal rights for Jews in the past. In the late 1960s, however, changes began taking place that would more and more rob the Jewish commitment to the Democrats of the sense it had formerly made. As I said in the Introduction to this book, I myself became so deeply involved in the struggles that developed over these changes that it would be disingenuous of me to go on speaking as I have mainly done thus far in the impersonal voice of the historian. I will therefore now shift gears and tell this part of the story in the voice and from the perspective of the active participant in it that I turned out to be.

PART TWO

WHY THE JEWS ARE STILL LIBERALS

18

THE GOLDEN AGE OF JEWISH SECURITY

In the spring of 1971, I was invited to address the Sixty-Fifth Annual Meeting of the American Jewish Committee (AJC). The invitation took me by surprise, and thereby hangs a tale.

The AJC, the oldest and most prestigious of the so-called Jewish defense organizations (the Anti-Defamation League, or ADL, is another), had been founded in 1906 by a group of eminent German Jews "to prevent the infraction of the civil and religious rights of Jews, in any part of the world." Since 1945, among its many other activities, AJC had been sponsoring *Commentary,* a monthly magazine of which, at the time it invited me to address its annual meeting, I had been the editor for a little over eleven years. In that capacity, I enjoyed complete editorial independence, which meant, quite simply, that I and my staff, and we alone, without interference of any kind from the Committee, had the power to decide what to publish and what not to publish in the magazine.

Once in a while, as might have been anticipated, this led to the appearance in *Commentary* of articles that conflicted sharply with the AJC's position on this or that issue, or that caused it embarrassment with this or that constituency. The leaders of the Committee were not exactly happy when such articles appeared, but they were willing to live with it. Having at the outset decided that they wanted something livelier and more intellectually distinguished than a house organ, and having understood that the only way to achieve this was by giving the new magazine editorial independence, they considered the occasional discomfort that the arrangement inevitably entailed a price worth paying.

I doubt that there has ever been another organization that was willing and principled enough to subsidize a magazine it did not, at least to some extent, control. This, however, was not the only feature that made *Commentary* unique. Although it had been designed as a Jewish magazine, it differed from all other Jewish magazines, past or present, in having a mandate to range beyond subjects of particular Jewish concern, and as widely over the entire political and cultural landscape as the editor saw fit. Under the aegis of this mandate, Elliot E. Cohen, *Commentary*'s founding editor and my immediate predecessor, had produced a predominantly Jewish magazine with a special interest in the world at large; the "New *Commentary*," as it came to be known shortly after I took over in January 1960, was a predominantly general magazine with a special interest in Jewish affairs.

There was another difference between Cohen's *Commentary* and mine, and that was political. Under Cohen, *Commentary* had been a liberal magazine, and in this respect, there was very little daylight between its point of view and the AJC's and very little occasion for the leaders of the Committee to regret having accorded him editorial independence. In my early twenties, I had also been a liberal, but by the time I became the editor of *Commentary* at the age of thirty, I had (as I indicated earlier) moved to the Left in my thinking, and I had also become closely and visibly identified with the nascent radical movement that still had no name but that would within a few years be dubbed the New Left.

Nowadays the term *liberal* is stretched to encompass almost anything to the left of center (as when Andrea Mitchell of NBC refers without being contradicted to "the net roots, the left wing of the [Democratic] party, the liberal wing of the party"). But in those days a distinction was still being drawn between liberalism and radicalism. Unlike the Communists in their popular-front phase of the '30s, the radicals of the '60s (myself included to a large extent) did not present themselves as "liberals in a hurry." On the contrary: they identified liberalism with the "establishment" they were trying to topple and which they blamed for everything they believed had gone wrong with America. A vivid expression of this point of view was a speech about Vietnam delivered in 1965 by Carl Oglesby, who was then the president of Students for a Democratic Society (SDS), the flagship of the New Left:

> The original commitment in Vietnam was made by President Truman, a mainstream liberal. It was seconded by President Eisenhower, a moderate liberal. It was intensified by the late President Kennedy, a flaming liberal. Think of the men who now engineer that war—those who study the maps, give the commands, push the buttons, and tally the dead: Bundy, McNamara, Rusk, Lodge, Goldberg, the President [Johnson] himself. They are not moral monsters. They are all honorable men. They are all liberals.[1]

The "honorable men" was a sly allusion to Mark Antony's characterization of Julius Caesar's assassins ("Brutus is an honorable man, / So are they all, all honorable men"),[2] and Oglesby intended it to carry the same ironic force. But the New Left's denunciations of the liberal establishment were rarely so classy, let alone so subtle. More often they were rhetorically brutal ("LBJ, LBJ, how many kids did you kill today?") and even more often they were couched in obscenity ("Up against the wall, Motherfucker!").

Neither I as a writer, nor the writers I sought out or discovered and then edited for publication in *Commentary*, ever used language like that. But in our own "highbrow" style we were just as rough on the liberal establishment as the students demonstrating on the campuses and on the streets. Moreover, we were frequently ahead of them in identifying the issues that demanded critical analysis. This was notably true of Vietnam.

Hard as it is to believe that what would grow into one of the prime obsessions of American history should ever have been almost completely ignored, the fact was in the first two years of the Kennedy administration, Vietnam was just another "underdeveloped" country in which only academic specialists took any interest. It was one such specialist, a political scientist named Joseph J. Zasloff, then a visiting professor at the University of Saigon, who in late 1961 sent me a paper he had written on the situation there, which (in de-academicized form) eventually appeared in *Commentary*. Here is how it began:

> While Laos and then Berlin and then Katanga have been domi-nating the front pages in recent months, a situation of equally critical proportions has been building up in South Vietnam, where the government of President Ngo Dinh Diem is struggling for survival against well-organized strongly sustained guerrilla forces—the Vietcong—inspired and supported by the Commu-nist Viet Minh government of the North.[3]

As though to confirm Zasloff's description of how little attention was being paid to Vietnam, his article attracted hardly any notice. Neither did a follow-up piece by the much better known Hans J. Morgenthau that we published shortly after a small number of American military advisers had been sent to Vietnam.

Some years later, the antiwar movement would violently attack the idea that fighting Communism was a good and necessary thing for the United States to do. But few if any of the early critics of American intervention in Vietnam went that far. Thus, like Zasloff, Morgenthau assumed without argument that it was important to prevent the Com-munists from taking over South Vietnam. What he, again like Zasloff, directed his fire against was what he saw as the emphasis in American policy on military means. "The only effective defense against Commu-nist subversion," he argued, was "a viable political order," and he urged that we resort to our "manipulative skills" in restoring such an order to South Vietnam. He then issued a warning that would turn out to be astonishingly prescient:

> If the present primarily military approach is persisted in, we are likely to be drawn ever more deeply into a Korean-type war. . . . Such a war cannot be won quickly, if it can be won at all, and may well last five or ten years. . . . Aside from the military risks

to which it will give rise . . . , such a war would certainly have a profound impact upon the political health of the nation. McCarthyism and the change in the political complexion of the nation which the elections of 1952 brought about resulted directly from the frustrations of the Korean war. The American people are bound to be at least as deeply affected by the frustrations of a Vietnamese war.[4]

Nor was it for Vietnam alone that the radicals of the '60s—again myself largely included—held the liberal establishment responsible. As the mantra that became familiar in the '60s had it, "war, racism, and poverty" were America's three great afflictions, and even on the questionable assumption that the liberal establishment was interested in curing racism and poverty (what, we demanded, had it done in all the years it had been running the country?), the tepid policies it had to offer were only allowing the diseases to metastasize.

As with war, so on the issue of poverty, too, *Commentary* took the lead, with two powerful articles by the economist Oscar Gass on the first year of Kennedy's "New Frontier." Gass was no radical, but he was deeply disturbed by the discrepancy between the administration's rhetoric and the reality of what it was actually doing to assist the poor, and he proceeded to demonstrate, point by point, that

always and running through everything, there is the characteristic New Frontier polarity of portentous general language and modest specifics.[5]

On racism, the third item of the mantra, the position of the liberal establishment was that the way to solve the "Negro problem" was through "integration," and against this idea, too, we radicals mounted an assault. Even, we said, if it was possible to get whites and blacks to live and work harmoniously together, it would take much too long, and even then the pervasive racism of American society would remain and would resort to more devious means to keep the Negroes down. There was no unified position on the Left as to a viable alternative. The still small but growing "Black Power" movement was beginning to push for separation; another faction was advocating "positive discrimination" or, in its later iteration, "affirmative action"; and I myself notoriously concluded that only "the wholesale merger of the two races" could solve the problem.[6]

Curiously enough, it was on these, and not on any specifically Jewish issue, that I first gave the AJC cause for regretting that I had been granted editorial independence. The occasion was a visit to the White House by a group of AJC leaders. Before they were ushered in to see the president, one of Kennedy's assistants demanded to know why their organization was so opposed to the administration. Puzzled, they answered in effect that they had no idea what he was talking about. Your magazine, he replied, has been attacking us month after month on everything we have been trying to do. When they responded by telling him that *Commentary* did not speak for the Committee, and by assuring him that they and their fellow members of AJC had the greatest respect for President Kennedy, he flashed a cynical grin: so far as he was concerned, he who paid the piper called the tune.

In spite of this incident—and there were a number of others as well—the worst that happened to me was a perfectly reasonable request or two to think twice before publishing anything that I knew might cause the Committee trouble. But there was more to this than AJC's steadfast commitment to the principle of editorial independence. For the fact was that "establishment" liberals in general, like the leaders of AJC, were uneasy about the contempt in which they were being held by "the young" (often their own children, who were accusing them of lacking the courage to act on their professed political values). They therefore tended to be indulgent of the "understandable excesses" of the radicals.

This was even true of certain key members of the Kennedy administration itself. For example, Kennedy's court historian, Arthur Schlesinger Jr., who would become violently hostile to me after I broke ranks with the Left in the late '60s, was very cordial in my radical days: "What mischief are you up to now?" he would ask with a conspiratorial smile whenever we met. Another future enemy, Kennedy's national security adviser, McGeorge Bundy, was also friendly. So was John Kenneth Galbraith, who had taken time off from his labors as an economist on the Harvard faculty to serve as Kennedy's ambassador to India (though unlike his friend Schlesinger, Galbraith would never cease being civil even after my apostasy). They were all eager to show that they were on the same side as the radicals. Or, as Schlesinger once put the case, the main difference between the radicals and people like himself and his colleagues in the Kennedy administration lay not in the goals being pursued but in the fact that we represented the utopian stream in American thought as against the pragmatic tradition for which they spoke.

As the decade wore on—with the foreign policies of the establishment liberals being discredited in their own eyes by ever angrier demonstrations against the war in Vietnam, and their domestic policies undermined by more and more riots in the black ghettos of the North—their eagerness to demonstrate solidarity with the radicals became veritably desperate. It was out of this desperation that something analogous to the sanitizing "liberals in a hurry" concept of the '30s first began being applied to the radicals of the '60s.

At the same time, however, something had also been happening to the radical movement itself. It had been born (as Schlesinger rightly perceived) out of the utopian ambition to perfect American society by closing the gap between its professed ideals and the realities of its practices. But the stubborn refusal of the country to change as quickly and as drastically as the movement demanded and expected had given rise to an increasingly violent hatred of "Amerika" (spelled in that way to suggest an affinity with Nazi Germany). Along with this change of heart had come the correlative conviction that nothing short of a revolution could eradicate the evils that were now seen not as deviations from the country's ideals but as manifestations of its very essence.

In the last two or three years of the '60s, I and a number of other intellectuals on the Left were finding ourselves increasingly repelled by this development (just as I had been in 1948 by the anti-Americanism of the Wallace campaign). So much so, indeed, that it provoked us into a reexamination of the ideas and attitudes behind the movement that we had been instrumental in launching and whose ideas we had taken the lead in propagating. In the process we were transforming *Commentary* into a passionate critic of those very ideas and attitudes. But there was a positive side to this coin as well. For along the way we also found ourselves rediscovering—and in some cases learning to appreciate for the first time—how rare and precious were the traditional American institutions that had in recent years come under such ferocious attack, and how desperate was the need for a sophisticated intellectual defense against this assault and a wholehearted affirmation in the teeth of it. Such a defense—combined with a new emphasis on the danger posed by the spread of Communist totalitarianism as embodied most powerfully and aggressively in the Soviet Union—is what we set out to provide.

But just as we were breaking ranks with the Left on the nature and quality of American society, establishment liberals like those in the AJC were moving in the opposite direction—toward the formation of what was in effect a new and updated Popular Front. And in a replay of what had occurred the first time around, the liberal label was being applied to and accepted by radicals who (like Carl Oglesby) had previously scorned it.

Under these circumstances, the grief I had brought the AJC from the Left was as nothing compared to the embarrassment I was now causing as a result of my evident conversion to (dread word) conservatism or rather (in the derogatory coinage of recent vintage that was being applied to leftists like me who had "sold out" to the Right) "neoconservatism." Consequently the last thing I thought the Committee would have wanted was to call more attention to what I was up to. Which was why it came as a surprise when its (very liberal) executive director invited me to explain my change of direction in an address to its annual meeting.

In accepting this challenge, I decided to meet it by speaking explicitly as a Jew to what was after all a Jewish defense organization. I say "after all" because AJC, like a number of other Jewish organizations, had in recent years been devoting more of its energies to the civil rights movement than to the defense of Jews against any and all forces intent on doing them harm.

What mainly accounted for this phenomenon was the steep decline of anti-Semitism in the two decades following the end of World War II.

Anti-Semitism still existed, but so besmirched had it become through its association with the name of Hitler that no one who aspired to respectable status in American public life dared voice anti-Jewish sentiments openly or dared make any use of them in appealing for the support of others. For the penalty was instant banishment from the world of acceptable opinion. This, for example, was why Senator Joseph McCarthy, sensitive to the vulnerability of any right-wing movement to accusations of anti-Semitism, and fully aware of the damage such accusations could do, went out of his way to appoint two Jews with markedly Jewish names (Roy Cohn and David Schine) as his chief assistants. Even the more extreme John Birch Society declared that anti-Semites were unwelcome in its ranks and the organization went so far as to expel members who were unable to restrain their frisky anti-Semitic passions when writing or speaking in public. Whether or not, then, the actual level of anti-Semitic feeling had declined in America, the sheer number of anti-Semitic statements, or even of statements hostile to Jews in any way or to any degree, all but disappeared from the public prints, the airways, political speeches, and possibly even private conversation.

Along with this decline in the open expression of anti-Semitic sentiments and ideas went a precipitous drop in discriminatory practices against Jews. Of course, pockets of discrimination continued to exist. There were business enterprises that would not hire Jews or, if they did, would keep them out of the executive suite. There were areas in which Jews were prevented from buying homes. There were cooperative apartment buildings—even in New York—from which Jews were tacitly barred. There were resorts and private social clubs to which Jews were not admitted. But between 1945 and 1967 most of these practices became illegal, and if this did not cause them to disappear entirely, it made them harder to follow and easier to fight where the will to fight was aroused.

It was this same period that saw the apparent end of quotas restricting the number of Jews who could be admitted into the elite colleges and the better professional schools. Such quotas, often operating under cover of the search for geographical and social balance, had been in existence since the early 1920s, and in an informal way they had also governed the hiring of faculty. By 1960 they seemed to have become almost entirely a thing of the past.

But to say merely that open anti-Semitism virtually disappeared and that discrimination against Jews declined would be to describe the situation too negatively. The truth is that the American climate of the first two postwar decades was not only less hostile to Jews than it had formerly been; it was also more congenial. Not only were obstacles removed, but invitations were issued. Not only were Jews less and less excluded from more and more places; they were also made to feel more and more welcome, more and more at home. Having, for example, always considered itself—without thinking about the matter very much—a Christian country, the United States was now extending recognition to Judaism as, along with Protestantism and Catholicism, one of the three major American religions. The rabbi became an obligatory partner of the minister and the priest on every ceremonial occasion, and though this development was not without its problems, the fact remained that Jews as Jews were being invited in, no longer alienated to that most literal extent.

Another and perhaps more telling example of how positively congenial the American climate became to the Jews in the period under consideration was the interest that developed in Jewish writers and artists and intellectuals, and the sympathy that began to be shown for their work. Formerly, Jewish novelists, poets, playwrights, and critics had played only a minor role in American letters, but now, all at once, they began finding an audience for the things they had to say. Furthermore, in the past only "non-Jewish Jews," who were in effect passing in literary terms as Gentiles, could succeed in entering the cultural mainstream, but this was no longer the case. For instance, where novelists were concerned, the more they wrote about Jewish life in particular—and the more they wrote in a style that betrayed its connections with Yiddish and with the contours of immigrant life—the bigger and more appreciative the audience would turn out to be. The enthusiastic response to Saul Bellow, Bernard Malamud, Philip Roth, and many others could not have contrasted more sharply with the complete neglect of such of their predecessors as Henry Roth (no relation to Philip) and Daniel Fuchs.

The literary world was not the only world in which Jews were able to benefit from and take advantage of a newly benign environment. Everywhere they seemed to be prospering. "Jews without money" (to borrow the title of a very popular book of the 1930s by the Communist writer Mike Gold) there continued to be, especially in the bigger cities. But the Jews who lived in poverty were in some ways even more invisible than the socialist writer and activist Michael Harrington famously said their nonwhite counterparts had become, if only because the Jewish community as a whole was in so vivid a state of economic bounteousness. The Jews were doing well, and so were most of their children, so many of whom were going to college that the exceptions came to be looked on as strange, almost, even, as a species of social deviant. "A Jewish dropout," went a joke of the period, "is a Jewish boy without a Ph.D." Those who did not have Ph.D.'s had MDs and law degrees, and the newly minted lawyers were being hired by firms that had only yesterday excluded even the best of Jewish applicants.

Last but not least, more Jews than ever were running for elective office, including such high offices as governor and United States senator, and more of them were getting elected than ever before. Despite the greater visibility of Jews on the political scene, moreover, the taboo on the use of anti-Semitism in electoral campaigns continued to be rigidly observed.

Take them for all in all, then, the two decades that followed the end of World War II constituted what some of us were calling a "Golden Age of Jewish Security." That this was in itself a happy development went without saying, but it naturally had the effect of severely curtailing the amount of work the Jewish defense agencies had to do. To the extent that they still spent time on anti-Semitism, they largely devoted it to attacking the "radical Right" and its Christian allies. Yet in an article titled "The Radical Right and the Rise of the Fundamentalist Minority,"[7] David Danzig, then the program director of the AJC, could find no open or outright anti-Semitism in either the secular or religious components of this movement. He simply took it for granted that such a movement must necessarily represent a danger to Jews. It was an assumption that fit in well with *The Authoritarian Personality,* a study sponsored by the AJC in 1950 in which the authors, in investigating the psychological roots of totalitarianism, focused entirely on the political Right and never even bothered to consider whether the same qualities might exist on the political Left (which they most certainly did).

To most of the leaders of the defense agencies (and even more so the staffs they employed to put their policies into practice) the decline of anti-Semitism was of course a wonderful thing in itself, but it also provided an additional justification for moving beyond the constrictions of Jewish particularism and into the "universalism" that in any case most of them believed to be the true essence of Judaism. Thanks to the new situation, instead of being mainly confined to the fight against anti-Semitism, they were now freer than ever to fight bigotry of every kind; and instead of being limited to preventing "the infraction of the civil and religious rights of Jews," they could now devote themselves to struggling for the "human rights" of all peoples everywhere.

All of which explains why my decision to speak as a Jew addressing his fellow Jews, and to bring some very bad news to boot about the resurgence of anti-Semitism in a new form and in an unexpected quarter, was bound to result in unpleasantness and trouble. But even knowing this, I would discover that I did not know the half of it.

SOMETHING NEW UNDER THE JEWISH SUN

In the last few years, my talk began, "some of us" (by which I meant a number of contributors to *Commentary*) had been surprised to find ourselves feeling "a certain anxiety"[1] about the Jewish position in America. For expressing these feelings, we were being accused of paranoia—or, in the words of a left-wing social scientist named Melvin M. Tumin (who was himself Jewish) of "sniffing an anti-Semite under every rock." Was he perhaps right? Or were we responding like healthy animals to a real danger lurking up ahead? Instead of trying to answer that question in the abstract, I said, I wanted to look at the two traumatic events that, coming by a diabolical coincidence together at roughly the same time, had led us to feel the way we did.

The first of the two events was the Six-Day War of 1967—not so much the war itself as the period leading up to it and the one following its conclusion.* About two weeks before the shooting started, the president of Egypt, Gamal Abdel Nasser, had closed off the Straits of Tiran, thereby instituting a blockade of the port of Eilat, Israel's only outlet to the Red Sea. Such a blockade had been instituted by Egypt

---

* Because memory of those events was still fresh when I gave my talk, I did not find it necessary to go into as much detail in my account of the Six-Day War as I do in what follows. So, too, with the New York City teachers' strike that I discuss below.

before, and breaking it had formed one of Israel's motives for joining with England and France in the ill-fated Suez campaign of 1956. When it was over, President Eisenhower and his secretary of state, John Foster Dulles, demanded that Israel give up the gain it had made in driving the Egyptian army out of the Sinai Desert, and they had promised in exchange for an Israeli withdrawal that American action would be taken against any future efforts to close the Straits. Yet in 1967, for two weeks after Nasser did close the Straits, President Johnson could not bring himself to honor his predecessor's commitment.* As the United States dithered, the armies of the Arab countries bordering Israel maintained themselves in a state of full mobilization, and Nasser and other Arab leaders issued a steady stream of bloodcurdling threats to destroy Israel and drive its Jewish inhabitants "into the sea."

Thus, for the second time in the twentieth century, and only a quarter of a century after the first, a major community of Jews was being threatened with annihilation, actual annihilation, and once again the world, as it seemed, was standing complacently by. Finally, persuaded that it was too risky to wait any longer for the blow to fall, Israel launched a preemptive strike, and in six short days went on to win one of the most brilliant victories in military history.

One might have thought, I continued, that this spectacular feat of arms would have lessened the sense of Jewish vulnerability that had been so sickeningly revivified by the run-up to the war. For many Jews it did indeed have this effect, but not for those of us who were taken

---

* In my talk I did not go into the reasons for Johnson's failure to act, but here is the explanation I gave many years later: "There was a kind of sick-joke aspect to Johnson's uncharacteristic passivity. According to Lucius D. Battle, who had been the Assistant Secretary in charge of the Middle East under Dulles, the U.S. in 1967 was 'unable to find the record of the meetings and the discussions of the 1956 period,' which, he said, 'were, for economic reasons, stored in the Middle West—Cleveland, I believe—and were therefore not available when we needed them.' Thus 'the obligations that Mr. Dulles undertook at the earlier time were unclear and unknown.' Battle recalled Dulles's assurances as 'vague,' but he acknowledged that the Israelis, whose 'records of the conversations' were, unlike the U.S.'s, 'readily available,' also 'proved accurate.' Nevertheless, he added, 'These assurances were weak reeds and meaningless in the face of crisis.' Indeed they were." ("The United States and Israel—A Complex History," *Commentary,* May 1998.)

aback by the response of the many nations and the many churches to which the Israeli victory gave anything but cause for celebration. Worst of all, perhaps, were my fellow intellectuals.

In going on to discuss them, I raised what was already becoming a highly contentious issue and would remain so for years to come: the extent to which "what pleased to call itself anti-Zionism" was in fact a cover for anti-Semitism. In bringing this question up, I took care to stipulate that "anti-Zionism" was not necessarily yet another mutation of anti-Semitism. But I also took care to say that the distinction between the two was often invisible to the naked eye. Furthermore, anti-Zionism was serving to legitimize the open expression of a good deal of anti-Semitism that would otherwise have remained subject to the taboo against it that had prevailed from the end of World War II until, roughly, the Six-Day War. More than anything else, it was the breaking of that taboo against the open expression of hostility to Jews that had caused me and others to feel as anxious as we did. It was so long since overt hostility to Jews had been regarded as a permissible attitude in America that we simply could not tell what consequences might follow from the weakening of this inhibition.

But of course, I continued, it was not only in connection with Israel and not only among intellectuals that the taboo no longer remained in force. It had also been broken among blacks. And this brought me to the second of the two traumatic events that had caused some of us to worry about a resurgence of anti-Semitism in America—the New York City teachers' strike of 1968.[2]

This strike was a long and complicated affair, but, briefly, it had broken out when the administration of Mayor John Lindsay backed the demand—made in the name of "community control" and self-determination—of a group of black teachers in Brooklyn to be promoted despite the fact that they lacked seniority under the rules of the contract between the New York Teachers Union (NYTU) and the city. It was to all intents and purposes a dispute between management (in this case the city of New York) and a labor union acting to protect the interests of its members. But this was not how it was interpreted by the "Black Power" radicals who immediately rallied to the side of the city. To them, the strike was nothing more and nothing less than a struggle for power between blacks and Jews. Never mind that the NYTU was not a Jewish organization with a Jewish agenda: all that mattered was that many of its members were Jewish. Never mind, too, that they were all devout liberals, and that the president of the union, Albert Shanker, had a long record of active support for the civil rights movement. In spite of such considerations, the press, along with leftist periodicals like *The New York Review of Books* and *The Nation,* accepted and circulated the canard that the legitimate demands of oppressed blacks were being blocked by a gang of racist Jews.

In those days it was still startling to hear good Jewish liberals being accused of racism. But the brazen ferocity with which this charge was expressed by the black radicals, and the naked anti-Semitism that accompanied it, were even more shocking—as in a little poem that was read over the radio during the strike:

Hey Jew boy, with that yarmulke on your head,
You pale-faced Jew boy—I wish you were dead;
I can see you, Jew boy—you can't hide,
I got a scoop on you—yeh, you gonna die.[3]

In my talk, I said that there were two points that needed to be made about the teachers' strike. The first was that it brought black anti-Semitism into widespread public view. There were, I acknowledged, surveys showing that blacks were less anti-Semitic than whites, or at least no more so.* This finding might well be true, but it did not mean that the anti-Semitism that did exist among blacks was anything other than anti-Semitism, or that it was any the less odious, or any the less a potential threat to Jews than the anti-Semitism that existed among whites. Those who tolerated black anti-Semitism were tolerating anti-Semitism. Those who apologized for black anti-Semitism were apologizing for anti-Semitism.

---

* What I did not say was that the same surveys were showing that, in Sachar's summary, "While anti-Semitism tended to decrease among educated whites, it appeared to increase among educated blacks—essentially, younger, middle-class blacks" (Howard M. Sachar, *A History of Jews in America* [New York: Vintage Books, 1993], p. 812).

Yet—and this was the second point—the anti-Semitism that had surfaced among blacks during the New York teachers' strike was in fact more often tolerated, more often explained, more often "understood" than it was ever forthrightly and straightforwardly condemned. Worse yet, instead of being discredited or otherwise penalized—as they would have been only yesterday—the black radicals voicing blatantly anti-Semitic sentiments and ideas were actually being rewarded, with patronage from the city and grants from the Ford Foundation.

What this revealed was that the friendliness toward Jews that had existed in certain quarters could no longer be taken for granted. On the contrary, in these quarters there was a readiness to discard just those social mechanisms and processes under whose aegis the Jews had been able to escape the grosser discriminations that had been directed against them in an earlier day—specifically the mechanisms of the merit system in civil service employment and in university admissions. The merit system had neither been invented by Jews nor had it come into being for the sake of Jews. Yet Jews had prospered under an arrangement based on the traditional American principle that all persons were to be judged and treated as individuals without regard to "race, color, creed, or place of national origin." Even if this principle might be more honored in the breach than the observance, it was enormously important that we go on honoring it.

I then quoted the warning of Daniel P. Moynihan (who, although a Democrat, was at that point in his career serving in the White House as Nixon's chief adviser on domestic affairs) that if, under the guise of "affirmative action," the merit system were replaced by a system of proportional representation according to race or ethnic origin, the Jews, constituting a mere 3 percent of the population, would be "driven out." Yet such a replacement was precisely what was being advocated in powerful circles that continued to regard themselves as impeccably liberal in outlook. To put the matter brutally, in the name of justice to blacks, discriminatory measures were to be instituted once more against the Jews.

Having made the case against the charge of paranoia, I concluded with a section rebutting the accusation—with which, as I well knew, most of my audience agreed—that those of us feeling "a certain anxiety" were advocating a mean-spirited and selfish parochialism. Nothing, I insisted, could be further from the truth. Far from withdrawing into an ethnocentric enclave, we had been propelled into a newly aggressive affirmation of the institutions and the values of the traditional American system, and a newly militant defense of that order against the ideas of those who were devoting their energies, either ignorantly or innocently or in full nihilistic awareness, to damaging or destroying it. For in trying to determine the ideological source of the threat now being posed to Jewish security, we had arrived at the realization that it came from the very same forces that in recent years had been mounting an assault on America itself: the forces of the radical Left to which I myself had until recently belonged.

Because it was in this part of my talk that I arrived at the heart of the matter, I think it would be better to quote the exact words I used instead of summarizing and paraphrasing:

[O]nce upon a time the worst enemies of the Jews were to be found on the ideological Right, and the time may very well come when this will be true again. But it is simply not true today. The main source of anti-Semitic propaganda in the world today is not a fascist country like Nazi Germany but a socialist one, so-called: the Soviet Union. In the Middle East the most intransigent enemies of Israel are not Arab conservatives like King Hussein but Arabs of the revolutionary Left, and the more ardently revolutionary they are, the more violent is their hatred of Israel and the more determined they are to destroy both the State and its Jewish population. In Europe, it is the radical Left and not the Right which chants such slogans as this lovely bit from the SDS in Germany:

Macht den Nahen Osten rot,
Schlagt die Zionisten tot.
(Make the Middle East red,
Beat the Zionists to death.)

And in America—in America we find publications of the ideological Right like the *Alternative** warning against and deploring the growth of anti-Semitism, while publications of the Left like the *Village Voice* blithely go on expressing or apologizing for anti-Semitic sentiments and ideas.

I did not end with a call for the Jews of America to join the ideological Right (in fact, I added, there was no chance that "a people so overwhelmingly liberal in its political views [would] ever really move to the Right"); all I asked was that Jews recognize the ideology of the radical Left for what it was: an enemy of democratic values in general and a threat to the Jewish position in particular, both in America and in Israel.

To say that this talk fell on deaf ears would be a gross understatement. As the question period made even clearer than the tepid round of barely polite applause I received, the reaction ranged from stunned silence to a furious anger that could not contain itself. The first member of the audience to be recognized by the chairman was a high-ranking AJC professional who rose not to ask a question but to announce that never would he have believed that such things could be said at a meeting of the Committee. Therefore, rather than dignify my outrageous talk with a response, he intended to walk out in protest, which he proceeded, stormily, to do.

Others, however, were only too eager to take me on. Foreshadowing a charge I would hear a thousand times in the years ahead, one "questioner" without a question denounced me for trying to silence any and all criticism of Israel by equating it with anti-Zionism or, worse, anti-Semitism. In vain did I reply that I had explicitly stipulated that this was not necessarily the case.

Another "questioner" attacked my interpretation of the teachers' strike. It was not, he angrily declared, the blacks who had injected anti-Semitism into the dispute, but the president of the union who, in order to discredit the legitimate demands of the black community, had

---

* It would later change its name to *The American Spectator*.

done everything in his power to publicize the rantings of one or two marginal "kooks" who would otherwise have gone unnoticed. To this I replied—again in vain—with a few citations showing that the anti-Semitism that had surfaced during the strike was anything but marginal among the Black Power radicals, and that to blind oneself to it was tantamount to apologizing for it.

But it was a third such questioner who clearly spoke for the entire audience when he expressed his incredulity at my contention that the Left was a greater threat to democratic values and to Jewish security than the Right. Had I forgotten Hitler? And how could I have ignored the Christian fundamentalists and their "fascist" allies in the John Birch Society and other fanatically anti-Communist organizations on the radical Right? If these people succeeded in their efforts to tear down the wall of separation between church and state, we Jews would be turned into a barely tolerated minority, with worse to follow. Before I could answer this outburst, I had to wait for the thunderous applause it elicited to die down. When it did, I repeated what I had already said about this issue in my talk, but the fuming liberals arrayed before me were no readier to listen than they had been the first time around.

NIXON AND ISRAEL

About six months after the text of my talk had been published in *Commentary* under the title "A Certain Anxiety," I wrote a follow-up piece for the magazine with the deliberately provocative title "Is It Good for the Jews?"[1] There I argued explicitly that the end of the Golden Age of Jewish security and "the brassier age aborning" made it necessary for Jews to begin looking "at proposals and policies from the point of view of the Jewish interest." I had no illusions about how any such appeal to self-interest—even when accompanied by the assurance that it did not mean withdrawing into an ethnocentric ghetto—would be received by the "universalists" who staffed most of the Jewish organizations. To them, speaking in the name of Jewish interests smacked of crassness and parochialism, and I expected them to reject the appeal for that reason, among others. Which, of course, they did.

I was not alone in taking note of this "universalist" phenomenon. Richard Perle, for one, recalled a day in 1972 when, as an assistant to the ardently pro-Israel Democratic senator Henry ("Scoop") Jackson, he was working to round up support for a bill that would provide crucially needed aid to Israel:

The telephone rang, and it was the Washington representative of one of the Jewish organizations. I figured he was calling in with a report on the response of some Senators to our lobbying efforts. He wanted to talk about [William] Rehnquist [who had just been nominated by Nixon to the Supreme Court]. I said, "Jesus Christ, don't you know we're in the middle of a crisis?" And he said, "Well, I also wanted to talk about that," and I said, "Well, what do you know?" And the other crisis he had in mind was Bangladesh. Here was the son of a bitch running around on Rehnquist and Bangladesh at the crucial moment we were trying to bring on board the necessary support for this rather substantial appropriation, and that's typical. The principal representatives of the Jewish organizations in town all are interested in other things.[2]

Another senatorial aide said that the Washington representative of one of the other Jewish organizations was

very good in working on what amounted to very marginal Jewish interests. These are the traditional liberal interests in civil rights, integration, housing, and all that. As far as the gut issues—Israel and Soviet Jewry—are concerned, his input has been zero.[3]

On the other hand, the realities of the "brassier" new age were forcing a previously overlooked segment of the Jewish community into the spotlight precisely because it was taking up the cudgels in behalf of its own interests. This segment consisted (in the words of the historian Sefton D. Temkin) of

the poor shopkeeper, the schoolteacher, the Orthodox Jew whose life centered around his synagogue. . . . While the sheltered suburbanites . . . tended to maintain their traditional liberalism, those in violence-prone neighborhoods began to feel less sympathy for the minorities who, while struggling to better themselves, were bringing a good deal of hardship into the lives of lower-middle-class Jews.[4]

When these Jews tried to fight back, they found themselves being vilified. This was what happened in the Forest Hills section of Queens, where the Lindsay administration proposed to build low-income housing that would mostly go to people on welfare. When the lower-middle-class Jews living there protested—with much evidence to back them up—that the new housing would bring crime and violence into the neighborhood, they were denounced as racists by many of their more affluent coreligionists, who of course lived in the tonier parts of Manhattan and the well-protected suburbs to its north and east.

Episodes like the teachers' strike and the uproar in Forest Hills, in tandem with the ideas being developed and advocated by the "*Commentary* crowd," raised the question of whether the Jews might, *mirabile dictu,* be moving to the Right. Or, if this would be too much to expect, that enough of them might at least be abandoning their commitment to liberalism to leave the community as a whole with (as Tumin disapprovingly put it)

> a normal distribution of political opinions along the same spectrum and in the same proportion as non-Jews.[5]

If such a possibility was deeply disturbing to socialists like Tumin, it also aroused hope in others. As the presidential election of 1972 drew closer, the Republicans began to see a chance for Richard Nixon to get a bigger slice of the Jewish vote in his campaign for reelection than the paltry 17 percent he had managed to attract in 1968. Those prospects became even more promising when the Democrats nominated George McGovern. Unlike Hubert Humphrey, who had run against Nixon four years earlier, McGovern was not known as a great friend of Israel. "In a real crisis in Israel," an anti-McGovern Democrat quipped, "McGovern would send in a battalion of the Peace Corps, and then go to the UN wearing a yarmulke."[6]

To brighten Nixon's prospects even further, Yitzhak Rabin, then Israel's ambassador to the United States, made no secret of his preference for Nixon. He told a radio interviewer that Israelis

must see to it that we express our gratitude to those who have
done something for Israel and not just spoken on behalf of
Israel.

And in case there was any doubt as to which candidate he meant,
Stephen Isaacs of the *Washington Post* dispelled it by reporting that he
"traveled Washington's cocktail party circuit openly plumping for
Nixon's reelection."[7]

But McGovern's tepid attitude toward Israel was not the only thing
wrong with him from the point of view of Jewish interests. There was
also the issue of affirmative action or (in the words of a *Commentary*
article exposing the reality being covered up by such euphemisms)
"quotas by any other name."[8] The same AJC official who a year earlier had stormed out of the room to protest against my talk now wrote
a letter to the McGovern campaign warning that Jews like those in
Forest Hills were not alone in worrying about quotas:

> In the long pull, even more important than the Israel issue, key
> Jews will be turned off on George because of his statements on
> appointments to the administration on a proportional popula-
> tion basis. . . . It has already turned off some very good associ-
> ates of mine, . . . and I know the alarm is spreading fast. Many
> of them see this as a fundamental threat to the kind of society
> we have and cherish.[9]

Even though this resulted in a letter by McGovern to the American
Jewish Committee disclaiming any support for "quotas," he continued
promising to implement them under the name of proportional representation.

With so much going against him, McGovern's share of the Jewish
vote (65 percent) was 16 points less than Humphrey's (81 percent). That
"only" two-thirds of the Jewish vote went to McGovern, and that Nixon
did twice as well with Jewish voters (35 percent) as he had in 1968
(17 percent), was taken by some to mean that the Jews were indeed moving to the Right. But Rabbi Arthur Hertzberg of the American Jewish
Congress was much closer to the mark in his reading of the results:

The fact about this election that everybody missed is that the Jews were still more than 60 percent for McGovern, and in a very bad year. They were the only white group still for him, which says not how reactionary Jews have become, but says something about the "liberal" tradition of Jews. The Jews were still the only white "have" group voting for him, despite the fact that he intimated, in an unguarded moment, that he'd give in with a quota system, that Jews didn't trust what he said about Israel, and so forth. They were willing to swallow even him. I see this as a continuing stability for the kind of Jewish politics I stand for.[10]

While agreeing with Hertzberg's analysis, I drew a very different conclusion from it—which was that in 1972, when it no longer made sense from the point of view of Jewish interests to vote for the Democratic candidate, a large majority of Jews (described by Isaacs as "the middle-class suburbanites and the well educated") nevertheless did vote for him, with only what Isaacs called "the more ethnic Jews" going in relatively significant numbers for the Republican.[11] Furthermore, what this said about "the 'liberal' tradition of Jews" (as, by putting the word in quotes, Hertzberg himself seemed to have recognized) was that identifying themselves as liberals had become so important to most American Jews that for the sake of it they "were willing to swallow" even ideas and policies that were virtually the opposite of the ones that had only yesterday been defined as liberal by the Democratic Party itself, and that had been as good for the Jews as they were for America.

To wit: whereas the Democratic Party since Roosevelt had stood for internationalism in foreign affairs, McGovernism (as heralded by the campaign slogan "Come Home, America") was isolationist in all but name; whereas the Democrats had believed in treating individuals as individuals without regard to "race, creed, color, or country of national origin," McGovernism's embrace of quotas translated into treating individuals entirely *with* regard to race, creed, and color; and whereas the Democrats had interpreted the idea of equality as meaning of opportunity for individuals, McGovernism took it to mean equality of results for groups.

From the point of view of Jewish interests, Nixon was not exactly the ideal alternative to McGovern. Although he took a firm rhetorical stand against quotas, his own administration had been implementing an affirmative-action program requiring the building unions to hire more black workers (the "Philadelphia Plan") that could easily have been subsumed under the general rubric of "quotas by any other name." Nor, as of 1972, were the reasons for Rabin's gratitude toward him altogether obvious. And on the other great cause for which the American Jewish community was now mobilizing to fight—the right of Soviet Jews to emigrate—his position was still unclear.

From my own point of view, moreover, Nixon was even less ideal as an alternative to McGovern. In those days I still regarded myself as a Democrat—in fact, I had been one of the founders earlier that year of the Coalition for a Democratic Majority (CDM), whose purpose was to take the party back from the McGovernites who had captured it and return it to the principles and positions it had formerly held. But if voting for McGovern was out of the question, I also had serious misgivings about Nixon's policy of détente toward the Soviet Union, which I saw as verging on appeasement. After much to-ing and fro-ing in my own head, I finally voted for him (my first vote ever for a Republican), mainly because I decided that the more resoundingly McGovern was defeated, the better chance we of CDM would have to break his grip on the party. But it was because of what Nixon did when the Yom Kippur War broke out in 1973, less than a year after his reelection, that I came to feel that voting for him had been the right thing to do.

Having been caught off guard by a coordinated two-front attack by the Egyptians and the Syrians, the Israelis suffered great losses in the first few days of the war. At that point they urgently requested that the United States resupply them with the arms they would need to stave off defeat, but the Nixon administration was slow in deciding how and when to do so. A controversy broke out then over whether it was Henry Kissinger, the secretary of state, or James Schlesinger, the secretary of defense, who bore the responsibility for delaying the resupply. At the time, I thought it was Kissinger, but I have since been persuaded by several Israeli officials who were involved that

Schlesinger was mainly to blame. Be that as it may, one thing is certain: that it was Nixon who made the decision and who then forced the pace. Here is his own uncontroverted account:

> By Tuesday, October 9, the fourth day of the war, we could see that if the Israelis were to continue fighting, we would have to provide them with planes and ammunition to replace their early losses. I had absolutely no doubt or hesitation about what we must do. I met with Kissinger and told him to let the Israelis know that we would replace all their losses, and asked him to work out the logistics for doing so.[12]

Nixon then checked "almost hourly with Kissinger to see how our resupply effort was coming." When Kissinger said that Schlesinger was "putting up all kinds of obstacles," Nixon told him to "tell Schlesinger to speed it up." He had no intention of letting Israel "go down the tubes" when "a massive Soviet airlift of weapons and supplies was under way to Syria and Egypt."*[13] The next day, when he learned that there were additional bottlenecks, he called Schlesinger and ordered him to get the transport planes going: "Whichever way we have to do it, get them in the air, *now*." Finally,

> when I was informed that there was disagreement in the Pentagon about which kind of plane should be used for the airlift, I became totally exasperated. I said to Kissinger, "Goddamn it, use every one we have. Tell them to send everything that can fly."[14]

Thanks to Nixon's exasperation, the airlift finally got under way, and it saved Israel from a defeat that could have spelled the extinction of the state. Nixon thereby bestowed a retroactive vindication on both Rabin's "gratitude" and the judgment of the Jews who had voted for

---

* In his own account of the airlift Kissinger also stresses the need "for a demonstrative counter to the Soviet airlift" (Henry Kissinger, *Years of Upheaval* [Boston: Little, Brown, 1982], p. 505).

him because they feared that if Israel were to be plunged into a serious crisis McGovern would indeed "send in a battalion of the Peace Corps, and then go to the UN wearing a yarmulke."

In 1976, however, the Democrats nominated Jimmy Carter, who as a graduate of Annapolis did not seem to harbor the McGovernite suspicion of anything military. Conversely, his Republican opponent, Gerald Ford (who had acceded to the presidency in 1974 when Nixon, disgraced by the Watergate scandal, was forced to resign), did not seem as ready as his predecessor to do what it might take to keep Israel from going (in Nixon's phrase) "down the tubes."[15] Nor, in the contest between Carter and Ford, did any issue of special Jewish interest arise.

True, Kissinger (whom Ford kept on as secretary of state) and Scoop Jackson had been involved in a big fight over whether economic pressure was the best way of forcing the Soviet Union to drop its restrictions on Jewish emigration. In proposing to do just that through an amendment he had cosponsored with Congressman Charles Vanik, Jackson had the backing of the most passionate activists within the Soviet Jewry movement, as well as the support of the leading Jewish "refuseniks" within the Soviet Union itself. Kissinger, fearing that the amendment would undermine his policy of détente with the Soviet Union, incurred the wrath of both groups when he held out for quiet pressure behind the scenes. So great was this wrath that it blotted out the memory of what Nixon had done for Israel in the Yom Kippur War. Hence the Jewish vote was free to return to its heavily Democratic default position. But before it could do so, the problem represented by the Democratic candidate himself had to be overcome.

CARTER: "JOINING THE JACKALS"

In the Democratic primaries of 1976, Carter was the least favored by Jews of all the candidates (largely, according to Milton Himmelfarb, because he was so unfamiliar). Yet running against Ford in the general election, he did better with the Jews (71 percent) than McGovern had (65 percent). He probably would have fared better still if not for the paradoxical fact that he seemed *less* liberal in foreign policy than Ford. For Ford was staunchly loyal to the détente with the Soviet Union that had been initiated by Nixon and Kissinger, while Carter seemed committed to the tougher strategy of containment that had been the traditional Democratic position. It was for this reason that I, as a "hard" anti-Communist who had been a fierce critic of détente, made the worst political mistake of my life in voting for Carter. But it was surely the other way around for a certain number of "anti-anti-Communist" Jewish liberals who favored the more conciliatory approach to the Soviet Union represented by détente.

In a preelection piece, Himmelfarb ended by saying that "Carter need not worry very much about his Jewish vote," but he then added, "I hope Jewish voters need not worry very much about him." It was a hope that would be so badly disappointed by Carter's performance in office that, running for reelection against Ronald Reagan in 1980, he became the first Democrat since James M. Cox in 1920 to win less than a majority (45 percent) of the Jewish vote. This was only slightly better than the 40 percent he managed to get from the electorate as a whole. John Anderson, a liberal Republican who ran as an independent, provided an alternative to both major-party candidates for 14 percent of Jewish voters (but only 6 percent of the electorate as a whole).

If we are to understand this extraordinary Jewish defection from a Democratic candidate, we have to look first at what Jewish voters may have had in common with other Americans, and then we have to analyze what may have driven them as Jews.

Like most other Americans, Jews discovered from his performance in office that the Jimmy Carter who had conducted so successful a campaign was very different from what he had seemed to be. Both in the primaries and the general election he had run not so much against Gerald Ford or even the Republican Party as against "Washington." By this he meant, and was taken to mean, that he no more belonged to the Democrats with their taint of McGovernism than to the Republicans with their taint of Watergate.

As it turned out, however, he *did* belong to (or perhaps was captured by) the Democrats, and specifically to the McGovernite or leftist wing of the party. His vacillations and inconsistencies may have confused some, but to those with ears to hear, the fundamental themes of his presidency were always audible and they were always in harmony with the music of the new leftist liberalism.

For example, in his first major speech on foreign policy as president, he congratulated the nation on having overcome its "inordinate fear of Communism," thereby revealing himself as an anti-anti-Communist, and when he promised to exercise "restraint" (his word) in both the maintenance and the deployment of American power, he revealed his suspicion of the military. In the area of domestic policy, the McGovernism was a little less visible, but it was there in his continued resort to quotas with their built-in hostility to individual merit and initiative.

More generally, what Carter and his people and his apologists told us was that we were a country in decline. There was then nothing especially controversial or provocative about the idea that our military power was declining in relation to the Soviet Union and that our economic power was declining in relation to the Japanese. Many conservatives were saying the same thing. The question was what had caused us to lose so much ground and whether there was anything we could do to arrest or reverse it. Carter's answer was that our new condition was the result of vast historical forces, that we had no choice but to make peace with it, and that when we finally did we would wind up in a better and more secure position in the world. To resist, to attempt anything else, was "immature" and "simplistic."

But then (in 1979) came the storming of our embassy in Iran by the new Islamist rulers of that country, and the seizure of seventy American hostages. Nothing could more blatantly have exposed the hollowness of the idea that we would be better off for the decline of American power than this incredible insult to our nation, Carter's inability to do anything about it for fourteen long months, and the humiliating failure of the attempted rescue operation he finally decided to authorize.

By the time Carter found himself running for reelection against Ronald Reagan in 1980, however, he had dropped the declinist line and had once again disguised himself as something other than a McGovernite. In the wake of the Soviet invasion of Afghanistan that followed hard upon the heels of the seizure of our hostages in Iran, he had begun acting, or at least talking, more like Harry Truman than like George McGovern. But his born-again hawkishness was so inconsistent with his earlier policies and so hesitant in implementation that not even many Democrats were convinced of its seriousness.

Among the unconvinced were the white ethnics who before 1972 had never voted for a Republican in their lives but whose inability to stomach McGovern had given Nixon his landslide victory. Now these voters, having discovered that Carter represented the second coming of McGovernism, deserted the Democrats once again. As for the Jews, more than half of those who had voted for Carter in 1976 now voted for Reagan in 1980. In this respect they were acting for once like the other traditionally Democratic white ethnic groups, only more so. "No other group," Milton Himmelfarb wrote in his analysis of the exit polls, "changed so much in 1980 as the Jews."[1]

Thus, when the 14 percent of the Jewish vote that went for Anderson was added to the 39 percent that went for Reagan, it turned out that Jews had been even a bit more anti-Carter (53 percent) than

Catholics (50 percent). The reason in all probability was that a more strictly Jewish consideration—namely, the Carter administration's attitude toward Israel—had come into play.

In his post-presidential phase, Carter has been openly and virulently hostile to Israel. Possibly he himself had not yet come to feel this way while in office, but whether or not he had, his foreign-policy team was made up of people who were decidedly unfriendly to Israel. All of them—Cyrus Vance, his secretary of state; Zbigniew Brzezinski, his national security adviser; and Andrew Young, his ambassador to the UN—took the view that "Israeli intransigence" was the main, if not indeed the only, obstacle to peace in the Middle East, and that the Palestinians were blameless victims of Israeli expansionism. From this it followed that the United States ought to ratchet up the pressure on the Israelis in order to force them into withdrawing from the territories they had conquered in 1967 and turning them over to a new Palestinian state that would inevitably be ruled by the PLO.

The difficulty was that the United States had formally promised the Israelis (in an official Memorandum of Agreement sent to them by Kissinger in 1975) that we would not deal directly with the PLO so long as it refused to recognize the existence of Israel. Andrew Young considered this policy "ridiculous,"* and in the hope of moving toward its abrogation, he met secretly with a PLO representative. When it came out that our ambassador to the UN had acted in violation of an American commitment, Young was forced to resign. Released now from the "restraints" under which he had operated at the UN, he denounced Israel as an oppressor of the Palestinians and as "an expansionist power" engaged in "terroristic" raids.[2]

Even apart from this incident, it was at the UN that the degree of hostility toward Israel within the Carter administration was most fully manifested. Between 1977 and 1980, the United States either voted for, or failed to oppose, a series of viciously anti-Israel resolutions. These measures built on and furthered the campaign that had begun in

---

* So did Brzezinski, who had long been on record as approving a Palestinian state, and when years later I asked a former high official of the Carter administration if he, too, had secretly favored statehood back then, he answered with a big grin, "You bet I did!"

1975 with the passage by the General Assembly of the resolution declaring that Zionism was a form of racism. In making this equation, the UN was effectively endorsing the charge that the state of Israel was an illegitimate entity. It was saying that the very idea of a sovereign Jewish state in the Middle East (Zionism), let alone the actuality of one (Israel), no matter where its boundaries might be drawn, was by *definition* criminal (racist). In the eyes of this resolution, Israel could cease to be criminal only if it ceased to be both Jewish and sovereign— if, in other words, it ceased to exist. Returning to the boundaries of 1967 or even the boundaries of 1948 would make not the slightest difference: the resolution did not concern boundaries or occupied territories; it concerned the right of a sovereign Jewish state of *any* size or shape to exist in the Middle East.

As the Ford administration's ambassador to the UN when the Zionism-racism resolution was passed in 1975, Daniel P. Moynihan had voted against it with a speech pointing to its purpose and meaning.* A Democrat who subsequently became the junior senator from New York in the same election that sent Carter to the White House, Moynihan was appalled by the record on Israel that an administration of his own party had compiled at the UN—a record he angrily characterized as "joining the jackals."[3] He also considered this abysmal record a factor in Carter's defeat in 1980, in no small measure because it cost him heavily with Jewish voters in several key states (including New York, which had always been reliably Democratic but had just been carried by Reagan).

Granted, Carter had presided over the peace treaty between Israel and Egypt that was hammered out at Camp David in 1978 by Prime Minister Menachem Begin and President Anwar Sadat. But whether he deserved credit for this was another matter, since he had originally opposed a separate peace between Egypt and Israel. What he had called for instead was a conference under UN auspices that would be

---

* For the record, the speech was largely written by me, as Moynihan was generous enough to acknowledge several times in public. I was an old and very close friend of his at the time, and he had been appointed to the UN on the basis of an article I had edited and published in *Commentary* ("The United States in Opposition," March 1975).

cochaired by the United States and the Soviet Union. This came as a great shock to Sadat, who, having in the wake of the Yom Kippur War expelled the Soviets from his country and then aligned himself with the United States, now found the United States proposing, of all incredible things, to bring the Soviets back into the picture. Moynihan:

> To Sadat, the meaning of this was clear: a veto in the hands of the radical forces, immediate stalemate, ultimately perhaps his overthrow. And so to avoid going to Geneva, he went to Jerusalem (where, he had every reason to know, a deal was waiting to be struck with the Begin government). This set in motion the events that ended with the Camp David accords of 1978, and the Egyptian-Israeli peace treaty of 1979.[4]

Moynihan called this Carter's greatest achievement, but in reality—as his own account definitively demonstrated—the only credit Carter deserved was for unintentionally frightening Sadat into the visit to Jerusalem that got the process going. If Carter had had his way, there would have been no visit and no deal, and it was only when he realized that there was no stopping Sadat and Begin that he inserted himself between them in the hope of reaping political benefit at home.

All this formed the basis of my own belief that the barely concealed hostility to Israel pervading Carter's administration was what drove the majority of Jews, insofar as they were voting *as* Jews, to desert him in 1980. And it was because of this belief that I could not agree with the many commentators who saw in the 39 percent of the Jewish vote for Reagan the start of the long-delayed move of the Jews to the Right and into the Republican fold.

THE 1980 ELECTION

On the other hand, I did think that the 1980 election signified the emergence of a "new majority"[1] that had coalesced around Reagan's promise to work toward the restoration of American power. I also thought that to a certain extent those Jews who had voted for him did so because, like most other Americans (myself emphatically among them), they, too, wanted to see the country becoming great again. This supposition was supported by Milton Himmelfarb's analysis of the exit polls, which showed that "more than anything else, foreign and military affairs determined Jewish voting in 1980." Asked to agree or disagree with the proposition that "we should be more forceful in our dealings with the Soviet Union, even if it increases the risk of war,"[2] a majority (53 percent) of the Jews who answered said that they agreed. The result for all voters was 64 percent. Though Jews were less hawkish than other Americans, then, more of them were hawkish than not, or than they had been in 1976.

But it seemed clear that insofar as the Jews had voted *as* Jews, they had an additional reason of their own for backing Reagan. This, too, was borne out by Himmelfarb, who concluded that the Jews interviewed by the exit pollsters had "used questions about foreign and military affairs to express their anxiety about American support for Israel."[3] For they now remembered what they had learned from

Nixon's airlift in the Yom Kippur War—which was how vital American power was to the security, and even the survival, of Israel; and they (or at any rate the men among them*) had come to realize as well that there was something very wrong about opposing defense spending while advocating military aid to Israel.

On this point, they had been given a tutorial by Moynihan in his campaign for the Senate in 1976. After months of urging him to run, I became his behind-the-scenes adviser, and the best piece of advice he got from me was to keep insisting to Jewish audiences that there was a direct contradiction between caring about the survival of Israel, as the leftist congresswoman Bella Abzug, his main opponent in the Democratic primary, professed to do, and voting, as she also consistently did, against the defense appropriations out of which vital military aid to Israel had to come.

Following this advice played no small part in his razor-thin margin of victory over Abzug, for ever since the near calamity of the Yom Kippur War, anxiety about the fate of Israel had moved to the top of the list of Jewish concerns. Not only had such anxiety deepened among Jews who already suffered from it, but it had also widened to include even those groups within the community who as late as 1973 had still been harboring the feelings that had driven them to oppose the establishment of a sovereign Jewish state in the first place. Gone now was the anti-Zionism that in the pre-state period had made bizarre bedfellows of some Reform rabbis (for whom the Jews were "no longer a nation, but a religious community," and who therefore did not look forward to "a return to Palestine"); some Orthodox Jews (those who then believed that sovereignty in the Holy Land must wait upon the coming of the Messiah); and some socialist intellectuals (those who considered Zionism a form of reactionary bourgeois nationalism). Gone as well was the "non-Zionism" of the American Jewish Committee and other such groups, who had been less violent than the anti-Zionists in their opposition to the founding of a Jewish state but who had shared the same (prescient) worry about the accusations of dual

---

* Himmelfarb: "Reagan's excess over Carter was . . . 25 percent greater among Jewish men than among Jewish women," who remained as dovish as before.

loyalty that the existence of such a state might provoke. And gone, finally, was the indifference of those highly assimilated Jews who had no interest in anything Jewish, and who, if they thought about it at all, regarded the idea of a Jewish state as a parochial embarrassment.

Thanks to the virtually complete disappearance of all these sentiments, the polls showed that an almost unbelievable 99 percent of American Jews had now become Zionists, at least in the limited sense of backing the existence of a sovereign Jewish state. This "Zionization of American Jewry," as I called it at the time,[4] had been brought about by the realization that, given the determination of the Arab world and its allies to wipe Israel off the map, opposition or indifference became tantamount to "joining the jackals" and inescapably acquiescing in their genocidal objective.

I did not say or think, and neither did Moynihan, that the Carter administration actually wanted Israel to be destroyed. But what we both thought and said was that, in "joining the jackals," Carter and his foreign-policy team were contributing to a campaign whose purpose—as they should have known—was to delegitimize the Jewish state as a first step toward destroying it. That they deceived themselves about this cannot be doubted, any more than it can be doubted that the Jews who voted for Carter in 1980 similarly deceived themselves. But the Jews who did not deceive themselves could not possibly have voted for Carter, and so almost 40 percent of them voted for Reagan, while those who were unable to bring themselves to vote for so "reactionary" a candidate voted instead for Anderson.

As I confessed above, I had voted for Carter in 1976 on the chance that he would take the Democratic Party back from the Left, but by 1979 I had come close to deciding that this was a lost cause. What finally clinched it for me was a meeting with Carter to which I, as part of a delegation from the Coalition for a Democratic Majority, had been invited shortly after the invasion of Afghanistan. The White House had arranged the meeting in the expectation that it would assuage our skepticism about the claim—vital to Carter's chances of beating Reagan—that the invasion had brought him around to a point of view on the dangers of Soviet expansionism much the same as ours. (Having, as we have seen, previously repudiated the belief of hawks like us that "Soviet expansionism was almost inevitable and must be contained," Carter now said that the invasion had wrought a "dramatic change" in his "opinion of . . . the Soviets' ultimate goals.") But the meeting had the opposite effect. He seemed oblivious to the reasoning behind and the implications of our position, and he responded very angrily to the questions arising from it (his face grew red and the veins in his neck bulged so visibly that I feared they might burst). Leaving that meeting, I no longer had any doubt that I was going to vote for Reagan, and neither did most of the others who had been there.

Unlike a few of them, however, in supporting Reagan I was not only repudiating Carter; I was also giving up on the hope for the Democratic Party that had led me to help found the Coalition for a Democratic Majority. The majority, of which I now saw myself as a member, was not the one for which CDM claimed to speak. It was "the new American majority" that had coalesced around an entirely different hope—the hope that Reagan would inaugurate a great effort "to reverse the decline of American power."

Those were the words I used as the subtitle of *The Present Danger,* a little book I had written a year or so before the election, and also before Reagan had won the Republican nomination. My purpose was to warn of the danger posed by the weakness that had overtaken American policy toward the Soviet Union, and to call for a resumption of our original determination to contain the spread of Communist power. It was a theme I had been sounding loudly since 1970, both as a writer and as the editor of *Commentary;* and—with Scoop Jackson having tried and failed to get the Democratic nomination and Moynihan having refused even to try—Reagan turned out to be the only viable candidate for the presidency in either party whose point of view was much the same as the strategy my fellow neoconservatives and I had been advocating for the past decade.*

Israel did not figure at all in *The Present Danger,* although I had long since come to believe that there was a happy harmony between its

---

* This was why, after winning the nomination, Reagan issued a statement urging "all Americans to read this critically important book." Gratifying though his endorsement of *The Present Danger* was, it created the false impression in some quarters, especially abroad, that I was one of his advisers, and a close one at that.

security and my "hard" anti-Communist perspective on the cold war. Yet so far as I could tell, this was not how most Jews felt. While I agreed with Milton Himmelfarb that a degree of hawkishness had gone into the Jewish vote for Reagan, I felt sure that it was a temporary product of the recoil from Carter. I therefore thought that it would have no lasting political effect either on the Jewish attachment to the Democratic Party or the Jewish identification with the going liberal ideas and attitudes. Here, too, my impression was bolstered by the exit polling, which found that only 12 percent of Jews called themselves Republicans and that only about 18 percent called themselves conservatives.*

Even more striking evidence came from the Jewish position on such social issues dear to the liberal heart as abortion and the Equal Rights Amendment (which was then very hot). Sachar writes:

> An NBC poll in 1980 found that 69 percent of Jews favored the Equal Rights Amendment, compared with 45 percent of others. Asked about abortion, 89 percent of Jews felt that the choice should be left to the woman, compared with 74 percent of Protestants and 61 percent of Catholics.[5]

Another very hot issue of the day was prayer in the schools. Just how hot it was for Jews I discovered on the book tour I took to promote *The Present Danger*, in the course of which I had occasion to speak in synagogues all over the country. In almost every one of them, I would be challenged less on the "present danger" of Soviet power than on how I felt about the much greater and more present danger, as my Jewish audiences saw it, of prayer in the schools. All American liberals were exercised over the matter, and it was the nonsectarian American Civil Liberties Union that was leading the fight against this allegedly unconstitutional breach of the separation of church and state guaranteed by the First Amendment. But there could have been none so passionate about this issue as the Jewish audiences I was addressing.

---

* The 18 percent figure represented an average of the finding of two different exit polls.

Without exception, they were convinced that it was the opening wedge in a campaign by the religious Right and its secular allies to turn all non-Christians, and especially the Jews, into second-class citizens.

In a lighthearted effort to allay their fears, I would generally respond by telling them about (and sometimes, if the mood was upon me, even doing a rendition of) the hymn I had sung every morning in the elementary school I attended as a child growing up in Brooklyn in the 1930s:

> Holy! Holy! Holy! Lord God Almighty!
> Early in the morning our song shall rise to Thee:
> Holy, Holy, Holy! Merciful and Mighty!
> God in Three Persons, Blessed Trinity.

Yet, I would then say, so little impression did the daily singing of this very Christian hymn make on me that it was only when, already well into adulthood, I heard it on the radio that I realized for the first time what the words signified. Surely, then, they were taking the whole thing too seriously.

This reassurance had about as much effect on them as the singing of the hymn had left on me. As the ensuing discussions made unmistakably obvious, the ancestral fear of Christianity was still alive in their nervous systems, and it was still so powerful that it blinded them to the growing evidence of a change within the two branches of Christianity that had traditionally been the most feared of all: Catholics and "Bible-belt" or evangelical Protestants.

I could make no headway in arguing how far the Catholic Church had come in its attitude toward the Jewish people when in 1965 it had formally and officially absolved "all the Jews then living" as well as "the Jews of today" of blame for the death of Jesus, and had also "deplore[d] the hatred, persecutions, and displays of anti-Semitism directed against the Jews at any time and from any source."[6] The only thing the Jewish audiences I was addressing seemed to know or care about this Declaration was that it had been watered down from an earlier and stronger draft. When I countered by saying that compared to the recent past, let alone earlier periods, even the admittedly watered-down version represented an enormous step forward, all I got in response was a roomful of rolling eyes and heads shaking at me in disgust.

Equally futile was my reminder that conservative Protestants were at least as passionate in their support of Israel as the Jews themselves. The one thing my Jewish audiences thought they knew and that they cared about was that the Protestants of the religious Right were pro-Israel only because they believed that Jewish sovereignty in the Holy Land was a precondition for the Second Coming of Christ and the conversion of all Jews to Christianity. It did no good to point out that this was the view of only one Protestant sect, and that the support of all the others for Israel was based not on any such millenarian expectations but on the promise God makes to Abraham in the Bible (which, as fundamentalists, they took literally and as absolute truth):

I will make of thee a great nation, . . . and I will bless them that bless thee, and curse him that curseth thee.[7]

To this the response would invariably be the same disgusted shaking of heads. So, too, whenever I quoted the witty comment by the original "godfather" of neoconservatism, Irving Kristol, that if the Second Coming ever came, we would discover whether the Christians had been right, but in the meantime there was no reason for us Jews not to embrace them as allies.

Pastor John Hagee of Christians United for Israel put the same idea even more humorously:

When we're standing in Jerusalem and the messiah is coming down the street, one of us is going to have a very major theological adjustment to make. But until that time, let's walk together in support of Israel and in defense of the Jewish people, because Israel needs our help.[8]

Yet even though, as a result of all these factors, I strongly doubted that the 1980 election marked the start of a Jewish migration either to the Right or to the Republican Party, the irony was that some were blaming and others crediting the neoconservative intellectuals, and me in particular as the editor of *Commentary,* precisely for having led the way to such a shift. Naturally I would have been happy to think so, since it would have meant that the Jews of America were finally beginning to acknowledge that the Left had largely become enemy territory and that their political friends were increasingly to be found on the Right. But if this was ever to be, the day had not yet arrived. It was true that in 1980 (as Sachar writes) "a far larger proportion of Jews declined to pull the Democratic lever than at any time since the first Eisenhower election of 1952."[9] Yet if (in Himmelfarb's words) "for the first time most [Jews] . . . experienced in their own flesh that the right hand need not wither if it strays from the Democratic lever,"[10] fewer of them would turn out to be ready for a second taste of this novel experience.

Thus, in 1984, instead of going up, Reagan's share of the Jewish vote went down, from 39 percent to 31 percent, and once again the Jews reverted to their traditional position, giving a big majority (61 percent) to his Democratic opponent, Walter Mondale. Compared with all the Democratic candidates who had preceded him in the past sixty years (except for Carter in 1980, whose running mate he had been), Mondale did poorly with Jewish voters. But compared with how he did with the electorate as a whole (40.6 percent), and with the two major Christian groups (Protestants: 27 percent; Catholics: 44 percent), his 61 percent slice of the Jewish vote amounted to a veritable landslide.

There were two reasons for the decline in Reagan's share of the Jewish vote. The less important of the two involved the widespread Jewish fear of the religious Right and the conservatives associated with it. This fear had been calmed to some degree during Reagan's first term by the failure of the campaign for prayer in the schools to win the support either of Congress or the courts. But it was reawakened with a vengeance when the story got around that copies of the Bible omitting the Old Testament and containing only the New had been distributed to the delegates at the Republican National Convention of 1984.

No greater gift could have been handed to the Jewish partisans of

Mondale. They gleefully seized upon it as proof positive that the Republicans, as well as Reagan himself, had been taken over by the religious Right whose secret agenda included removing Judaism from its place of honor in the "Judeo-Christian tradition." It was a waste of breath for us Jewish supporters of Reagan to argue yet again that the vast majority of evangelical Protestants disavowed any such intention. Nor did it help us to point out for the thousandth time that on Israel, the most important issue of Jewish concern, the religious Right was on the side of the angels. The plain fact was that not even anxiety about the security of Israel could trump the suspicion harbored by many Jews that deep in the heart of the religious Right lay the determination to abrogate by reinterpretation the First Amendment's prohibition of "an establishment of religion" and to get the United States officially declared a Christian country.

Nor were they in the least bit reassured by the persistent affirmations of commitment to the separation of church and state that conservative Christian leaders like Pat Robertson and Jerry Falwell had made. As Robertson once put it:

Despite claims to the contrary, I have never suggested or even imagined any type of political action to make America a "Christian nation." While it should never mean that religious ideals and ideas are to be excluded from political discourse, I agree that church and state should be separated because the separation of church and state is good for religion, religious institutions, and the religious liberty of believers. These are not merely words of acquiescence to the acrimonious writings of a few— they are the enunciation of my most personal beliefs and my most fundamental convictions.[11]

The sincerity of this statement seemed, and seems, obvious to me. Yet even if it and others like it were meant to conceal the true agenda of the Christian Right, it would still have taken a greater miracle than any in the Bible for the Supreme Court—even in the equally miraculous event that it were composed of five Antonin Scalias and four

Clarence Thomases—to read the First Amendment's prohibition of "an establishment of religion" as sanctioning the establishment of Christianity as this country's official religion.

None of this meant, however, that anxiety over the security of Israel played no part in depressing Reagan's share of the Jewish vote in 1984. It most assuredly did—but from a wholly unexpected direction.

REAGAN AND ISRAEL

After leaving office, when he had nothing to gain politically from professing a great concern for Israel, Reagan wrote:

> I've believed many things in my life, but no conviction I've ever held has been stronger than my belief that the United States must ensure the survival of Israel.[1]

And again:

> My dedication to the preservation of Israel was as strong when I left the White House as when I arrived there . . .

But the rest of this sentence ended with the words:

> . . . even though this tiny ally, with whom we share democracy and many other values, was a source of great concern to me while I was President.[2]

The concern was mutual, and it arose on both sides in his first few weeks in office over the proposed sale to Saudi Arabia of several of the flying radar stations, known as AWACS, that (in Reagan's own description) could "spot incoming aircraft and missiles and direct the launching of defensive or offensive missiles."[3]

Reagan was convinced that the sale would not change the balance of power in the Middle East, but that it would demonstrate that American support of Israel did not preclude a friendly consideration of the interests of the "moderate" states within the Arab world. So far as Saudi Arabia in particular was concerned, the underlying purpose of this policy was (Reagan would later write) to prevent it from becoming "another Iran."[4] Not much was said in public about Iran in the protracted and heated debates over the AWACS, but that it played a serious part in Reagan's decision I discovered when, around this time, I happened to run into his secretary of defense, Caspar Weinberger.

In sharp contrast to the strongly pro-Israel Alexander M. Haig, then the secretary of state, Weinberger (despite, or perhaps because of, the fact that, although not Jewish himself, he had Jewish roots) was notoriously hostile toward Israel. He was, however, very cordial toward me because I held the same hard-line position as he did on the Soviet threat, and for this he was willing to forgive me my position on Israel. Taking advantage of this friendly feeling on his part, I quixotically taxed him about the AWACS sale, expecting that he would justify it as a way of reducing Soviet influence in the Middle East. But to my surprise, he said that the main reason for the AWACS deal was that it would give the Saudis the ability to "peep into Iran," and to help us keep an eye on what the Khomeini regime was up to.

In any event, Menachem Begin (who in 1977 had become the first prime minister in the history of Israel who was not a member of the Labor Party) violently disagreed with Reagan both about the balance of power and about the putative moderation of the Saudis. I shared Begin's view of the matter as well as his passion about it, and so did most American Jews, even though, unlike me, they were very uncomfortable to find themselves politically in bed with a right-winger like him.

In this they were reflecting the attitude toward Begin that had been prevalent on the Israeli Left ever since his accession to power. To the political and intellectual establishment in Israel, which was made up almost entirely of men of the Left, Begin was a hated figure. Interestingly, the feelings of the Israeli establishment toward him bore a striking resemblance to the feelings of the liberal establishment in America about Richard Nixon. Liberal hatred of Nixon had deep roots, going all the way back to his role in the Hiss case; in like fashion, the hatred of Begin in Israel went back all the way to the ideological and political wars of the pre-state period between the Labor Zionists on the Left and the "Revisionist" disciples of Vladimir Jabotinsky on the Right of whom Begin was a leader. In America this hatred of Nixon as the ancestral enemy was widened and deepened by the chagrin of the liberals over his success in mobilizing the so-called silent majority to usurp the power that they were convinced rightfully belonged to them; and it was much the same in Israel, where the socialist Zionists were in a heightened rage over Begin's success in riding the Sephardi and the Orthodox vote to power over them.

But if this made most American Jews uneasy, I had no such problem. Besides, in fighting against the AWACS sale, I was appealing to Reagan as one of his supporters, and on the basis of his own professed determination to do nothing that would jeopardize the survival of Israel. A little while later, I would attempt something similar through an article titled "The Neoconservative Anguish Over Reagan's Foreign Policy,"[5] in which I pointed to the many discrepancies between his ideas about the threat posed by the Soviet Union and the strategy he was pursuing toward it. (This elicited a phone call from him explaining that he meant to win by squeezing the Soviets economically. I remained skeptical, but it was exactly what he went on to do through the Strategic Defense Initiative.)

The main argument that I—along with most of its other opponents—advanced against the AWACS sale was that the justification for it rested on a fantasy. Summarizing that justification in his diary, Reagan wrote:

> We are striving to bring stability to the Middle East and reduce
> the threat of a Soviet move in that direction. The basis for such
> stability must be peace between Israel and the Arab nations. The
> Saudis are a key to this. If they can follow the course of Egypt
> the rest might fall in place.[6]

As against this line of reasoning we maintained that in reality the Saudis were no less determined than "frontline" Arab states like Syria and Iraq to wipe the Jewish state off the map. Consequently the AWACS would more likely serve as an intelligence weapon against Israel in the event of another war than as an inducement for the Saudis to "follow the course of Egypt." Reagan, however, could not be swayed, and this gave those Jews who had refused to vote for him another golden opportunity to claim vindication while leaving those of us who had supported him disappointed and abashed.

Then, in the midst of the AWACS furor, relations between the United States and Israel were strained even further when, on June 7, 1981, the Israelis launched a surprise air attack on the nuclear reactor that was being built by Saddam Hussein in Iraq.

A time would come when it would be very widely acknowledged that if not for this spectacular military operation, Saddam Hussein would shortly thereafter have developed a nuclear arsenal through which he could have deterred any such effort as was successfully made in the Gulf War of 1991 to stop him from taking over the oil fields of the entire region. But in 1981, far from being thanked, Israel was universally condemned for—in the language of the resolution passed by the Security Council with the acquiescence of the United States—its "clear violation of the Charter of the United Nations and the norms of international conduct."

To me, it was appalling that the Reagan administration should have voted for this infamous resolution when it had the veto power to prevent its passage—and all the more so because the American arm that was raised in support belonged to my friend and fellow neoconservative Jeane Kirkpatrick. Like Pat Moynihan before her, she had been appointed ambassador to the UN on the strength of an article that, as with his, I had edited and then published in *Commentary*.[7] A number of other contributors to *Commentary* (including Eugene V. Rostow, Richard Pipes, William J. Bennett, and Elliott Abrams) had also been given important positions in the administration, but she was the most visible as well as the one most widely known to be associated with the magazine and with me. Consequently I—like every other Jew who had backed Reagan—was even more embarrassed and abashed by the vote she cast for the resolution than I had been over Reagan's support for the AWACS sale.

I knew Kirkpatrick to be so passionately pro-Israel that it was inconceivable to me that she agreed with the resolution she had voted for. When I remonstrated with her, she told me that she had done so only after ensuring that the resolution would not entail sanctions. I replied that I still thought she should have insisted on exercising the veto but, convinced that she had done a good job under the circumstances, she stuck to her guns. Subsequently I learned that Haig, who shared her feelings about Israel, thought so well of the compromise she had worked out that he claimed credit for it. And Reagan, too, was so pleased that he called Kirkpatrick to congratulate her.[8] He would later write that "some cabinet members wanted me to lean hard on Israel," and as a sop to them,

> we sent a note to the Israeli government criticizing the raid, and delayed shipment of several additional military aircraft as a show of our displeasure.

Even so, Reagan "had no doubt that the Iraqis were trying to develop a nuclear weapon" and he "sympathized with Begin's motivation and privately believed that we should give him the benefit of the doubt."[9]

All this was very well, but it still left a bitter aftertaste that lingered on long enough to do its share in depressing the Jewish vote for Reagan in 1984. But what caused even more trouble between Reagan and the American Jewish community was his response to the Israeli incursion into Lebanon in 1982.

The original purpose of this move was to drive the PLO out of the "state-within-a-state" it had created within Lebanon, in an area of some twenty-five miles bordering on the north of Israel and from which it had relentlessly been shelling nearby Israeli towns. But after accomplishing that limited objective—which the Reagan administration had tacitly supported—the Israelis decided to go further, with the intent of forcing the PLO out of Lebanon altogether. In the course of pressing their way toward the Lebanese capital of Beirut, the Israelis also attacked Syrian missile sites in the Bekaa Valley and dealt a stunning blow to the Syrian air force to boot. When, however, they reached the outskirts of Beirut, into which the PLO forces had retreated, the Israelis reckoned that it would be too costly to go in and dig them out with ground troops. Hence they laid siege to the city and proceeded to bombard sites within it in which, according to their best intelligence, the PLO forces were holed up. The Israelis took great care to minimize civilian casualties, but there was no avoiding them entirely since the PLO had resorted to the usual terrorist tactic of hiding behind civilians.

Under international law (specifically Article 28 of the Geneva Convention of 1948), "the presence of a protected person may not be used to render certain points or areas immune from military operations," and the responsibility for civilian casualties or damage rests on the party, in this instance the PLO, who thus uses protected persons or areas. What the other side, in this instance Israel, was required to do was exactly what Israel did: that is, warn the civilians in advance so that they would have a chance to leave the area or otherwise protect themselves.

Nevertheless—and not for the last time—it was not the PLO but the Israelis who were universally condemned for violating international law, and for the "slaughter in Beirut" they were perpetrating through the

relentless and indiscriminate bombardment of neighborhoods filled with Lebanese civilians who had absolutely no role in the Israeli-PLO dispute.

The strong words I have just quoted were Reagan's own,[10] but they were mildness itself compared to what he said directly to Begin. "I told him," Reagan recorded in his diary, that

[the bombing and shelling] had to stop or our entire relationship was endangered. I used the word "Holocaust" deliberately and said the symbol of his country was becoming "a picture of a seven-month-old baby with its arms blown off."[11]

Begin, as might be imagined, did not take kindly to this equation of an attack on the PLO strongholds in Beirut with the slaughter of six million Jews by the Nazis, and word of it certainly contributed its share to the decline of the Jewish vote for Reagan in 1984. Yet in making that equation Reagan was echoing what innumerable commentators—the overwhelming majority of them, ironically, on the Left—had been saying almost from the first minute the Israelis had crossed into Lebanese territory.

For the war in Lebanon triggered an explosion of invective against Israel that in its fury and its reach was unprecedented in the public discourse of this country. Although some of it came from the Right, the lion's share emanated from prominent liberal columnists like Anthony Lewis of the *New York Times,* Richard Cohen of the *Washington Post,* Mary McGrory also of the *Post,* and William Pfaff of the *International Herald Tribune.* A respectful hearing was also being given to Edward Said, the most famous academic apologist for the PLO, who was offered space on the Op-Ed page of the *New York Times* to accuse Israel of pursuing "an apocalyptic logic of exterminism."[12]

The comparison with Nazi Germany that Said evoked with the word *exterminism* became the main theme of the left-wing attacks on Israel. "Incident by incident, atrocity by atrocity," wrote the columnist Nicholas von Hoffman, "Americans are coming to see the Israel government as pounding the Star of David into a swastika."[13] Similarly, William Pfaff, who began one of his columns on the subject by declaring that "Hitler's work goes on," and then concluded with the prediction that Hitler might soon "find rest in Hell" through "the knowledge that the Jews themselves, in Israel, have finally . . . accepted his own way of looking at things."[14]

No military action taken by Israel could have been more "disproportionate" than these condemnations of Israel, and the very need they created for a refutation of what should have been self-evidently preposterous seemed to me a measure of the intellectual and moral swamp into which the liberal community had sunk in its attitude toward the Jewish state.

ANTI-"ZIONISM"

In "J'Accuse," the article I wrote about the liberal response to Lebanon—and in which I was forced by the very act of refuting it to dignify the disgusting charge that Israel had become the moral equivalent of Nazi Germany—I said that the only honest way to characterize such wildly irrational attacks on Israel was to call them anti-Semitic. In justifying the use of so loaded a term, I pointed out that historically anti-Semitism had taken the form of labeling certain vices and failings as specifically Jewish when they were in fact common to all humanity: Jews were greedy, Jews were tricky, Jews were pushy, Jews were clannish—as though Jews were uniquely or to an exceptional degree guilty of all those sins. Correlatively, Jews were condemned when they claimed or exercised the right to do things (like working hard to better themselves, or looking after their own) that all other people were accorded an unchallengeable right to do, and were even praised for doing. Now the same charges that anti-Semites had always hurled at Jews living in the Disaspora were being translated into the language of international affairs and applied to the Jewish state.

Thus, whereas all other peoples were entitled to national self-determination, when the Jews exercised this right, they were committing the crimes of racism and imperialism; and whereas, according to

Henry Kissinger, no other "sovereign state could tolerate indefinitely the buildup along its borders of a military force dedicated to its destruction and implementing its objectives by periodic shellings and raids,"[1] when Israel exercised the right to use force under such circumstances, it was committing the crime of aggression.

I went on to stress that criticisms of Israel based on this double standard, and only such criticisms, should be called anti-Semitic—even when they were mouthed by Jews or, for that matter, Israelis. That being Jewish or possessing Israeli citizenship guaranteed immunity from anti-Semitic ideas might seem a plausible proposition, but it was not borne out by experience. Like all other human beings, Jews were influenced by the currents of thought around them; and like all other minority groups, they often came to see themselves through the eyes of an unsympathetic or hostile majority. Jews were of course the majority in Israel, but the state itself was isolated among the nations, and subjected to a relentless barrage of moral abuse aimed at its delegitimation. This seemed finally to be taking the inevitable psychological toll in the appearance among left-wing Israelis of the term *fascist* in talking about their own society, when by any universal standard it was among the two or three countries in the world least deserving of this epithet.

Knowing all too well that I would once again be accused of trying to suppress any and all criticisms of Israel by stigmatizing them as anti-Semitic, I took care to add (not that it did any good) that criticisms based on universally applied principles and tempered by a sense of balance in the distribution of blame were entirely legitimate, even if they could be shown to be mistaken or dangerous to Israel. As an example, I cited the editorials published on Lebanon in the *New York Times*. They had been harsh on Israel, they had often been unfair, and they had pointed toward policies that would jeopardize Israel's security. But they had not been guided by the usual double standard, and therefore, I said (and meant it), they could not and should not be regarded as anti-Semitic.

I also went out of my way to make it clear that it was the *ideas* that were being spread about Israel in general, and its move into Lebanon in particular, that I was calling anti-Semitic and not the people (or at least not most of them) who were spreading those ideas. I was even willing to concede that in some, or even most, cases, they were unaware of the anti-Semitic pedigree of the ideas they were spreading.

But this could not have been true of Reagan. Having, as he would later admit, "consciously used the word *holocaust* to describe the indiscriminate bombing of Beirut because I knew it would have a special meaning for Begin,"[2] he could not have been acting in ignorance when he made this equation between what the Nazis had done to the Jews and what Israel was now doing to Beirut.

Yet so far from being an anti-Semite was Reagan that an FBI dossier had once portrayed him

> as an emotional foe of anti-Semitism who denounced persecution of the Jews in radio broadcasts and nearly came to blows at a party with a guest who said that the Jews had profiteered from the war.[3]

And so far was he from being hostile to Israel that Shimon Peres, one of the leading Israeli political figures of the period, could say: "Israel was one of those issues about which . . . [Reagan] was unshakable— he was a staunch supporter."[4] Jerry Falwell, then the head of the Moral Majority, would go even further:

> I discussed Israel with him many times. Once at the White House . . . I said, "Mr. President, I believe that God deals with nations in regard to how those nations deal with Israel. . . . There are a number of reasons why God has blessed this country, but one of them is that we blessed Abraham. So if there is any one thing that you as a President must never compromise, it is our commitment to Israel." And he didn't hesitate; he said, "I believe that."[5]

Further confirmation would come from Lou Cannon, one of the closest and more objective students of Reagan's presidency:

> Reagan operated on the assumption that U.S. interests were linked to those of Israel. . . . While his views on most other

subjects changed during his metamorphosis from liberal Democrat to conservative Republican, Reagan remained staunchly pro-Israel. As a liberal, he felt that U.S. protection of Israel was owed to the survivors of the Holocaust. As a conservative, he came to regard Israel as a strategic bulwark against Soviet intervention in the Middle East. "The crucial element determining the success or failure of American policy [in the Middle East] is the fate of Israel," Reagan said in a policy paper issued early in his 1980 campaign.[6]

With these feelings and this conviction, how could Reagan have said what he did to Begin? The answer, I believe, is that even he had been influenced by all the talk in the air equating Israel with Nazi Germany. Notoriously susceptible to what he saw on film, he was hit especially hard by the television footage that provided a highly exaggerated picture of the extent of the damage being done to Beirut—a picture those of his own advisers who were unfriendly to Israel not only did nothing to correct but accepted totally at face value. ("I can't be a part of this anymore, the bombings, the killing of children," said one of his closest aides, Michael Deaver, who threatened to resign unless Reagan forced Begin to stop.[7])

As if this were not enough, Reagan was misled into believing that many Jews felt much the same way. For several groups within the Jewish community—especially those on the Left who had only grudgingly dropped their original opposition to Jewish statehood—were now being driven by Lebanon to reconsider the "Zionization" they had undergone as a result first of the Six-Day War of 1967 and then of the Yom Kippur War of 1973.

In both of these earlier wars, because Israel's survival was imminently threatened, they had rallied to its side. However, as the Sinai campaign of 1956 had demonstrated, and as Lebanon once again showed, if Israel resorted to arms when its total destruction was not the immediate alternative to war, their support could not be counted on. In general, indeed, only when Israel behaved in what they considered an exemplary fashion, beyond any and all liberal reproach, were they prepared to stand fast against the relentless efforts of the "jackals" to define it as a criminal state, to rob it of legitimacy and therefore of the right to exist. What the Six-Day War of 1967 and the Yom Kippur War of 1973 had done for these conditional friends of Israel, the war in Lebanon of 1982 now undid.

A few, but only a few, went so far as to join the jackals themselves by openly returning to the anti-Zionist position they had held in the past. But when the leftist opposition within Israel, driven by an undying hatred of Begin, began hurling epithets like "fascist" at him, and when a line like "In our matzah is the blood of Palestinian children" could appear in an Israeli poem, encouragement was given to those American Jews in whom repressed doubts about the value and validity of Jewish statehood were now returning with a vengeance.

Although these (more or less) de-Zionized Jews were a small minority (I estimated it at 15 percent of the community as a whole), the liberal media—seeking Jewish cover for its own virulent response to Lebanon—made full use of its power to create the impression that they represented at least half of the American Jewish community. Scarcely a day passed without a story in the newspapers and on television playing up statements by prominent Jews who denounced the Israeli invasion of Lebanon as everything from an unwise resort to force to an act of imperialist aggression. To remain unaffected by all this, Reagan would have had to be, so to speak, more Jewish than the Jews.

This is not to deny that hostility to Israel also existed on the Right. It did, as exemplified by Caspar Weinberger at the Pentagon and in the White House by Reagan's vice president, George H. W. Bush, and James Baker, his chief of staff, not to mention the Arabists in the State Department (by no means all of whom, however, were on the Right). There were also a number of conservative pundits like Patrick J. Buchanan and the columnist team of Rowland Evans and Robert Novak whose hostility to Israel was a match for the enmity of liberals like Mary McGrory.

Nevertheless, there could be no doubt that the staunchest—and almost the only—defenders of Israel in the media during Lebanon were also conservatives, whether to the manner born (like the columnist George F. Will, the editorialists of the *Wall Street Journal,* and most contributors to *The American Spectator*) or converts from the Left (like the neoconservatives who wrote for *Commentary*).

Even the unflinchingly pro-Israel Charles Krauthammer, then associated with the professedly liberal *New Republic*, was already showing signs of the neoconservatism he would later embrace as a widely syndicated columnist; and it was often said of Martin Peretz, the editor of *The New Republic*, who was second to none in his passionate championship of Israel, that one of the reasons he kept insisting on calling himself a liberal was that his magazine's main rival, *The Nation*, was always trying to smear him by charging that the political line of *The New Republic* was indistinguishable from the neoconservatism of *Commentary* (which, on Israel but not on Israel alone, it often very nearly was).

The upshot is that, with a few exceptions duly noted, the reversal of roles between Left and Right on issues of Jewish interest—and on Israel above all the rest—grew even more pronounced in the responses of the two sides to Lebanon than it had been when it first became noticeable in the aftermath of the Six-Day War of 1967.

THE CASE OF *THE NATION*

Speaking of *The Nation,* it would before too long provide a vivid picture of the extent to which "anti-Zionism" had metastasized on the Left since 1967. The occasion was the publication of an article by the famous writer Gore Vidal that appeared in a special issue commemorating the magazine's 120th anniversary.

Titled "The Empire Lovers Strike Back,"[1] Vidal's piece impressed me and many other people as the most blatantly anti-Semitic outburst to have appeared in a respectable American periodical since World War II. *The Nation* was a left-wing magazine run by an editor, Victor Navasky, who was himself Jewish. Yet one reader (who happened not to be Jewish) wrote in a personal letter to Navasky that he could not recall encountering "that kind of naked anti-Semitism" even in papers of the lunatic-fringe Right, which specialized in attacks on Jews; to find its like, he said, one had to go back to the Nazi gutter press.

Actually, however, it was not the crackpot racism of Julius Streicher that Vidal was drawing on, but sources closer to home. Prominent among these was Henry Adams, about whom Vidal had written admiringly and with whom he clearly identified. As we have seen, Adams was given to anti-Semitic outbursts so violent that they shocked even his closest friends. One of these outbursts—"The Jew has got into the soul. I see him—or her—now everywhere, and wherever he—or she—goes, there must remain a taint in the blood forever"—seemed to have made a particularly strong impression on Vidal.

In Vidal's own diatribe there was no explicit mention of blood, but there was its functional equivalent in the idea that Jews—even those born in the United States!—were all foreigners living here by the gracious sufferance of the natives. Incorrigibly alien though the Jews were, however, they exercised enormous and malevolent power over the politics of what Vidal, conjuring up the long-discredited spirit of nineteenth-century nativism, did not hesitate to call "the host country."

In the days of Henry Adams, the great power of the Jews was supposedly used in the interests of world Jewry; but after 1948 it was generally said to be deployed in the interest of the Jewish state, which Vidal, taking up this line, characterized as a "predatory" nation "busy stealing other people's land in the name of an alien theocracy."[2]

Here was Vidal's version of how the conspiracy worked:

> In order to get Treasury money for Israel (last year $3 billion), pro-Israel lobbyists must see to it that America's "the Russians are coming" squads are in place so that they can continue to frighten the American people into spending enormous sums for "defense," which also means the support of Israel in its never-ending wars against just about everyone.

As befitted this resurrection of two of the classic themes of anti-Semitic literature—the Jew as alien and the Jew as the conspiratorial manipulator of malign power dangerous to everyone else—Vidal's tone was poisonous. His every word dripped with contempt and hatred, and underlying it all was a strong note of menace. The Jews had better watch out if they wished "to stay on among us"—not that "we" would necessarily permit them to stay even if they did begin minding their manners. Why should "we," when their only purpose was "to make propaganda and raise money for Israel," thereby impoverishing the rest of us and bringing the world closer and closer to a nuclear war?

As I would later write,[3] I could hardly believe my eyes when I first read this article. What amazed me was not the fact that I and my wife,

Midge Decter, had been singled out by Vidal as representative examples of the phenomenon he was claiming to expose. I had known Vidal personally for many years, and had followed his career, so I was well aware that he believed in getting back at anyone who had the temerity to criticize him—a crime that Midge Decter and I had each recently committed.

So a retaliatory strike, or even two, was to be expected from Vidal. Why then was I amazed when it came? It was because neither of the two pieces Vidal was pretending to answer so much as mentioned Israel or had anything whatever to do with the particular concerns of the American Jewish community. One of them (mine) was about the attitudes of the American literary world toward the United States; the other (my wife's) dealt with the American role in Mexico, Hawaii, Puerto Rico, and the Philippines. By gratuitously dragging the issue of Jewishness into such a discussion, Vidal was recklessly exposing himself to the charge of anti-Semitism. For who but an anti-Semite would attempt to refute an opposing political position by interpreting it as a Jewish conspiracy against the rest of "us"?

But Vidal did more than merely introduce the "Jewish question"— as his anti-Semitic forebears liked to call it—into an unrelated discussion. He did more than sound two classic themes of anti-Semitic literature. He did all this without even bothering to conceal his true feelings. For example, in response to my statement that in America "the blessings of freedom and prosperity are greater and more widely shared than in any country known to human history," he said that I was wrapping myself in "our flag" and wearing it "like a designer kaftan." Again, in taking up Midge Decter's detailed challenge to his conception of American imperialism, Vidal countered that "she is [an Israeli] propagandist (paid for?), and that is what all this nonsense is about." And to make certain that his meaning would not be mistaken, he called us both an "Israeli Fifth Column."

So it went, literally ad nauseam.

I was confident that a storm of protest would be unleashed against Vidal and *The Nation,* but I was certainly not expecting anyone to defend me or my wife. What I hoped for was that the protest would come from people sympathetic to *The Nation*'s left-wing political position, who would say that while they detested everything Norman Podhoretz, Midge Decter, and all the other neoconservatives stood for, and while nothing made them happier than seeing us raked over the coals, they were outraged by the reintroduction of anti-Semitism into American political discourse in general and their own political community in particular.

And indeed, about a week after Vidal's piece appeared, just such a protest emerged from the very heartland of that community, the *Village Voice*. Under the rubric "Jew Roasting," its press critic, Geoffrey Stokes, wrote:

> Happy 120th Birthday, *Nation*! On the other hand, what the *hell* was Gore Vidal's anti-Semitic screed doing in the special anniversary issue? Not even clever, . . . Vidal's piece . . . had the unsettling effect of making me briefly sympathetic to Podhoretz.

Gratifying though this was, however, it was followed by complete silence from the Left. In *The Nation* itself, three issues went by with no letters to the editor, and when an inquiry was made to its editorial offices, the answer was that the mail on Vidal's piece had not been unusually heavy, that it was split evenly pro and con, and that some of it would eventually be run.

Growing impatient, I had a letter sent out from my office to twenty-nine friends and supporters of *The Nation* whose names were selected both from the magazine's masthead and from the congratulatory messages that had appeared in the anniversary issue. It read as follows:

> In connection with a projected article, we are asking a number of friends and supporters of *The Nation* whether they have seen fit to protest against the contribution by Gore Vidal to the 120th anniversary issue ("The Empire Lovers Strike Back"). Could you let us know whether you have made such a protest, either in private or in a letter for publication?

In the four weeks that followed the mailing of this letter we received only seven replies. By that time *The Nation* had also begun running letters in its correspondence columns, of which three were from people who had been on our list. Eliminating overlaps, this came to a total of eight out of twenty-nine. Of the eight, only five said they saw anything wrong with the article or with *The Nation*'s decision to publish it. Of the others, two attacked our letter as an impropriety, while either saying nothing about Vidal at all or explicitly denying that his article was anti-Semitic. The third, the journalist Roger Wilkins, writing to *The Nation* for publication, called Vidal's piece "splendid" whereas the attacks on it as anti-Semitic were "ugly mumblings," a species of McCarthyism, and a threat to the First Amendment. Striking a note that had repeatedly been sounded in response to "J'Accuse," and that would be heard over and over again from defenders of Vidal, Wilkins declared:

> Scoundrels have many last refuges. One is to attack as anti-Semitic any criticism of the policies of any given government of Israel or of any supporters of Israel, no matter how frothing those supporters may be.

But Wilkins was not content with defending Vidal against the charge of anti-Semitism. He even denied that the piece was anti-Israel. Like himself, Wilkins wrote, Vidal believed that

> one [could] criticize an Israeli government policy or one advocated by a supporter of Israel as being both dangerous to peace and to Israel's security without being either anti-Israel or anti-Semitic.

In other words, the critics of Israel were allowed to say anything they wanted, no matter how vile, about the state and its supporters, but it was McCarthyism and a threat to the First Amendment to criticize *them*. To put the same idea another way: it was permissible to make anti-Semitic statements, but it was impermissible to call such statements anti-Semitic. Yet if anyone was erasing the line between legitimate criticism of Israel and anti-Semitism, it was precisely the likes of Wilkins who were doing so by their unwillingness or inability to distinguish between the former and a clear case of the latter like the Vidal article.

But what of the twenty-one who did not respond to our letter? What did their silence mean?

Some weeks later, after the controversy had attracted a great deal of publicity, both in America and many other countries, three of the twenty-one finally got around to communicating their dislike of Vidal's piece directly to me. All three, however, said that they felt no compelling reason to protest against its publication. As for the other eighteen, not a one was ever heard from.

In short, a large number of prominent Americans on the Left who had publicly associated themselves in one way or another with *The Nation,* and whose names had appeared in one capacity or another in the very issue containing so blatantly anti-Semitic an article, had not been sufficiently outraged to register disapproval or to express a protest. Nor did many others on the Left respond by (to borrow an image Vidal had used in congratulating himself for candor) calling a spade a spade: by, that is, denouncing Vidal's article as a vile anti-Semitic outburst and expressing dismay or disgust at the fact that a magazine professedly devoted to liberal ideals should have given house room to such a piece.

After nearly a month of waiting for a serious protest to materialize, I finally came to realize that things were even more ominous than they had seemed at first. It was bad enough that a presumably reputable author should see fit to write a blatantly anti-Semitic article; it was even worse that a magazine calling itself liberal should see fit to publish such an article; but what was worst of all was that so few of the magazine's friends and admirers had been willing to raise their voices against it.

I had up to this moment been very reluctant to weigh in on Vidal myself, mainly because I feared (rightly, as it would turn out) that my arguments would be dismissed as nothing more than the complaints of an aggrieved interested party. But I now felt that I had no choice but to write something, and to make the piece I proceeded to do as impersonal as possible, I emphasized the theme of liberal silence:

a silence as deep as the moral pit into which the *Nation* itself
has fallen in welcoming the unabashed return to American
political discourse of a murderous poison against which the only
antidote is the revulsion of decent people.

This piece first appeared in the *New York Post,* and then a day later
in the *Washington Post,* at which point a veritable storm broke out.
Before it subsided two months or so later, at least twenty articles had
been published about the controversy in American newspapers and
magazines, and nearly half as many again in other countries, including
England, France, Germany, Australia, and Israel. The majority sided
with Vidal, and the rest divided into two camps. One refused to take
the dispute between us seriously (it was nothing more, declaimed
Newsweek, than "a big-league literary feud"). The other, equating an
anti-Semitic article with a protest against it, called down a plague on
both our houses (writing in the *Los Angeles Times,* Jody Powell, a former adviser to Jimmy Carter, "steadfastly refused to choose" between
us because it was "impossible to attack one without appearing to be
allied with the other").

It would have been hard to find better evidence than this entire
episode for the case I had been trying to make since 1967 that anti-
Semitism had now found a comfortable and hospitable home on the
Left. But what about the other side of this coin—the argument that
anti-Semitism was becoming more and more unwelcome on the Right?
By a lucky coincidence, the answer to that question was given by *The
Nation*'s opposite number on the Right, *National Review,* when
around the same time it became embroiled in a similar controversy of
its own.

26

THE CASE OF *NATIONAL REVIEW*

Joseph Sobran was nowhere near as famous or as influential as Vidal, but he had standing and a respected position on the Right as a senior editor of *National Review,* a syndicated columnist, and a commentator on CBS radio. For some years, and especially since the Lebanon war, when he had joined the jackals on the Left who were attacking Israel, he had become increasingly hostile to the Jewish state. Remonstrations had been privately made to him by friends about how far he was going in those pieces, and a number of angry letters were printed in one of the small-town newspapers that carried his column.

To all this Sobran responded by defending himself against what he indignantly denounced as Jewish attempts to intimidate and silence him. He would not, he vowed, be intimidated; he would not be silenced. And he was as good as his word. Over the following months, he seemed to let no opportunity slip for attacking Israel and American support for Israel. As bitter an opponent of the Left as could be found, he was even driven to seize on a book attacking Zionism from the Left as a vehicle for the amazing declaration that he had never seen a good case made, except by Jews (whose arguments, of course, could not be trusted), for the American alliance with Israel.

This was far from the only instance when the issue of Israel drove Sobran into making common cause with people or positions he would normally have been the first to attack. The most egregious example was his criticism of a strike ordered by Reagan on Libya in retaliation for an act of terrorism in which American soldiers had been killed. This was so uncharacteristic a stance for a hard-line conservative hawk like Sobran to take, and so inconsistent with his general world-view, that it could only cause his regular readers to wonder how he had come to such a pass. But demonstrating his fearless disregard of the "gas-chamber rhetoric" that would no doubt be thrown at him, Sobran provided the materials for dispelling that wonder:

> The Israeli lobby is, of course, the most powerful lobby in America. That is ultimately why Congress so quickly endorsed a direct military strike against Libya, while it quibbles endlessly about whether aid to the *contras* in Nicaragua might lead, someday, to American military involvement in Central America. Qaddafi is an enemy of Israel. Communist Nicaragua isn't. It's an enemy of America, period. So we fight Qaddafi, and maybe, the administration hints, Syria and Iran as well. Ostensibly the issue is "terrorism," but that sounds more and more like a surrogate word for enemies of Israel.[1]

Of course the Sandinistas ruling Nicaragua—who had declared that "the PLO cause is the cause of the Sandinistas"—*were* enemies of Israel. But Sobran would not permit so elementary a fact to stand in the way of his theory that the Jews first manipulated Reagan into bombing Libya, and then manipulated the Congress and the media into applauding him for doing so.

As if all this were not enough, Sobran in his syndicated column took the occasion of the pope's visit to a synagogue in Rome earlier that year to dredge up canards against the Jews as a people and Judaism as a religion that had rarely been heard since the Middle Ages:

> Millions of Jews chose to migrate to Christian Europe. They lived there for centuries. If Christians were sometimes hostile to Jews, that worked two ways. Some rabbinical authorities held that it was permissible to cheat and even kill Gentiles. Although

the great Jewish theologian Moses Maimonides insisted that it was as wrong to kill a Gentile as a Jew, it seems strange that this should ever have been a matter of controversy, and Maimonides was in some quarters regarded as a heretic.

The ignorance here, and the malicious use to which Sobran put it, was breathtaking. Never mind the preposterous lies about rabbinical permission to cheat and kill Gentiles or the suggestion that the reason Maimonides was regarded "in some quarters" as a heretic was that he considered it wrong for a Jew to kill a Gentile. Never mind the ludicrous moral judgment that (in another passage of the same column) equated Christian "hostility" to Jews—manifested, as detailed in Part One of this book, in mass expulsions, pogroms, forced conversions, and denial of civil or political rights—with the Jewish refusal to accept Jesus as the Messiah and the correlatively derogatory Jewish attitude toward him. The point to be stressed was that in this column, although Israel came in at the beginning and the end, the issue was not Zionism, or rather anti-Zionism, but Jews and Judaism throughout the ages. Anti-Semitism, in other words: naked and unashamed.

There was no problem, then, over how to characterize Sobran's writings about Israel and the Jewish community in general, but there was a problem of what to do about it. With the Vidal controversy still raging, it seemed reckless to open up, so to speak, a second front. On the other hand, to let Sobran's pieces go by without protest might only make it seem that while we neoconservatives were all too ready to attack anti-Semitism on the Left, we were perfectly content to tolerate it on the Right. After thinking about it for a while, we hit on the idea of writing a very tough letter to Sobran himself and to send copies to a number of mutual friends and political allies. *Mutatis mutandis,* then, just as members of Vidal's political community had been asked for their reaction to his piece in *The Nation,* so Sobran's political friends were now being asked how they felt about his column on Israel and the Jews. But there the similarity ended.

In contrast to the Vidal-*Nation* case, none of the clearly anti-Semitic Sobran columns had appeared in *National Review*. In spite of this, the editor of *National Review,* William F. Buckley Jr., responded to our letter, and to the urgings of nearly all the people to whom it had been sent, by deciding to publish an editorial dissociating the magazine from Sobran on this issue. Written by Buckley himself with the concurrence of all the other senior editors of *National Review*, the editorial affirmed that while his colleagues were sure that Sobran was not in his heart an anti-Semite, anyone who did not really know him

> might reasonably conclude that those columns were written by a writer inclined to anti-Semitism. . . . Accordingly, I here dissociate myself and my colleagues from what we view as the obstinate tendentiousness of Joe Sobran's recent columns.

Buckley also expressed confidence that Sobran would in the future respect the "welcome" structure of "prevailing taboos concerning Israel and the Jews."

It would be pleasant to report that this was the end of it. Unfortunately, Sobran himself and a number of his other friends and allies sprang to his defense in terms very similar to those used by Vidal and his apologists. They denied that the columns in question were anti-Semitic; they complained that anyone who "criticized" Israel was smeared with accusations of anti-Semitism; they charged that the Jewish lobby was trying to silence them; they invoked the First Amendment.

From Vidal's political friends on the Left, then, mainly denial, and from the editor of *The Nation*, stonewalling. From Sobran's political friends on the Right, mostly outrage (with the exceptions noted above), and from the editor of *National Review*, dissociation and repudiation of anti-Semitism.

What emerged from this dramatic contrast between the two cases was further evidence that anti-Semitism had largely if not entirely been banished from its traditional home on the Right, while, especially in the guise of anti-Zionism, it was meeting with more and more toleration, and sometimes even approval, on the Left.

Meanwhile, large segments of the American Jewish community (like the liberal community as a whole) were persistently refusing to take this momentous phenomenon seriously. So reluctant were even the Jewish defense organizations to register outrage at what *The Nation* had done that several weeks passed before they could get themselves to speak up. A reporter from an Israeli newspaper, who later went around trying to find out why these agencies had been so quiet, discovered that the feeling was that "Norman can take care of himself." But the issue was not "Norman," and to define it in those terms was to turn an anti-Semitic assault into "a personal quarrel" and thereby to evade facing up to the immensely important change it so clearly revealed and the reversal of political alliances for which it so urgently called.

27

GEORGE H. W. BUSH AND ISRAEL

I have speculated that Reagan's policy toward Israel—as reflected in the AWACS sale, the American vote on the Israeli raid on the Iraqi nuclear plant, and his anger about the military tactics Israel was using in Lebanon—helped to lower his share of the Jewish vote in 1984. If, as seems more than likely, the Jews who had voted for Reagan in 1980 but who then switched to Mondale in 1984 did so because they believed that the Democrats behind Mondale (as opposed to those behind Carter) were more pro-Israel than the Republicans behind Reagan, it soon became clear that they had been mistaken.

A few months after the election, the passengers on a TWA plane that had been hijacked by Hizbollah were being held hostage at the Beirut airport. In the midst of this crisis, an ABC News–*Washington Post* poll asked a representative sample of Americans whether they agreed or disagreed with the proposition that "the U.S. should reduce its ties to Israel in order to lessen the acts of terrorism against us in the Middle East." The findings were as follows: among those who "approved of the way Ronald Reagan is handling his job as President" (presumably consisting of conservatives), the percentage who opposed reducing ties to Israel outnumbered the anti-Israel group by 35 points (61 percent to 26 percent). Among the anti-Reagan group (presumably made up of liberals), however, the margin in favor of Israel was only

2 points (45 percent to 43 percent). Measured by party affiliation, among Republicans the pro-Israel group outnumbered the anti-Israel group by 29 points (57 percent to 28 percent), whereas among Democrats the pro-Israel margin was only 13 points (50 percent to 37 percent).[1]

The discrepancy between these numbers and the opinions expressed in the *National Survey of American Jews* conducted in the first half of 1984 by the sociologist Steven M. Cohen was startling. Asked which groups they thought were anti-Semitic, 29 percent of Cohen's respondents answered Republicans as against 6 percent who named Democrats, while 35 percent pointed the finger at conservatives as against 7 percent who named liberals. Yet only a few months after the survey was completed, the mostly liberal delegates to the Democratic National Convention (pleading procedural obstacles but not unreasonably suspected by many of fearing to offend the black leader Jesse Jackson and using those obstacles as an excuse) would refuse even to consider a proposed resolution condemning anti-Semitism, while the mostly conservative delegates to the Republican convention would loudly applaud Reagan and Jeane Kirkpatrick when they made a point of denouncing anti-Semitism and praising Israel.*

In short, if what drove the Jews who had voted for Reagan in 1980 back to the Democrats in 1984 was their expectation that Israel would fare better under a Mondale administration than it had during Reagan's first term, they were acting out of the same refusal to recognize the great change that had come over the liberal community with respect to Israel that would show up in that community's response to the Vidal scandal.

It was also close to unimaginable that a Mondale administration would have done as much on the other issue that had come to the fore

---

* According to a report in the *New York Times* (October 30, 1984), the Democratic Party claimed that "its rules precluded the adoption of a resolution that had not been approved by a standing committee." But three weeks later, after Reagan had made this a campaign issue, Mondale tried to defuse it by getting the executive committee of the Democratic National Committee to adopt a resolution repudiating "people who promote all forms of bigotry, racism and anti-Semitism." In addition to being prudently evenhanded, this belated statement was never made "part of the party platform."

in the 1970s and had now begun to rival Israel in importance to the American Jewish community—the plight of Soviet Jewry—as the Reagan administration did in its second term. The main objective of the Democrats was to improve relations with the Soviet Union, and they would therefore have been very reluctant to take any steps that might rile the Soviets. But Reagan was out not to placate but to defeat the Soviets, and he had no compunctions about making demands on them when he considered it both politically and morally necessary. This very much included the plight of Soviet Jewry, in which, according to Yitzhak Shamir, who would later become prime minister of Israel,

> Reagan's interest . . . was immense; it was close to the first issue on the American agenda and was part of the confrontation between the two superpowers.[2]

Reagan's second secretary of state, George Shultz, grew equally impassioned as the years wore on, and he never ceased pressing the Soviets to allow those Jews to emigrate who wanted to do so, and to give those who wanted to stay the right to practice their religion without being hampered or harassed. These relentless efforts paid off in the gradual lifting of restrictions both on Jewish emigration and on Jewish religious practice.

In 1988, Reagan's vice president, George H. W. Bush, running against the Democrat Michael Dukakis, drew a larger share of the Jewish vote (35 percent) than the 31 percent Reagan had received in 1984. Even so, this did not in my opinion give any good reason for the hope or the fear, as the case might be, that the Jewish tie to the Democratic Party was resuming the loosening trend that had seemed to set in with Reagan in 1980. For even to so unprepossessing a Democrat as Dukakis, the Jews gave two-thirds (64 percent) of their vote, or nearly 20 points more than the 45.6 percent he received from the electorate as a whole.

Still, the Jewish vote for Bush was surprisingly high. According to one explanation, he was helped by the role he had played as vice president in engineering Operation Moses, the first airlift of Ethiopian Jews to Israel.[3] But it may also be that some of the credit for how much the Reagan administration had done for Soviet Jewry had rubbed off on him. Conversely, it seemed that none of the blame had rubbed off on Bush for the visit Reagan made at the beginning of his second term to a German military cemetery in the town of Bitburg. When he had first promised the German chancellor, Helmut Kohl, that he would go to Bitburg, Reagan did not know that SS men were buried there. But once this fact came to light, it engendered a storm of protest—and not from Jews alone—against the proposed visit. Lou Cannon reports that he was tempted to cancel it, but after Kohl told him that "he would be politically and personally embarrassed . . . and that his government might fall"[4] if the visit were called off, Reagan felt that he had no choice but to keep his promise.

Inevitably this gave more ammunition to the Jewish liberals who continued to insist that the Republicans were still at best indifferent and at worst hostile to Jewish concerns. Yet the amount of ammunition they got from Reagan's visit to Bitburg would be as nothing compared to what they were about to get when Bush succeeded him as president.

It began with the First Gulf War of 1991 ("Desert Storm") that was launched to force Saddam Hussein out of Kuwait, which he had invaded a few months earlier in what was widely seen to be a first step toward a takeover of all the oil fields in the Middle East, including those of Saudi Arabia. For this purpose Bush put together a coalition that included most of the Arab states but from which Israel was pointedly excluded. Yet almost immediately after Desert Storm was launched, Saddam Hussein began making good on the threat he had issued earlier to rain Scud missiles—possibly armed with chemical warheads—into Israel. I was in Jerusalem at the time, rushing night after night into a sealed room with a gas mask on, and I well remembered how desperately the Israelis had wanted to retaliate. They had three excellent reasons for chafing at the bit.

First, as a matter of national self-respect, they did not want American soldiers shedding blood on their behalf. Second, they were afraid that their passivity in the face of these attacks would undermine the deterrent effect of their long-standing policy of retaliation. And third, they believed—with good cause, given the specialized training their bomber pilots had received to execute just such missions—that they themselves could have done a better job of eliminating the Scuds than was being done by the United States and its coalition partners.

Knowing all this, Bush still insisted that (as he reportedly said in private) the Israelis would come in "only over my dead body." Supposedly his theory was that their entry would drive out at least some of the Arab members of the anti-Iraq coalition. Yet he must also have known that the Egyptians, the Saudis, the Kuwaitis, and even the Syrians, the most anti-Israel of the Arab states in the coalition, had indicated, not once but several times, that they would stay put if Israel were to take defensive retaliatory action against Iraq.

Why then was Bush so adamant about keeping Israel out? Some Israelis were derided at the time for the "paranoid" suspicion that, as a way of exerting pressure on Israel to make territorial concessions that most Israelis considered dangerous to their security, he was planning to throw it up to them that Americans had risked their lives in order to defend the Jewish state. But it was these "paranoid" Israelis who turned out to be right, as Bush proved when, in a press conference after the war, he did precisely what they had feared:

> Just months ago, American men and women in uniform risked
> their lives to defend Israelis in the face of Iraqi Scud missiles,
> and indeed, Desert Storm, while winning a war against aggres-
> sion, also achieved the defeat of Israel's most dangerous adver-
> sary.[5]

Yet when he made that statement, Bush also knew that the Israelis had never asked Americans or anyone else to defend them; all they ever asked for was help in equipping their own people to defend themselves. If things were different in the Gulf War, it was because, and only because, Bush himself had forcibly prevented the Israelis from assuming direct responsibility for their own defense against the Scud attacks. (That is, he had refused to give the Israeli Air Force the "friend or foe" codes its pilots would have needed to escape being shot down when flying over American-dominated airspace on their way to the Iraqi desert.)

In general, this press conference introduced a new tone toward Israel into the air. It was a tone ranging from ordinary coldness to the outright animosity that was on display in Bush's description of himself—the president of the United States!—as "one lonely little guy" up against "something like a thousand lobbyists on the Hill." The lonely little guy, he would have all the world understand, wanted to convene a new conference to resolve the Arab-Israeli conflict, but the Arabs would not attend unless the Israelis met certain conditions (first and foremost a freeze of new settlements in the West Bank). In order to force Israeli compliance with these conditions, the lonely little guy had asked Congress to delay a previously promised loan guarantee needed by Israel to house Jewish immigrants from the Soviet Union, and it was this that the putative army of lobbyists on the Hill was working to prevent.

For thus playing into the canard that the American alliance with Israel was based on the illegitimate manipulation of domestic politics by an all-powerful Jewish lobby, Bush won his delay. But he also called forth an avalanche of congratulatory mail so egregiously anti-Semitic that it reportedly caused him to regret his use of this squalid tactic.

The worst of it from the Israeli point of view was that the United States, far from eliminating the Iraqi missile threat, had failed to locate most of the Scud launchers during the war and had succeeded mainly in destroying decoys. Nor had any missiles been shot down by the Patriot interceptors that the United States had hurriedly sent in for that purpose. Consequently, finding themselves vulnerable once again in case of a renewal of hostilities, and now being able to operate without "friend or foe" codes, the Israelis undertook a series of reconnaissance flights over Iraq.

In response, Saddam Hussein protested to the United Nations, to which the White House, instead of dismissing this as a piece of arrant chutzpah, replied by expressing its "concern about the Israeli overflights . . . to the Israeli government at the highest level." These overflights, explained the president's spokesman, might "disrupt the peace process," and besides they were unnecessary because the United States was already providing Israel with intelligence on Iraq. Yet in view of the very fact that Iraq had emerged from the war with so many Scud launchers and missiles intact, the Israelis might have been forgiven for doubting that American intelligence was all that it should have been in this field, or all that was needed to keep Israel secure.

In addition to adopting a new tone in its relations with Israel, the Bush administration was going beyond any of its predecessors in the intensity of its preoccupation with the Arab-Israeli conflict. It was, indeed, a preoccupation that seemed to border on the obsessive. Thus, at a moment when Saddam Hussein was massacring Kurds and Shiites in one part of the Middle East, James Baker, the American secretary of state, was spending all his time shuttling back and forth from Jerusalem to Amman to Damascus to Riyadh in order to arrange for a peace conference in Madrid. Nor did such concurrent events as the breakup of the Soviet empire and the collapse of Communism within the Soviet heartland distract Baker's attention from what he and Bush evidently regarded as a more important priority.

Considering that the maintenance of stability in every part of the world was the chief goal of Bush's foreign policy (which was why he had notoriously urged the Ukrainians to forget about seeking independence even though the Soviet empire was no more), this obsession would have made sense if it had been true that the Palestinian problem was the main source of instability in the Middle East. Yet though this theory was almost universally accepted as gospel, the plain facts of the case made complete nonsense of it. Since the birth of Israel in 1948, there had been up to that point at least nineteen violent clashes in the region having nothing whatever to do either with the Palestinians or with the Jewish state. Among these were several major wars, most recently the one between Iran and Iraq, the Iraqi invasion of Kuwait, and Desert Storm itself, not to mention such earlier examples as the five-year-long (1962–67) clash between Egypt and Yemen, the endless factional carnage in Lebanon, and several Syrian aggressions against Lebanon and Jordan.

In any event, the behavior of the Bush administration toward Israel in the aftermath of Desert Storm served to reinforce the impression already created during the war that he was no friend of Israel. And to top it all off, word got around that Baker had said that Bush need not worry about losing the Jews in his campaign for reelection in 1992:

"Fuck the Jews, they don't vote for us anyway." Baker had forgotten that an usually high percentage of the Jews *had* voted for "us" in 1988, but thanks in part to his remark, the percentage plunged from 35 percent to 11 percent (only one point less than the record low for a Republican since the days of FDR).

THE CASE OF PAT BUCHANAN

There was yet another factor that contributed to George H. W. Bush's dismal showing with the Jews in 1992—the prominent position that had been given to Patrick J. Buchanan at the Republican National Convention.

Buchanan had run against Bush in the Republican primaries, and he had done surprisingly well—so well that *Time* magazine had credited him with holding "hostage many of the angry 'swing' voters who are likely to pick the next President."[1] Which was why the Republican National Committee, with the acquiescence of Bush himself, decided to give him a prime-time slot at the convention. When Buchanan then seized upon the occasion to make a speech describing the coming election as a "religious war," he reignited the Jewish suspicion that the Republican Party had been taken over by the fearsome religious Right.

Yet even if Buchanan had delivered the usual anodyne speech of a defeated primary candidate calling for party unity, the very fact that he had been honored with a prime-time slot would have been enough, and more than enough, to frighten Jewish voters away from Bush. For as a columnist and as a television panelist Buchanan had already said a number of things that came within an inch or two of being as nakedly anti-Semitic as Gore Vidal's notorious piece in *The Nation.*

The first such statement he had made was on the *McLaughlin Group* television show during the buildup for Desert Storm:

> There are only two groups that are beating the drums . . . for war in the Middle East—the Israeli Defense Ministry and its amen corner in the United States.[2]

A few days later, he wrote a column in which he listed four members of the "amen corner"—the retired editor of the *New York Times* A. M. Rosenthal, who was then a columnist; former assistant secretary of defense Richard Perle; the columnist Charles Krauthammer; and former secretary of state Henry Kissinger. Just to make triply sure his point was getting across, he followed up with another piece in which he listed four "kids with names like McAllister, Murphy, Gonzales, and Leroy Brown"[3] who would do the fighting if the Jews of the "amen corner" were to succeed in dragging us into a war in the Persian Gulf.

But Buchanan's attitude toward Israel and its Jewish supporters was only one of the many pieces of evidence that cumulatively made it very hard for his defenders to exonerate him from the charge of anti-Semitism. In an article that provided perhaps the most thorough and painstakingly documented examination of the case, Joshua Muravchik would write:

> One definition of anti-Semitism, Patrick J. Buchanan observed in his syndicated column, . . . is "an embedded hatred of Jewish people, manifest in writing and conduct, . . . a grave sin, a disease of the heart, a variant of racism." But he also gave a second definition: "a word . . . used to frighten, intimidate, censor, and silence; to cut off debate; to . . . smear men's reputations."

After a lengthy and detailed analysis of Buchanan's writings on Jews and Jewish concerns, Muravchik concluded as follows:

> When a man falsely maintains that he is the victim of a "preplanned orchestrated smear campaign" by the Anti-Defamation

League; when he is hostile to Israel; when he embraces the PLO
despite being at adamant odds with its political philosophy;
when he implies that Jews are trying to drag America into war
for the sake of Israel; when he sprinkles columns with taunting
remarks about things Jewish; when he stirs the pot of intercom-
munal hostility; when he rallies to the defense of Nazi war
criminals, not only those who protest their innocence but also
those who confess their guilt; when he implies that the generally
accepted interpretation of the Holocaust might be a serious
exaggeration—when a man does all these things, surely it is
reasonable to conclude that his actions make a fairly good
match for the first, not the second, of Patrick J. Buchanan's two
definitions of anti-Semitism.[4]

It would be going too far to say that the Buchanan phenomenon
delighted the Jewish liberals who had been fighting tooth and nail
against the neoconservative argument that there was now more anti-
Semitism on the Left than on the Right. But it would not be going too
far to say that they felt vindicated by him. Many of them had long
been convinced—although few were willing to say so openly—that
even the more moderate and respectable wing of the Republican Party
represented by Bush and Baker was infected with anti-Semitism. But
by according Buchanan a place of honor at the Republican National
Convention, even after his anti-Semitic passions had proved powerful
enough to force their way out of the closet, the party lent credence to
the semi-secret liberal conviction that the Right was still, and as it had
ever been, bound and determined to "fuck the Jews."

Moreover, when Buchanan used the words *religious war* to characterize what was really just an ordinary American presidential election,
he also lent credence to the abiding Jewish fear of the Christian Right.
And not only the religious Right: for just as the remark made in an
unguarded moment by a Baptist leader that "God does not hear the
prayers of the Jews" was triumphantly cited by Jewish liberals as
affording a peek at what all Christian conservatives "really" thought
but considered it the better part of prudence not to say out loud, so
Buchanan's anti-Semitic effusions were taken as an open expression of

how the wider conservative movement, of which he had always been a respected member, "really" felt about Jews.

Those of us who had been trying for twenty-five long years to persuade our fellow Jews that the Right had become friendlier to Jews and Jewish concerns than the Left did not deny that pockets of anti-Semitism still existed on the Right. On the contrary: it was we who had taken the lead in exposing the anti-Semitism of right-wing writers like Sobran and Buchanan and right-wing publications like *Chronicles of Culture.*

Nor were we content with exposure alone. We also fought to persuade other conservatives that well-documented instances of anti-Semitism should be called by their proper name and denounced as such. As I once put it, some people were always complaining that false charges of anti-Semitism were just as bad as anti-Semitism itself, but for these people, virtually all charges of anti-Semitism were false. Their reasoning seemed to be that the accusation of anti-Semitism was so damaging that not even those who made blatantly anti-Semitic statements should be subjected to it. For some, nothing short of releasing gas into the showers of Auschwitz constituted anti-Semitism (assuming, as the most extreme of them might quickly go on to add, that such a thing ever really happened; or if it did happen, that it resulted in as many deaths as "the Jews" claimed it did).

In urging our fellow conservatives not to go along with this dodge in the case of Buchanan, we realized that we had our work cut out for us. It was far more likely that in some quarters we would be attacked for smearing Buchanan than thanked for calling attention to his anti-Semitic sentiments and ideas. There were, for example, his admirers at *Human Events,* a magazine in whose eyes he could say or do no wrong. There was the columnist team of Evans and Novak, who had sided with him on the Gulf War and were at least as hostile to Israel as he was. And there were the so-called paleoconservatives, a group of *enragé* intellectuals then centered around *Chronicles of Culture* whose isolationist fervor predated his own and was even more extreme. The paleos were also fanatical nativists to whom immigration from anywhere except Western Europe (or perhaps only England) represented the greatest of all threats to the health and integrity of American society—a view Buchanan had increasingly come to embrace in recent years. Last but far from least, like Buchanan himself, who in this as in other respects had for all practical purposes become one of them, the paleos regarded us neoconservatives as liberals in disguise who had succeeded in kidnapping and corrupting the conservative movement.

On the other hand, we felt confident that *National Review,* which was still the flagship of the movement, would join us in acknowledging that Buchanan was a carrier of anti-Semitic sentiments and ideas and that on that ground alone he could have no claim on conservative support. Buckley had by then retired as editor of the magazine, but John O'Sullivan, his successor, was cut from the same cloth, and we had no reason to expect that he would deviate from the precedent set by the case of Sobran.

To our amazement and mortification, however, *National Review* announced that it had decided to endorse Buchanan in the Republican primaries. Its rationale was that Bush—first in raising taxes after his famous promise ("Read my lips") that he never would, and then in signing a civil rights bill that was bound to promote quotas (after speaking out strongly against them)—had betrayed the Reaganite principles to which true conservatives remained loyal. They had a duty, therefore, to mount a challenge to him from the Right, and since Buchanan was the only candidate in the field willing to do just that, they had a correlative duty to support him.

Yet quite apart from the issue of anti-Semitism, this rationale made no sense in its own terms, for Buchanan—who had by now become an outspoken and fervent isolationist as well as a protectionist—was a greater apostate from Reaganite principles than Bush himself. O'Sullivan and his colleagues acknowledged—how could they not?—that Buchanan was an isolationist and a protectionist, but for a number of sophistically convoluted reasons, they did not consider this enough to disqualify him as the only alternative to Bush. If he were anti-Semitic, they added, that *would* be enough, but they disposed of this objection simply by denying that Buchanan was guilty as charged.

Though no longer the editor of the magazine, Buckley still owned it, and he certainly had the power to prevent his successors from supporting any candidate he himself opposed. And so we were doubly surprised and mortified when, for some reason incomprehensible to us, he not only refused to override the magazine's "tactical" endorsement of Buchanan in the early primaries but acquiesced in it.

Nor was *National Review* alone among Reaganite conservatives in failing to oppose Buchanan with the forthrightness his apostasies—not to mention his anti-Semitism—might have been thought to demand of them. In private, many such conservatives had long been expressing their dismay over Buchanan's desertion of Reaganite principles; and a few who had known him for years had no hesitation in acknowledging that he had become anti-Semitic (why, as I was told more than once, they could not understand). In public, however, the statements of opposition from some leaders of conservative organizations within the Reaganite camp tended to be weak and ambiguous, rather like the way liberal Democrats in 1988 danced around Jesse Jackson's embrace of Yasir Arafat and his reference to New York City as "Hymietown."

One reason these Reaganite conservatives were so inhibited in their criticisms of Buchanan was that they and their constituents had come to loathe George H. W. Bush and were in no mood to lend him aid and comfort by undermining his only challenger from the Right. Another reason was that Buchanan was apparently drawing a good deal of support from the conservative grass roots, and especially from the young activists of the movement. Consequently, as David Keene, the chairman of the American Conservative Union (ACU), told the *Wall Street Journal,* "a lot of conservatives" were afraid to "stand up and speak out against Pat." (As he would soon prove by defying his own board, Keene was not one of them.)

But if, by their refusal to dissociate themselves from Buchanan, these conservatives gave no aid and comfort to the partisans of Bush, they gave a great deal of both to our antagonists within the Jewish community, who were only too happy to use them as additional proof that we had all along been dead wrong in claiming that anti-Semitism had largely been driven out of the Right.

Of course we fought back. As I said in one of several articles I wrote on the subject,[5] a formidable collection of conservative political leaders and intellectuals had strongly contested Buchanan's claim to the Reaganite mantle, and while denying (as one of them put it) that

Buchanan was "personally" anti-Semitic, declared that he *was* "practicing political anti-Semitism." I also pointed out that the editorial page of the *Wall Street Journal,* perhaps the most influential exponent of Reaganite principles in the country, as well as its editor, Robert L. Bartley, had made their opposition to Buchanan abundantly clear (in, among other ways, inviting me to write about him for them).[6] So, in no uncertain terms, had Malcolm S. Forbes Jr., editor in chief of *Forbes,* America's most widely read, and very conservative, business magazine. And another important conservative journal of opinion, *The American Spectator,* and its editor, R. Emmett Tyrell, came out strongly against Buchanan—and with no waffling on the issue of anti-Semitism.

One more heartening item of good news was a letter to *National Review* signed by thirteen eminent conservative intellectuals—all non-Jewish—who expressed their dismay at the magazine's "tactical" endorsement of Buchanan in spite of his anti-Semitism.[7] When in his reply O'Sullivan reiterated his denial that Buchanan was an anti-Semite, Richard John Neuhaus, one of the signatories of the letter, published an editorial in his own magazine, *First Things,* which concluded with the following sharp retort:

> In recent decades, the line against anti-Semitism has been held by the conservative movement, by neoconservatives, by the Christian New Right, and by *National Review* under the leadership of William F. Buckley, Jr. That line of defense is now weakened by the attack of the Randolphites [a paleoconservative group in the Buchanan camp]—an attack inadvertently aided by the inept response of *National Review* to their candidate.[8]

In his own reply to the protest letter from the thirteen conservatives, Buckley seconded O'Sullivan's claim that "we would not have endorsed Mr. Buchanan if we had believed him to be anti-Semitic." Yet he himself had only just written, after a long and careful review of the record in his book-length essay "In Search of Anti-Semitism," that he found it impossible to defend Pat Buchanan against the charge that what he did and said during the period [leading up to the Gulf War] amounted to anti-Semitism, whatever it was that drove him to say and do it.[9]

In an open letter to Buckley about "In Search of Anti Semitism,"[10] I took him to task for thus piling contradiction upon contradiction. I also tried to show that (among several other failings I saw in his essay) he had not yet fully come to grips with the degree to which anti-Semitism was now disguising itself as anti-Zionism. Referring to a passage about me in "In Search of Anti-Semitism," I told him:

Even though you now defend me against the canard that in my eyes "mere opposition to an Israeli policy constitutes anti-Semitism," you still seem to resist what logically follows from my "logically sound" point namely, that criticisms of Israel . . . rooted . . . in the ancient traditions of anti-Semitic propaganda, deserve to be stigmatized as, quite simply, anti-Semitic.[11]

For all its flaws, however, I thought that Buckley's essay was a very good sign. It seemed to me that the willingness of the universally acknowledged intellectual leader of the conservative movement to call Pat Buchanan's descent into anti-Semitism by its true and proper name outweighed the craven refusal of lesser leaders to do so, and it would inevitably override Buckley's ephemeral confusion over Buchanan's candidacy.

At the beginning of "In Search of Anti-Semitism," Buckley recalled that at its founding in 1955, *National Review* had

declined association with anti-Semites, and indeed on one occasion went a generic step further. When it became clear, in 1957, that the direction the *American Mercury* was headed was anti-Semitic, I ruled, with the enthusiastic approval of my colleagues, that no writer appearing on the *Mercury*'s masthead, notwithstanding his own innocence on the subject, could also appear on *National Review*'s.[12]

Take it for all in all, "In Search of Anti-Semitism" represented another "generic step" in Buckley's campaign to keep anti-Semitism out of the conservative movement.

Since anti-Semitism when recognized as such was still disreputable in America, Buchanan was hurt by our exposure of him; and by the extremism of his ideas and his willingness to reach down into the fever swamps of American politics for support, he more and more marginalized himself as an influential force. Nevertheless, by seeming to confirm the bred-in-the bone and never entirely dormant Jewish suspicion of the Right as inveterately anti-Semitic, the Buchanan phenomenon did great damage to the prospect of a significant move by Jewish voters in a more conservative direction. It also hampered our struggle to focus Jewish attention on the absence of any comparable effort within the Left to discredit Jesse Jackson, its own counterpart to Buchanan. And finally, by their policy toward Israel and their attitude toward the Jews, Bush and Baker quashed whatever chance there might have been in the foreseeable future of a significant Jewish move away from the Democrats and into the Republican Party.

CLINTON, THE RELIGIOUS RIGHT, AND THE JEWS

The net effect of Bush's record was a very heavy Jewish vote for Bill Clinton, the Democratic candidate who ran against him in 1992. Not only did Clinton's 80 percent share far exceed the totals achieved by McGovern (65 percent), Carter (71 percent and then 45 percent), Mondale (67 percent), or Dukakis (64 percent), it even came within a hair of Humphrey's 81 percent in 1968. Yet while winning by landslides among Jewish voters, neither Humphrey (in defeat) nor Clinton (in victory) was able to attract more than 43 percent of the electorate as a whole.*

For reasons I spelled out earlier, the Jewish vote for Humphrey in 1968 was not especially noteworthy. But Clinton was on the whole an unknown quantity, and it is safe to assume that he owed his extraordinary success with Jewish voters to the well-deserved antagonism Bush and Baker had aroused among them.

I would say, then, that from the point of view of their interests *as* Jews, it made more sense in this particular instance to go big for the Democratic candidate—even an unfamiliar one like Clinton—than it had in any election since 1972. (I, however, suspecting Clinton of

---

* Humphrey's 43 percent in 1968 was narrowly exceeded by Nixon, but because Ross Perot, the third-party candidate in 1992, cut into Bush's support, Clinton's 43 percent was enough to give him a plurality.

being a moderate-sounding front for the McGovernite leftists who still dominated the party, could not bring myself to vote for him. But neither could I forgive Bush for his animus against Israel and "the Jews," and so I sat this election out.)

But did it make sense for Jews—to the extent that they were acting *as* Jews and as such passionately concerned over the issue of Israel—to go almost as big for Clinton (78 percent) when he ran for reelection in 1996? In 1992, he had benefited from being opposed by Bush, but there was no basis for thinking that his Republican opponent in 1996, Bob Dole, held views on Israel similar to those of the Bush-Baker team. In fact, Jews could easily have concluded the exact opposite from Dole's choice of Jack Kemp—than whom there was no greater supporter of Israel in American politics—as his running mate. Yet only a derisory 16 percent of the Jewish vote went to the Dole-Kemp ticket.

In 1992, in addition to being helped by the Jewish aversion to Bush, Clinton helped himself with Jews by giving the strongly pro-Israel Al Gore the second spot on his ticket, by keeping his distance from Jesse Jackson during the campaign, and by running as a "New" (i.e., non-McGovernite) Democrat. But like Jimmy Carter before him, the minute he was elected he veered sharply leftward. He even appointed two alumni of the Carter administration to head his foreign-policy team: Warren Christopher as secretary of state and Anthony Lake as national security adviser. Since both of them still harbored hopes of a complete Israel withdrawal from the West Bank and Gaza in favor of a Palestinian state run by the PLO, it was reasonable to conclude that Clinton himself did as well.

Meanwhile, the First Lady, Hillary Rodham Clinton, was letting it be widely known that her thinking about politics had been influenced by one Michael Lerner, the editor of the leftist Jewish magazine *Tikkun.* In the '60s, Lerner had been active on the New Left, but far from having outgrown the politics of his younger days, he now presumed to give them the imprimatur of Judaism. For example, to the sins listed in the Yom Kippur confessional prayer *Al Khet,* he added a few drawn from the updated catechism of the New Left, including the "sins" of "accepting the current distribution of wealth and power," "participating in a racist society," "not doing enough to save the environment," "not doing enough to challenge sexist institutions," and "turning our back on the oppression of gays and lesbians."[1] Naturally Lerner often sided with the Palestinians against Israel.

After a few months in office, and with the polls showing that the public regarded him as "too liberal," Clinton tacked to the Right on several issues. Among other moves in this direction, he "sinned" against the Left by backing away from his support of gays in the military and he withdrew his nomination of Lani Guinier, widely known as the "quota queen," to head the Civil Rights Division of the Justice Department. Thanks, however, to Israel's then prime minister, Yitzhak Rabin, no such course correction was necessary where the PLO and its leader Yasir Arafat were concerned.

Rabin had always refused to deal with the PLO on the ground that it was a terrorist organization openly dedicated to destroying the Jewish state. But in early 1993, he was suddenly presented with the elements of an agreement that was being hammered out (evidently without his authorization or even, some said, his knowledge) between representatives of his foreign minister, Shimon Peres, and emissaries of Yasir Arafat, meeting secretly in the city of Oslo. Under these "Oslo Accords," Israel would enter into negotiations with the PLO in exchange for its promise to renounce terrorism and to recognize Israel's right to exist. Rabin had serious doubts as to whether Arafat would honor these commitments but, impelled by various considerations that he felt gave him no choice, he decided to acquiesce in the Oslo Accords.

The United States had played no part in the Oslo Accords, but Clinton—never one to let a golden political opportunity slip by—invited Rabin, Peres, and Arafat to sign them in a ceremony on the White House lawn. And so, on September 13, 1993, Rabin, at Clinton's urging, and with a reluctance so visible that all the world noticed it, shook the hand of Arafat—a hand that, he had often rightly said, was drenched in Jewish blood.

Some of us rained on this triumphal parade by predicting from the start that Arafat's hand would soon be covered by even more Jewish blood, but so sacrosanct did Oslo become that to raise questions about it was to be excoriated as an enemy of peace. No wonder, then, that

Clinton, by making himself into a surrogate father to Oslo, should have achieved great popularity with the American Jewish community.

Nor did his popularity suffer in the coming years when he kept pushing the Oslo Accords even though the illusions about Arafat out of which they had grown were being shattered by a resurgence of the terrorism that he had pledged to give up. If anything, the futile efforts Clinton kept on making on behalf of Oslo earned him the reputation as the best friend Israel had ever had in the White House (an accolade that surely belonged to Richard Nixon, who had saved Israel from possible extinction, whereas Clinton was doing everything in his power to promote a "peace process" that led to another war).

Yet in my (admittedly speculative) opinion, Clinton's standing with the Jews of America did not rest entirely or even mainly on his identification with Oslo. I think it had more to do with the same factor that caused virtually the entire liberal community to spring to his defense when in 1999 he was impeached for lying to a grand jury about his sexual liaison with a young White House intern named Monica Lewinsky.

In order to appreciate how extraordinary this outpouring of liberal support for Clinton was, we have to remind ourselves that by then he had added conservative policies on welfare and crime to his earlier "sins" against liberalism on gays in the military and racial quotas. For this alone, liberals might well have felt betrayed by him, just as conservatives had felt betrayed by Richard Nixon over his embrace of liberal policies like wage and price controls, détente with the Soviet Union, and the opening to Communist China. Yet whereas Nixon was deserted in droves by conservatives when he faced impeachment, liberals rallied around Clinton to a man, and even to a woman, when he was in a similar situation.

The anomaly here was more confounding among women than it was among men. (As one female dissenter from her pro-Clinton sisters told an interviewer, "The CEO of a corporation wouldn't have had time to pack up his briefcase before he was fired" for doing what the president of the United States had done with Monica Lewinsky—and a number of other women as well). But I thought then, and I still think, that what accounted more than anything else for the support he got among both sexes was fear of the religious Right. Liberals tended on the whole to be secularists, even if they occasionally went to church or told pollsters that they believed in God, and some indeterminate number were positively hostile to religion. When these latter, whether self-proclaimed atheists or agnostics, thought of religion, what came into their minds was the fanaticism and intolerance they imputed to Pat Robertson and Jerry Falwell. Not only that, but they also attributed these unlovely qualities to irrationality and superstition, and associated them with intellectual and cultural backwardness. So far as they were concerned, nothing had really changed since one of their great heroes, the freethinking Clarence Darrow, had crossed legal swords with the fundamentalist William Jennings Bryan at the Scopes trial in the 1920s over the teaching of evolution in the schools.

In fact, many liberals were sure that the forces of benightedness, after a brief setback, had grown even stronger since then. Only a few liberals were reckless enough to say this explicitly in print, though plenty of them came close in their denunciations of Kenneth Starr, the special counsel who had been appointed to investigate Clinton and who (to their great good polemical fortune) happened to be an evangelical Christian himself. But in private, as I could testify from the talk at numerous dinner parties I had attended, there was almost no limit to the paranoia aroused by the Christian Right among liberals.

When, as we have seen, Barry Goldwater ran for president in 1964, the all-but-open liberal fear was that he would bring fascism to the United States. In the ensuing thirty-five years, the specter of fascism had been replaced by the conviction—the sincere conviction—that if the Christian Right ever got into power behind a Republican candidate fronting for it, we would face a contemporary version of the Salem witch trials.

One might have thought that such liberals would have been reassured by the presidency of Ronald Reagan. Despite Reagan's expressed sympathy with the religious Right, its influence on American life and culture during his administration was no more discernible than it had been under Jimmy Carter (himself a born-again Christian). But no. Liberals remained unimpressed. They still imagined that if a Republican were elected with a debt to the Christian Right, all hell (as liberals envisaged hell) would break loose. The sacred right to abortion would be taken away by the repeal of *Roe v. Wade;* the gay rights movement would practically be outlawed; artists writing about and depicting erotic acts would be censored; and children would be forced to intone the Lord's Prayer, or worse, in school every morning.

For all his sins against liberalism on other issues, it was, I have always believed, because Clinton seemed so solid a bulwark against the Puritanical jackboots the liberal community saw waiting menacingly in the wings that it rallied in its entirety to his defense. (His very nature as a libertine may even have contributed subliminally to confidence in him in this respect.) In trusting Clinton to protect them from the religious Right, Jews were like other liberals, only more so, in that they had the additional fear of being turned into second-class citizens by the Christian Right.

As I have already tried to demonstrate, this fear was even more devoid of support by the facts of the case than the one Jews shared with all other liberals. Although anti-Semitism still existed on the Christian Right—and I had the hate mail to prove it—the dominant trend, according to the authoritative testimony of Father Richard J. Neuhaus, was toward a new "understanding of Christianity's dependence upon Judaism"—not only

> the Judaism of what Christians call the Old Testament, but the living Judaism that continues in mysterious relation to God's election and unbreakable promise.[2]

And as for living Jews, all the polls showed a correlative trend among conservative Christians toward a repudiation of anti-Semitism.

Similarly with the political ambitions and the power of the Christian Right. Evangelical and fundamentalist Christians had formerly been content to render unto Caesar what was Caesar's and to concentrate on saving their own souls. What drew them into politics, first behind Jerry Falwell's Moral Majority and then behind Pat Robertson's Christian Coalition, was not any wish to impose their own views and mores on the rest of us. Far from being an aggressive move, it was a defensive one against the aggressions the liberal culture—with the aid of the courts, the federal bureaucracies, and the ubiquitous media—had been committing against *them*. Among other things, they were being forced to allow the spread of pornography into their own communities and to keep any trace of religion out of the schools their children attended, or (since it was forbidden to post the Ten Commandments on a classroom wall but permissible to teach girls how to unroll a condom over a cucumber or some other representation of an erect penis) both at once.

In trying to fight all this off, the Christian Right had failed—so dismally that some of the people who had persuaded them that political activism was the only way to defend themselves were now counseling an abandonment of that particular field and a return to the spiritual realm alone.

As to the William Jennings Bryan streak that repelled so many liberals, and perhaps the Jews most of all, Martin Peretz of *The New Republic,* speaking as a Jew to other Jews, would later write that the Republican camp

> is the camp of ignorance and bias. It is against science; it is against tolerance; . . . it is against religious and intellectual liberty. . . . Die-hard Republicans . . . are mostly not of our rational kin and their thinking is not in our spiritual ken.[3]

Yet even granting that a form of anti-Darwinism was still alive in the campaign to put creationism into the public-school curriculum, the plain fact to which Peretz resolutely blinded himself was that science, tolerance, and intellectual liberty had for the past forty years been up against a greater threat from the secular Left than from the religious Right or the Republican camp. "During my adult life," wrote the leading political scientist of our day, James Q. Wilson,

> I have been part of five institutions—the Catholic Church, the University of Redlands, the United States Navy, the University of Chicago, and Harvard University. If I were required to rank them by the extent to which free and uninhibited discussion was possible within them, I am very much afraid that the Harvard of

1972 would not rank near the top. In the last two or three years, the list of subjects that cannot be publicly discussed there in a free and open forum has grown steadily, and now includes the war in Vietnam, public policy toward urban ghettos, the relationship between intelligence and heredity, and the role of American corporations in certain overseas regimes.[4]

As the years went by, other such scientifically unresolved questions as the extent of human responsibility for global warming and the curative potential of embryonic stem-cell research were declared to have been settled and tacked on to this list of issues that could not be discussed in a free and open forum. In other words, what was true in 1972 was still true in 2008, when Wilson commented on the subject again:

> If you ask who in this country has prevented people from speaking on college campuses, they are overwhelmingly leftists. . . . If you ask who produces campus codes that infringe on free speech, they are overwhelmingly leftists. If you ask who invaded the classroom of my late colleague, Richard Herrnstein, and tried to prevent him from teaching, they were overwhelmingly leftists.[5]

Nothing daunted, even though as a member of the Harvard community he was well aware of these episodes, Peretz further asserted that

> the Republicans are people who don't believe in evolution or in genetics. For Jews, however, evolution and genetics tell at least half the story of our survival.[6]

But it was precisely for having written about the genetic component of IQ that Herrnstein, an eminent psychologist, was hounded by the Left; and it was precisely for asking whether the paucity of women in science might have a genetic basis that Lawrence Summers would later be made by an overwhelmingly liberal faculty to apologize and recant and would then be forced out of the presidency of Harvard.

None of these considerations, nor all of them together, could make more than a very small dent in the Jewish aversion to and fear of the Christian Right. If I had not already learned this from the violence of the opposition to school prayer I had encountered when speaking in synagogues all over the country to promote *The Present Danger,* I would have been left in no doubt of it by the even more violent response to an article I wrote some years later about Pat Robertson.[7]

The purpose of this article was to defend Robertson against the charge of anti-Semitism that had recently been revived by a report on the Christian Right by the Anti-Defamation League and a number of pieces in publications like *The New York Review of Books*. I did not deny that Robertson had subscribed to certain crackpot ideas originating in the eighteenth century about a conspiracy between Jewish bankers and Freemasons to take over the world. Nor did I conceal the fact that one of his books relied on several sources that were unquestionably anti-Semitic. And I also castigated him over a passage attacking a "strident minority" of "Jewish intellectuals and media activists" for having ridiculed and vilified the religious beliefs of the Christian majority. The complaint, I said, was justified, but the threatening tone in which he made it was reprehensible.

Nevertheless, I went on to argue, all this was trumped by Robertson's unwavering support for Israel. In this regard, *mutatis mutandis,* he resembled Aleksandr Solzhenitsyn, who had also been accused of anti-Semitism because of the bitterness he expressed in some of his writings over the contribution made by revolutionaries of Jewish origin in bringing Communism to Russia. But almost anything Solzhenitsyn might believe about the role of Jews in the past seemed to me academic by comparison with his consistently fervent support of Israel at a time when Israel had become *the* touchstone of attitudes toward the Jewish people, and anti-Zionism the main and most relevant form of anti-Semitism. Like Solzhenitsyn, Robertson, too, had befriended and defended the state of Israel when it was under relentless moral assault everywhere, and not least among liberal Christians, both Protestant and Catholic, who more often than not participated enthusiastically in the orgy of vilification. Hence even though Robertson's ideas about Jewish bankers derived from a lurid paranoid fantasy, while Solzhenitsyn's ideas about Jewish revolutionaries were based on an uncomfortable historical reality, Robertson was as deserving as Solzhenitsyn of acquittal on the charge of anti-Semitism.

Having demonstrated by my earlier attacks on Pat Buchanan and Joe Sobran that I was no apologist for anti-Semites of the Right, I thought I would be immune to the accusation in coming to the defense of Pat Robertson. Yet one of the many angry protests sent to *Commentary* and published in its correspondence columns declared, precisely, that I had "adopted a no enemies to the Right policy."[8] Another denounced the "unprincipled opportunism" exemplified by my "cynical argument that Robertson must be forgiven his anti-Semitic rantings because he supports Israel." An erstwhile admirer of my work was "flabbergasted" that I of all people should have written an "exculpatory article" on an anti-Semite like Robertson. A longtime subscriber to the magazine found "something disgustingly obsequious" about my "attempt to laugh off Pat Robertson's anti-Semitic mouthings, and to do so in the name of an alleged friendship toward Israel is simply absurd!"

And so it went, even among conservative Jews who—given their overall political orientation—might have been expected to understand how little they had to fear from the Christian Right and how much there was to appreciate not only in its support for Israel but also in the often lonely resistance it offered to the spread of relativism in our culture.

GEORGE W. BUSH AND ISRAEL

As fate would have it, almost exactly a year after the Senate had declared Clinton innocent of the articles of impeachment brought against him by the House, the issue of the Christian Right moved to the very center of American politics. The occasion was the exceptionally bitter battle in the South Carolina primary between George W. Bush and John McCain, the two leading contenders for the Republican presidential nomination in 2000. The *New York Times* reported that, shortly after losing to Bush in South Carolina,

> Senator John McCain intensified the battle over the political power of the religious Right. . . . In [a previous] speech . . . Mr. McCain called Pat Robertson and Jerry Falwell—both support-ers of Mr. Bush—"agents of intolerance." Today, he went further, criticizing them for "the evil influence that they exercise over the Republican Party."[1]

Judging from my own experience, I had no doubt that McCain would win over practically every Jewish Republican there was by por-traying Bush (in the words of the *New York Times*) "as deeply indebted to the leadership of the Christian Right" and by "casting himself as the one candidate who [could] rescue the Republican Party from religious leaders who . . . preach[ed] 'a message of intolerance and exclusion.' "[2]

As it was, the already small number of Jews who were likely to vote for Bush in the general election was probably diminished even further by McCain's attacks on him as—to use a term then in the air—a "stealth candidate" of the religious Right. When we consider that Bush was a born-again Christian; that he was the son of George H. W. Bush, whose animosity toward Israel and its American Jewish supporters had by no means been forgotten; that his Democratic opponent was Al Gore—not only a strong supporter of Israel but a very different political animal from the wild global-warming doomsayer he would later become; and that, in Senator Joseph Lieberman, Gore chose as his running mate the first Jew ever to make it to a presidential ticket—when we take all this into account, we can only wonder that Bush managed to get any Jewish votes at all.

What he did wind up getting was 19 percent, as against Gore's 79 percent. Bush's total, though very low, would have been even lower by one vote if not for me, and in toto it was higher than I would have predicted; and since he won the presidency by virtue of having beaten Gore in Florida by a tiny margin, he may for all we know have owed his victory to the few Jewish votes in Miami that went to him when they might confidently have been expected to go to Gore.

Be that dizzyingly ironic possibility as it may, no one, whether Jewish or Gentile, could have foreseen that the younger Bush would become friendlier to Israel than any president before him. When he entered office, there was little if anything to suggest that his conception of the American role in the world differed from his father's "realist" perspective in world affairs. This meant that he, too, would accept without question the totally *un*realistic idea that a resolution of the Palestinian problem was the "key" to stability in the Middle East (or even, as England's then prime minister, Tony Blair, would astoundingly declare, the most important issue in the entire world). Hence it also seemed unlikely that Bush's policy toward Israel would deviate from his father's. That is, it, too, would in all probability involve bringing unilateral pressures on Israel to withdraw from the West Bank and

Gaza. Yet when it came to the question of who would take control of those territories after the Israelis withdrew, it turned out that there was one very important respect in which George W. Bush was prepared to deviate from his father's policy.

In the elder Bush's time in office, both Israel and United States still formally opposed the establishment of a sovereign Palestinian state. The many American peace plans that had been floated from 1967 until Oslo envisaged either a return of the West Bank to Jordan and of Gaza to Egypt, a federation of some kind linking Arab Palestine with Jordan, or autonomy for the Palestinians (though not as a prelude to statehood). Nor before Oslo had Israel been willing to accept the PLO's claim to be "the sole legitimate representative of the Palestinian people" and to acquiesce in the eventual establishment of a Palestinian state run by the PLO (or, rather, the Palestinian Authority into which it had been transmuted by Oslo).

The stage had thus been set by Oslo for a change in American policy, and George W. Bush decided to make it. The original plan was to announce the change in September 2001, but 9/11 forced a delay, and so it was not until October that Bush became the first American president to come out openly in favor of a Palestinian state.

At that early stage, it seems, Bush had not yet fully factored 9/11 into his thinking about the new policy. In the months that followed, however, he obviously came to realize that there was a blatant contradiction between the war on terror he had now begun to wage and his support for a Palestinian state that would be run by terrorists like Yasir Arafat and his henchmen. Why should the United States wish to add another state to those harboring and sponsoring terrorism at a time when we were at war to rid the world of just such regimes?

Presumably it was under the prodding of this question that, about nine months later, on June 24, 2002, Bush removed the anomaly built into his new policy by adding a codicil to his endorsement of a Palestinian state:

Today, Palestinian authorities are encouraging, not opposing, terrorism. This is unacceptable. And the United States will not support the establishment of a Palestinian state until its leaders engage in a sustained fight against the terrorists and dismantle their infrastructure.[3]

To this he added the requirement that they elect "new leaders, not compromised by terror," which amounted to an implicit demand that Arafat be replaced.

Although he made an effort toward the end of this statement to seem evenhanded by challenging Israel "to take concrete steps to support the emergence of a viable, credible Palestinian state," Bush most emphatically did not follow the usual practice of blaming the persistence of the conflict on "Israeli intransigence." Instead, he took the unprecedented step of placing the onus on the Palestinian leaders and the Arab states backing them up. By saying up front that "there is simply no way to achieve . . . peace until all parties fight terror," he was blaming the absence of peace on the Arab states and the "Palestinian authorities" (who were "encouraging, not opposing, terrorism"), and he was exonerating the Israelis (who were being "victimized by terrorists," not supporting them).

Venturing even further in this unprecedented direction, Bush eschewed the usual practice of demanding that Israel take the first steps toward peace by making unilateral concessions. That responsibility he assigned not alone to the "Palestinian leaders" but also to "the entire Arab world," which he called upon "to build closer ties of diplomacy and commerce with Israel, leading to full normalization of relations" with the Jewish state.

It was an extraordinary statement, and in practice it would spell an end to the zigzagging from green light to red that had previously characterized Bush's position on Israel's right to defend itself by military and other means, including through the security fence beginning to be built by the then prime minister, Ariel Sharon. Under this new dispensation, Bush or one of his spokesmen might from time to time still chide the Israelis for going too far. But in those instances it was a yellow light that would be flashed rather than a red.

The Israelis greeted the June 24 statement with great enthusiasm, as did some of us within the American Jewish community who had already become admirers of Bush for the way he had responded to the 9/11 attacks. Yet not from that day to this did Bush's radically new approach to the Palestinians temper the antagonism that most American Jews, in common with all American liberals, felt toward him.

Jews had harbored this feeling all along, but it was soon to be exacerbated by Iraq. For contrary to the widespread allegation that "the Jews" (usually disguised as "neoconservatives") had dragged us into Iraq for no other reason than that it would serve the interests of Israel, the vast majority of American Jews came to be as violently opposed to Iraq as were all other American liberals. And contrary to the idea that Israel had wanted us to invade Iraq, most Israelis thought that it would have been better to go after Iran instead, and almost all Israelis thought that Bush was very naïve to imagine that Iraq could be democratized in the near future, or perhaps ever.

It should have come as no surprise, then, that the Democratic candidate in 2004, John Kerry, who received only 48 percent of the popular vote in losing to Bush, was showered with 76 percent of the Jewish vote. What did come as a bit of a surprise was that Bush (with 24 percent) did a little better with Jews in his bid for reelection instead of a little worse than he had done in 2000 (19 percent). There is no way of knowing for sure, but a possible explanation for Bush's improved showing may be that Kerry was less appealing to Jewish voters than Clinton and Gore, and/or that one out of every four Jewish voters had actually come to believe that Bush was not quite so demonic as the liberal community imagined. Or could it be that they had even come to agree with those few of us who were by now convinced that Bush was not only a great friend of Israel but would one day be recognized as a great president in the mold of Harry Truman, and that he richly deserved our support both as Americans and as Jews?

If so, their newfound confidence in him was soon to be shaken by the failure to find the weapons of mass destruction we had supposedly invaded Iraq to eliminate. And this confidence would then be altogether destroyed by the losing course we seemed to be following in Iraq against the coalition of die-hard Saddamists, domestic Islamofascists, and foreign jihadists who were murderously bent on preventing the democratization of the country. Like all other liberals, most Jews developed a veritably poisonous hatred of Bush in his second term, and doubts began to arise even among his few Jewish supporters about his Trumanesque stature.

With a lonely exception or two (myself loudly among them), those few Jewish supporters of Bush were not even reassured by what he did when in July 2006 war broke out between Israel and the terrorists of Hizbollah, who had steadily been firing Katyusha rockets across the border from their emplacements in southern Lebanon.

From the start, all the world rushed to condemn Israel in the usual terms—for "aggression," for using "disproportionate force," for "slaughtering" many thousands of innocent civilians. But Bush would have none of this. Again steering clear of the old moral equivalence between Israel and the forces trying to destroy it, he described its struggle against Hizbollah as yet another front in the "broader struggle between freedom and terror that [was] unfolding across the region." He also denounced Hizbollah as a creature of Iran and Syria, and as one of the instruments they were using in their long-standing campaign to wipe the Jewish state off the map.

Meanwhile, the Security Council was demanding a cease-fire before the Israelis could finish the job they had gone to war to do, which was to drive Hizbollah out of southern Lebanon and thus put their northern towns out of the range of its rockets. Here, too, refusing to go along, Bush authorized a series of diplomatic maneuvers to buy time for the Israelis. In the end, the government of Ehud Olmert (who had become prime minister after Sharon suffered a disabling stroke) botched the chance to take advantage of this additional margin, and thereby left Israel with, at best, a demoralizing standoff. This gave heart to the Hizbollah terrorists, who were able to claim that they had defeated the mighty Israeli army, and it disappointed Bush's hope that Israel would indirectly deal a decisive blow to Iran and Syria.

Yet in spite of everything Bush had done to help the Israelis, he got little if any credit from his few Jewish supporters. Some even perversely interpreted the maneuvering he did at the UN not as the effort it so obviously was to buy the Israelis time, but as pressure on them to appease Hizbollah.

More disillusionment set in about a year later, when the "Road

Map to a Permanent Two-State Solution to the Israeli-Palestinian Conflict" was published. This document was supposed to be a blueprint for implementing the principles of the June 24, 2002, speech, but the very fact that it had been produced by a so-called Quartet (the United States, the UN, the EU, and Russia) was enough to arouse suspicion and cause apprehension. Given that three of the four members of the Quartet were hardly known for friendliness toward Israel, and that the U.S. contingent was made up of State Department officials, how could this entity be expected to resist undermining the principles of Bush's June 24 speech while pretending to show how they should be put into practice? Surely the drafters of the Road Map would either ignore the president's tacit repudiation of the cult of moral equivalency, otherwise known as "evenhandedness" and at whose shrine the Arabists in the State Department worshipped, or else they would find a way to sneak it back in.

This was precisely what, after careful study of it, critics of the Road Map charged. It represented, they all agreed, not the fulfillment but (in the words of Robert Satloff and David Makovsky) "the antithesis of Bush's June 24 vision for peacemaking in terms of substance, sequence, and procedure."[4] Perhaps the worst of the many discrepancies they all found was the egregious example of "evenhandedness" that one of them described as the "sham, even indecent, parallelism between Palestinian and Israeli behavior." Thus the Road Map called on each side, in virtually identical language, to "cease violence" against the other, as if acts of terror and efforts to defend against them were commensurable. It also balanced a demand that "official Palestinian institutions end incitement against Israel" with one that "official Israeli institutions end incitement against Palestinians," even though there was not, nor ever had been, any such incitement coming from the Israeli side.[5]

I found these criticisms, unlike the attacks on Bush's handling of the Second Lebanon War, entirely convincing. As time went on, however, I gradually came to the conclusion that, despite the best efforts of the drafters of the document in the State Department, and contrary to what they probably imagined they had pulled off, they had failed to eliminate the most radical feature of the president's June 24, 2002, statement—namely, its insistence on putting the onus for peace on the Palestinians rather than on the Israelis.

Of course the State Department drafters made sure to place as much emphasis as they could get away with on the concluding section of the June 24 speech in which the president had reiterated the usual demands on Israel to do its part by "freezing settlement activity in the occupied territories"; by "permitting innocent Palestinians to resume work and normal life"; and by pulling its military forces out of areas heavily populated by Palestinians. Still, and in spite of this bone the president had thrown to the cult of "evenhandedness," the drafters of the Road Map simply could not sneak their way around the fact that he had made these demands on Israel contingent in the first place upon Palestinian action against terrorism.

But most of the erstwhile supporters of Bush within the Jewish community were not persuaded. Their skepticism then soured into outright dismay when Bush acquiesced in a new idea cooked up by his secretary of state, Condoleezza Rice, and warmly endorsed by Ehud Olmert. In accord with this idea, Olmert and Mahmoud Abbas (who had become president of the Palestinian Authority after Arafat's death) set out at a hastily convened conference in Annapolis to give the Palestinian people "new hope" by presenting them with an agreement specifying what they could expect if they followed the Road Map to a state of their own that would live in peaceful coexistence with Israel.

It was a foolish and futile undertaking because, even if Olmert and Abbas were to succeed in reaching such an agreement before Bush left office, they both lacked enough political support to do anything with it. Why, knowing this, Bush should still have given it his blessing was a mystery wrapped in an enigma. Nevertheless, even while endorsing the post-Annapolis negotiations, he went out of his way to dispel the impression that they represented an abandonment of the conditions he had attached to American support for the establishment of a Palestinian state. In a speech in Jerusalem on January 10, 2008, he unequivocally declared that "implementation of any agreement is subject to implementation of the Road Map," which for the Palestinians, he made sure to stress, required "confronting terrorists and dismantling terrorist infrastructure." He also reiterated, and in unmistakable terms, that American support for a Palestinian state still depended upon the fulfillment of that condition ("No agreement and no Palestinian state will be born of terror").

I for one took Bush at his word, and I argued that his successor would, even if reluctantly, be bound by his commitment to that condition (just as Jimmy Carter was bound by the analogous commitment Kissinger had made with regard to the PLO in 1975). But so few of the already tiny group of Jewish supporters of Bush agreed, and so betrayed by him did they feel (and not only on Israel), that if he had been able to run again in 2008, he might well have sunk to the near record low in Jewish support his father had achieved in 1992.

2008

But of course Bush could not run again. I was hoping that he would be succeeded as the Republican candidate in 2008 by Rudy Giuliani, whom I not only supported but served as a senior foreign-policy adviser. But it was Bush's old rival in the primaries of 2000 who emerged as the winner this time. The John McCain of 2008, however, was not the same candidate who had run against Bush eight years earlier by portraying him as a stealth candidate for the religious Right. The new McCain was intent on mending his fences with the conservative forces he had alienated before, and this was bound to arouse Jewish suspicion of *him* as the stealth candidate he had accused Bush of being in 2000. In particular, his long-standing pro-life position was bound to make him unacceptable to the overwhelming majority of Jewish women, who seemed to think that the absolute right to an abortion had been inscribed on the tablets Moses brought down from Sinai. And when he chose Sarah Palin, an equally adamant foe of abortion, to be his running mate, he guaranteed that hardly a Jewish woman in America would vote for him.

To make matters worse with Jewish voters of both sexes, McCain had once told an interviewer that, as president, he would consult on the Middle East with advisers like Zbigniew Brzezinski, who were not exactly friendly to Israel. One might have thought that this passing remark would be canceled out in Jewish eyes by the solid fact that it was not McCain but his Democratic opponent, Barack Obama, who had actually turned to Brzezinski (as well as a number of other like-minded "experts," including Robert Malley and Samantha Power) for advice on the Middle East. But one would have been wrong.

One would also have been wrong in assuming that McCain's position on Iran would weigh heavily in his favor with Jewish voters (as it certainly did with me). After all, the Iranian president, Mahmoud Ahmadinejad, had repeatedly pledged to "wipe Israel off the face of the map," and McCain's response was that he would if necessary use force to prevent Iran from acquiring the means to do so ("the only thing worse than bombing Iran is letting Iran get the bomb"). Obama, by contrast, evidently believed that if only the president of the United States would agree to sit down with Ahmadinejad "without preconditions," the Iranians could be talked out of developing nuclear weapons.

Yet the advantage McCain's hawkishness on Iran might have given him was neutralized by the aversion of Jewish voters to the use of military force—an aversion that, while somewhat lessened by the threat posed by Ahmadinejad, was still strong enough to prevail over the all too reasonable fear of another holocaust. Thus, even though 67 percent of the sample in the AJC's 2008 Annual Survey of Jewish Opinion described themselves as either "very close" or "fairly close" to Israel, the opponents of "taking military action against Iran to prevent it from developing nuclear weapons" still outnumbered the supporters by 47 percent to 42 percent.

Altogether, Israel was yet another issue about which a reasonable guess would turn out to be wrong. As was to be expected in a race whose outcome could well be affected by the Jewish vote in Florida and possibly one or two other swing states, both candidates made fervent statements of support for Israel. The Republican Jewish Coalition and other Jewish opponents of Obama did their best to cast doubt on the bona fides of his pro-Israel professions, but his Jewish backers were even more active on his behalf. Three hundred rabbis issued a statement all but declaring him to be a successor to the Hebrew prophets. A few well-known champions of Israel wrote articles explaining on rather convoluted grounds why they were backing Obama (Alan Dershowitz of the Harvard Law School, for example: "The election of Barack Obama—a liberal supporter of Israel—will enhance Israel's position among wavering liberals"[1]; Martin Peretz of *The New Republic*: "Israel's conflict with the Arabs . . . is mostly about history, and Obama is a student of history"[2]; and Martin Indyk of the Brookings Institution: "I believe Obama passes the *kishke* [gut] test"[3]). Finally, the popular comedy star Sarah Silverman even urged young Jews to organize a "Great Schlep" down to Florida to persuade their presumably racist grandparents (their *"bubbes* and *zaydehs"*) to vote for Obama.

Yet unlike McCain—whose campaign assurances to Jewish voters were consistent with his record—Obama's credibility was undermined by a history of involvement with anti-Israel associates. There was, most notoriously, his longtime pastor, the Reverend Jeremiah Wright. In addition to damning America, and honoring the blatantly anti-Semitic Louis Farrakhan, Wright was on record as believing that Israel had joined with South Africa in developing an "ethnic bomb" that would kill blacks and Arabs but not whites; he had accused Israel of committing genocide against the Palestinians; and he had participated in a campaign to get American companies to "divest" from Israel. None of this, however, nor all of it together, had provoked Obama to leave Wright's congregation, where he stayed for twenty years, during which time Wright officiated at his marriage and baptized his children. Then there was Rashid Khalidi, holder of a professorship at Columbia named after his idol, the late Edward Said. As befitted a reverential disciple of the leading propagandist for Palestinian terrorism, and as himself a defender of suicide bombing, Khalidi regularly denounced Israel as a "racist" state in the process of creating an "apartheid system." Nevertheless, Obama had befriended him, had publicly acknowledged being influenced by him, and, as a member of the board of a charitable foundation, had also helped to support him financially. And there was also one of Obama's main advisers on national security, General Merrill ("Tony") McPeak, who subscribed to the canard that American policy in the Middle East was dictated by Jews in the interests not of the United States but of Israel.

Even though Obama either distanced himself from or repudiated the ideas of these men, he got around to doing so only when the political exigencies of his campaign left him no prudential alternative. One would therefore have been justified in assuming that Jewish voters would at a minimum judge Obama to be less reliable than McCain on Israel. To some—largely the Orthodox—this seems to have been the case. (Although there were precincts in which Orthodox Jews are heavily concentrated where Obama did about as well as Kerry in 2004, there were others where McCain beat him by more than 2 to 1.[4]) Apparently, however, it did not occur to most other Jewish voters that the real stealth candidate in this race—a stealth candidate, that is, for the anti-Israel Left—might be Obama. And so more than three-quarters (78 percent) of the Jewish vote went to him (25 points higher than the 53 percent he scored with the electorate as a whole).[5]

The Jewish vote for Obama was also a staggering 35 points higher than the pro-Obama white vote in general (43 percent), and it was even 11 points higher than the Hispanic vote (67 percent). Only with blacks, who gave him 95 percent of their vote, did Obama do better than with Jews. And the results were just as dramatic when broken down by religion as by race and ethnicity: Protestants gave 45 percent of their vote to Obama (33 points less than Jews), and Catholics gave him 54 percent (24 points less than Jews).

Early in the race, there was speculation that the state of black-Jewish relations had grown so strained that Obama might fare badly among Jews, especially the elderly. Ironically, however, if there had been a "Great Schlep" to Florida, it would have resulted in the grandparents persuading their grandchildren to vote for Obama rather than the other way around, for the late tracking polls showed that whereas three-quarters of Jews over fifty-five had decided to vote for Obama, "only" two-thirds of those under thirty-five were preparing to do so.[6]

Is it possible that the heavy Jewish vote for Obama signified a diminution of the community's concern over Israel? According to a poll conducted for the left-wing organization J Street,

when considered among the other issues facing the country, Israel is actually in the bottom tier of issues, and only 8 percent of Jews identify it as one of the top two most important issues in deciding their vote for President and Congress.[7]

Yet in the same poll, 58 percent of the respondents said that

> a candidate's position on Israel plays a big role in determining how I will vote for Congress and the president.[8]

This second finding is very hard to reconcile with the first, and is also more consonant with the results of the AJC survey for 2008 (the one in which 67 percent professed to be "very close" or "fairly close" to Israel). The AJC survey, in turn, is more consonant with a study issued only days before the election by Steven M. Cohen (in this instance collaborating with Samuel J. Abrams of Harvard). According to their findings,

> Among Jews 65 and over, 54 percent rate "high" or "very high" the Israel-Palestine conflict as a consideration in determining their vote for Obama or McCain.[9]

This was the very group that the late tracking polls showed was about to go more heavily for Obama than Jews under fifty-five (non-Orthodox Jews, that is), for whom the Israel-Palestine conflict played a comparably minor role. Cohen and Abrams may be right in seeing these results as pointing to "The Diminished Place of Israel in the Political Thinking of Young Jews." Yet the fact remains that most of the Jews who voted for Obama *did* care about Israel but, downplaying or dismissing or ignoring his anti-Israel associations, they voted for him anyway.

Thus it was that in the face of Iran's pursuit of nuclear weapons, which constituted the most serious threat ever mounted to the survival of Israel, the Jews of America stuck with the Democratic Party even though it had nominated a candidate for president who, so far as could be determined from his record, was less concerned about and less well equipped than his Republican opponent to do whatever might be necessary to prevent a second holocaust. Since it beggared belief that these American Jews were indifferent to the possibility of another holocaust, I could only interpret the way they voted in 2008 to mean that their commitment to liberalism, and to the Democratic Party as its principal political vehicle, was still so deep and so powerful that anything threatening to shake it would be fended off with willful blindness and rationalizations built on denial.

Then, as if to bolster this interpretation, yet another threat to the Jewish faith in the Democrats materialized shortly after the election when the Israelis, in a clear act of self-defense, finally hit back at Hamas, which had steadily been firing rockets from Gaza into nearby Israeli towns. According to a Rasmussen poll taken at the time, the Israeli action was supported by twice as many Republicans (62 percent) as Democrats (31 percent). Even more striking was that only 47 percent of Democrats blamed the Palestinians, whereas 73 percent of Republicans did. (As we saw in chapter 27, a similar disparity in sympathy for Israel showed up after the 1984 election when a TWA plane was hijacked by Hizbollah.) Furthermore, 75 percent of Republicans said that Israel was an ally of the United States, as against only 55 percent of Democrats who did—a gap of 20 points.[10]

A gap of twenty points also showed up between Republicans and Democrats in judgments about the tactics used by Israel in the war. In a Pew poll taken when there was much talk in the air about Israel's "disproportionate" military actions, nearly two-thirds of Republicans (65 percent) as against fewer than half of Democrats (45 percent) said that Israel's response in Gaza was "about right." Conversely, only a minuscule 8 percent of Republicans as against more than a third of Democrats (36 percent) believed that Israel had gone too far.[11]

Here, then, was a very vivid demonstration of how much less the Democrats could be depended upon to stand behind Israel in a crisis than the Republicans. But judging from the silence with which Jewish liberals greeted this latest threat to their identification with the Democrats, it, too, was successfully fended off with willful blindness and denial.[12]

AS LIBERAL AS EVER?

Strange as it may seem after the long story I have just finished telling, there are those who argue that the central premise of this book is not entirely valid. Despite all appearances to the contrary, they say, American Jews are not really all that liberal, and even if they were in the past, they have since the late '60s been taking a "rightward political turn."[1] Indeed, I myself, both as an individual and as a "godfather" of neoconservatism, am often singled out as a trailblazer on this path to the Right.

I would dearly love to take credit for so politically salubrious an influence, but alas, the evidence stands in the way. George Nash, the leading historian of American conservatism, says that my labors as the editor of *Commentary* made it "respectable . . . to be both a Jew and a conservative."[2] This may, for all I know, be true, and yet even if it is, there can be no serious doubt that most American Jews are still as wedded as they have been since 1928 to the Democratic Party in particular and to liberalism in general.

To recapitulate: in every presidential election since 1928—with the single exception of Jimmy Carter in 1980—the Democratic candidate has scored a landslide among Jewish voters even when defeated by a landslide among the electorate as a whole (George McGovern in

1972). No Democratic candidate in all those elections (again, except Carter) has attracted less than 60 percent of the Jewish vote, and the overall average since 1928 is a stunning 75 percent. Jews have not voted as consistently or as heavily for the Democrats in county, city, or state elections, but only because local issues have come into play. In congressional elections, on the other hand, Jews have shown much the same level of partisanship as they have in voting for president, with from two-thirds to three-quarters of them supporting Democratic candidates.[3]

When these numbers are broken down, they become even more extraordinary. Striking differences in Democratic partisanship between Jews and their non-Jewish counterparts show up not only in terms of income (i.e., that "Jews earn like Episcopalians and vote like Puerto Ricans"), but in almost every other respect as well. For example, basing themselves on exit polls and various opinion surveys, Greenberg and Wald tell us that between 1990 and 2000 only 39 percent of "white, college-educated, urban, middle-aged non-Jews" identified themselves as Democrats as compared with 60 percent of Jews with the same characteristics.[4] And as we have already seen, an even greater difference shows up between Jews and the other white groups who were their partners in the New Deal coalition. Unlike all other white groups, moreover, Jews of all kinds, with the partial exception of the Orthodox (about whom more later), hardly differed from one another in their attachment to the Democratic Party. Even in age and gender, the two categories where internal Jewish differences did show up, they were smaller than those within other groups. About the age factor, Greenberg and Wald write:

> We know . . . that younger Americans are generally less partisan than older Americans. But Jews exhibit fewer differences related to age. Young Jews appear less committed to the Democratic Party than older Jews, but they are *not* moving into the Republican Party. Instead, only 10 percent of Jews under thirty-five years old call themselves Republican, while 41 percent call themselves politically Independent, and 49 percent identify as Democrats.[5]

Judging by the size of the aggregate Jewish vote, however, it seems to me a safe bet that most of these "Independents" vote Democratic most of the time. (Writing in 1955, Lawrence H. Fuchs made very much the same point about the liberalism of Jewish "Independents"— and he, too, put the word in quotes, signifying skepticism as to its true meaning.) The only exception in this period—and even it amounted to only 9 percent—was 1992, when Ross Perot offered an anti-(elder) Bush alternative to Clinton.

Then there is the famous "gender gap." As with all their American sisters, between 1990 and 2000, Jewish women (with 64 percent) identified more strongly with the Democrats than did Jewish men (56 percent)—a gap of 8 points. Yet here again, if we add the self-described Independents to the self-described Democrats, we come up with a gap of only 3 points (87 percent for women; 84 percent for men).

To go by the annual Surveys of American Jewish Opinion commissioned by the American Jewish Committee, the one change of any significance took place in 2002, when the proportion of Jews who described themselves as Republican doubled (from 9 percent in 2000 to 18 percent in 2002). This was accompanied by a roughly commensurate decline in Democratic self-description from 59 percent to 48 percent (the other 2 percent went into the "Independent" column).* But thereafter the relative proportions varied only slightly from year to year. From 2002 to 2008, between 15 and 18 percent of Jewish voters identified themselves as Republicans, as against a Democratic share in the mid-to-high 50s, and an "Independent" proportion in the mid-to-high 20s. In 2008, to be precise, the numbers were 56 percent Democrat, 17 percent Republican, and 25 percent Independent.

In short, what one of the most astute students of Jewish voting patterns, Earl Raab, then of Brandeis University, said in 1996 was still true ten and more years later: "If you scratch an American Jew, you will find a Democratic voter." (I would add that if you scratch a liberal organization like the American Civil Liberties Union or the United Nations Asso-

---

* For some reason, the survey for 2001, unlike all the others, did not contain a question about party affiliation. The change in 2002 probably reflected the great popularity George W. Bush enjoyed in the immediate aftermath of 9/11.

ciation, you will find Jewish members and Jewish money sustaining it, and if you scratch a Jewish organization, you will find a liberal agenda.) But having made this unsurprising observation, Raab counterposed it to a commensurately surprising one: "The complicating news . . . is that if you scratch somewhat deeper, you will not always find a liberal."[6]

What Raab mainly meant was that a substantial percentage of Jews were describing themselves as "moderate" or "middle-of-the-road" rather than as liberal, and that these "moderates" were taking the conservative position on a number of issues. The examples he gave were the size of government, law and order, and affirmative action. On several other issues, including welfare reform and environmentalism, the Jewish "moderates" were also on the conservative side, though less strongly so.

Four years later, Murray Friedman (a maverick neoconservative on the senior staff of the American Jewish Committee) went even further. Referring to the same statement by Raab that I have just quoted, he wrote:

> His words still carry greater force today, when, at least at the local level, you are also decreasingly likely to find a Democratic voter.[7]

The signs of a possible realignment to which Friedman pointed included the election with heavy Jewish support of law-and-order Republicans like Rudolph Giuliani as mayor of New York and Richard J. Riordan to the same office in Los Angeles. He also cited the emergence of Jewish politicians like the Republican Stephen Goldsmith of Indianapolis, and the Democrats Joseph Lieberman of Connecticut and Ed Rendell of Pennsylvania, who "were uncomfortable with many of the old liberal dogmas."

But what Raab and Friedman failed to notice was that there was nothing new in the supposedly new trend they were spotting. In 1955, Lawrence H. Fuchs observed that

> the Jews have not been as kind to Democratic candidates running for lesser office as they were to Roosevelt, Truman, and Stevenson.[8]

Nor, as we can also tell from Fuchs, was there anything new about the tendency of Jews to see themselves as "moderates" and "independents" rather than as Democrats:

> Though the Jews have turned in very substantial pluralities for Democratic Presidential candidates, they do not consider themselves to be overwhelmingly Democratic. They prefer, rather, to think of themselves as independents. Whenever members of ethno-religious groups have been asked to designate their party affiliations in sample surveys, the percentage of self-designated independents is always much higher among Jews than in any other group.[9]

Moreover, it was a combination of local concerns and of what Friedman would later call "bellwether issues" (in Fuchs's days they were New Deal domestic policies and internationalism) that determined whether and when Jewish voters would desert a given Democratic candidate. Fuchs:

> It must be remembered that candidates for Governor and for Congress run on local as well as national issues, and a large number of Jews have not always found the Democratic position on local issues as compatible with their own views as the Democratic position on national and international questions.[10]

So it was with the Jewish voters of the late 1990s whom Raab and Friedman were writing about. As Friedman himself acknowledged, these voters (exactly like their forebears of the 1940s) were willing to back Republicans *only* so long as they adopted the liberal positions on "such bellwether issues . . . as immigration, abortion, gay rights, and the separation of church and state." But this alone—in addition to showing that there was nothing new about the tendency he and Raab thought they detected—demonstrated that, contrary to Friedman's conclusion, Jews were definitely *not* becoming less liberal.

We find further confirmation of the stubborn Jewish refusal to rethink the old political pieties in a paper titled "American Jewish Liberalism: Unraveling the Strands" by Steven M. Cohen and Charles S. Liebman, one of the most authoritative and sophisticated statistical analyses ever done of the subject.[11]

"In what ways and to what extent are Jews liberal?" ask Cohen and Liebman, and they search for an answer by stacking the attitudes of Jews toward a wide range of issues against those of all other Americans. The first category they look at is political identification, and there they find that 47 percent of Jews call themselves liberals, as compared with 28 percent of all other Americans. Then come church-state relations, and in particular our old friend, the issue of school prayer. More or less as I would have guessed from personal experience, Jews oppose it by a whopping 82 percent, whereas only 38 percent of non-Jews do. The third category Cohen and Liebman examine is civil liberties, and there it turns out that an equally whopping 81 percent of Jews provide liberal responses, as compared with, on average, 60 percent of non-Jews.

Moving on to government spending, the gap between Jews and non-Jews is also large. Here 74 percent of Jews versus 57 percent of non-Jews feel that not enough is being spent on health, education, and the environment. A wide gap also shows up on race. Seventy percent of Jews support policies on behalf of blacks, but only 58 percent of non-Jews do; and by a margin of 64 percent to 53 percent, Jews also take the politically correct position that discrimination (rather than such factors as the large percentage of female-headed households) is what accounts for the condition of the black community.

In spite of the evidence they themselves provide, however, Cohen and Liebman—out of annoyance, I suspect, with the self-gratulation that often pervades reports on this matter—bend over backward to bolster the argument of Raab and Friedman that Jews may not be as liberal as most people think:

> Jews may indeed earn like Episcopalians and vote like Hispanics; but, with respect to many key issues, they think like Episcopalians. In this respect, contrary to what others have argued, there is no anomaly of excessive Jewish liberalism.[12]

And yet, with all due respect to Cohen and Liebman, very few Jews have been thinking like Episcopalians even though the standard liberal agenda of recent years has conflicted sharply with their economic interests. What another of the most astute students of the American Jewish community, the sociologist Nathan Glazer of Harvard, wrote in 1980 was still valid—give or take a detail or two—in 1997, when Liebman and Cohen published their paper, and—give or take another detail or two—it remains valid in 2009:

> Jews have for decades numbered relatively few workers, so they
> shouldn't have cared about strengthening trade unions. There
> has been almost no Jewish lower class, so they shouldn't have
> cared about welfare. It's true that since Jews are such an aged
> population they want more social security and Medicare, and
> this is one interest that still links them to the liberal agenda, but
> that doesn't amount to much when one considers the interests
> that should lead them to oppose that agenda. Jews have been,
> disproportionately, businessmen and self-employed profession-
> als, who are also small businessmen. They should have been
> against higher taxes and government spending, for tax breaks to
> business, against government regulation of business. But what-
> ever the promptings of their *economic* interests, Jews have
> supported the party that wants to increase government spending,
> expand benefits to the poor and lower classes, impose greater
> regulations on business, support the power of organized labor.[13]

Much the same point can be made about affirmative action. Practi-cally every Jew in America had been raised to believe, and did believe, that one of the country's chief glories—one of the features that raised it above all other nations—was its commitment to the principle of treating individuals as individuals without regard to race or religion or national origin. Moreover, Jews had a clear interest in maintaining the meritocratic system that flowed from this principle and in opposing its replacement with a system based on favoritism toward certain groups (blacks and some other minorities to begin with, and then women). At first, most Jews did recognize that this new system of reverse discrimination would inevitably involve quotas, or proportional representation according to group, and that, being both tiny in numbers and no longer regarded as a minority, they were in danger of being subjected to a new wave of discrimination. But (as is shown by the statistics I have just cited on the position they take about special policies for blacks) their resistance to this danger proved short-lived. For not even the powerful combination of principle and self-interest could withstand their fear of being stigmatized as racists by their fellow liberals.

What is even more significant than the positions Jews take on political and economic questions is how they score on the issues that fall into the area of "social codes," where an "anomaly of excessive liberalism" becomes unmistakable and undeniable. These are the issues being fought out in the great culture war that in our day has fueled more political passion than the size of government or welfare reform or how best to deal with crime—and Cohen and Liebman themselves have the statistics to prove that Jews are at least as liberal as ever:

> Jews are firmly committed to permissive social codes, sexual codes in particular. The gap between Jews and others on the scale that measures attitudes toward nonmarital sexual behavior, marijuana, and divorce laws is quite substantial: 58 percent of Jews had liberal responses on these items as opposed to just 31 percent of non-Jews. In like fashion, huge gaps separate Jews from others on abortion (86 percent vs. 44 percent) and control of pornography (71 percent vs. 45 percent).[14]

On women's rights, Jews are in the liberal fold by the most whopping majority of all (89 percent), though here the gap separating them from non-Jews (with 75 percent) is somewhat smaller than on other issues.

But not only are Jews more liberal on these issues than non-Jews in general; they are even "decidedly more liberal" than non-Jews who resemble them in "socioeconomic factors and residence patterns":

> Holding constant for [these factors], we found that 24 percent more Jews than non-Jews approve of abortions for any reason;

21 percent more approve of legalizing marijuana; 7 percent
more assert that pre-marital sex is not wrong at all, 15 percent
more that extra-marital sex is not always wrong, and 26 percent
more that gay sex is not wrong at all. An analogous gulf divides
Jews from similarly situated non-Jews when it comes to church-
state relations: 37 percent more of the former oppose prayer in
the public schools—and . . . this opposition cuts across denomi-
national lines.*[15]

The issue of gay marriage had not yet come to the fore in the surveys Cohen and Liebman used, but according to the analysis of Greenberg and Wald, who were able to include it in theirs, Jews are twice as
likely as non-Jews to support its legalization.[16] More recently, in an
AJC survey of Jewish opinion, 49 percent support making gay marriage legal, 36 percent favor civil unions, and 74 percent oppose a constitutional amendment defining marriage "as a union only between a
man and a woman."

For Jewish attitudes toward suicide and euthanasia—another hotly
contested battleground of the culture war that neither Cohen and
Liebman nor Greenberg and Wald examine—we can turn to an even
more extensive and detailed report by Tom Smith of the National
Opinion Research Center at the University of Chicago. Smith tells us
that Jews overwhelmingly, and by a much larger percentage than any
other ethnic/racial or religious group, take the liberal side on this issue:

About 85 percent of Jews would allow suicide or euthanasia
when a person has an incurable disease, compared to 58–67
percent of non-Jews. . . . Support for suicide in the case of bank-
ruptcy, dishonoring one's family, or being "tired of living" is
backed by 22–33 percent of Jews and 8–15 percent of non-Jews.[17]

Finally, there is the question of how Jews feel about the military and
the use of military force. Cohen and Liebman provide no data on this

---

* Almost certainly the level of non-Jewish support on certain of these items—
especially premarital sex and gay rights—has by now gone up.

all-important liberal-conservative divide, and Greenberg and Wald touch on it only when they note that Jews, by a 2–1 margin, support military intervention for humanitarian purposes.

Greenberg and Wald do not, however, make it sufficiently clear that in doing so, the Jews are again taking the liberal position, since humanitarian considerations are (or were) just about the only justification liberals have come to accept for the use of military force. A good example is the difference between the opposition of most liberals (including the Jews among them) to the First Gulf War of 1991 and their advocacy a few years later of intervention in Bosnia and Kosovo to help save the Muslims there from being wiped out by the Serbs. Because the Gulf War was fought to secure a major source of our supply of oil, it was tainted by self-interest in the eyes of liberals. But to those same liberal eyes, no clear national interest or material advantage was visible in Bosnia and Kosovo. Hence the use of American military force became permissible.

So much for the exception. As to the rule, a solid majority of Jews oppose our use of force under almost any other conditions. This stems in part from their attitude toward the military. As we learn from Smith, of all fifteen groups in his survey, Jews rank at the very bottom—yes, fifteenth—for confidence in the military. We also learn: "Of all ethnic/racial and religious groups Jews have . . . the greatest support for gun control,"[18] from which we can infer that very few Jews are members of the National Rifle Association. By the same token, Jews have also consistently favored cuts in defense spending.

Clearly, then, Raab and Friedman were wrong in seeing a Jewish move away from liberalism, while Smith was right in concluding, after a meticulous review of the data, that

> counter to some claims that Jews have been becoming more conservative either generally or politically, with few exceptions, Jewish views have either held steady or, more often than not, grown more liberal in recent decades.[19]

This was what the data showed in 2005. Three years later, the picture remained much the same. In the AJC's Annual Survey of American Jewish Opinion for 2008, 44 percent described themselves as liberal, 30 percent as "moderate," and only 24 percent as conservative.[20]

Nor is there any sign of an impending Jewish break with the Democratic Party. We know this to a certainty from the Jewish vote in presidential elections, emphatically including the one in 2008. But we also know from the AJC's survey for 2008 that most Jews (in majorities ranging from 52 to 63 percent) still think that the Democratic Party is more likely than the Republicans "to make the right decision" on every single one of the five major issues they were asked about (terrorism, the economy, support for Israel, energy independence, and Iraq). And this, mind you, is *regardless* of how [they] usually vote."

Which, at long last, brings me to the question of why.

THE WRONG ANSWERS

Many attempts have been made to account for the stubborn persistence of Jewish liberalism. Some focus on historical experience, some on sociological factors, and some on religious influence. Let me examine each of these theories in turn.

Having spent most of this book trying to show that it is the historical experience of the Jewish people that turned them into liberals, I am not about to argue that the historical theory is wrong. Yet while it tells us why Jews were on the Left for much of the past, the historical theory does not explain why, under radically different conditions, they still are. Some say that it is because the Jews have long memories, but I find more illumination in the story of the guns of Singapore. Before the outbreak of World War II, these artillery pieces were pointed in the direction from which the island had last been invaded, and so they proved utterly useless against the Japanese, who simply invaded from the other side. "The guns of Singapore" thus became shorthand for the not uncommon phenomenon of fighting the last war instead of the one that needs to be fought now. For the Jews, the enemy had always been on the Right, and it was from there that he had only yesterday launched the most murderous assault on them in their long history. It may be understandable that they would keep looking for the enemy where he was last seen, but as the British defending Singapore discovered in 1940, fighting the last war can only bring defeat in the new war that has just broken out.

What, then, of sociological factors? The first of these on which exponents of the sociological theory generally zero in is the "minority group status" that leads to a feeling of "marginality," and worries about anti-Semitism.

One might think that American Jews, being so successful by every measure, would no longer be suffering from a sense of marginality (they are no longer even thought of by others as a minority), but it seems that they still do. According to the 2008 AJC survey, 86 per-cent[!] of American Jews think that anti-Semitism in America is either "a very serious problem" (23 percent) or "somewhat of a problem" (63 percent). At the same time, "most look to the liberal camp to pro-tect them from the anti-Semites, who are perceived as being on the Right more than on the Left."[1] But this only confirms what we already know without helping to explain it. If anything, indeed, it deepens the mystery. For when 98 percent of American Jews tell the AJC pollsters that they think more anti-Semitism now comes from the Muslim world than from anywhere else, and when 86 percent think that more anti-Semitism now also comes from Muslims than from any other group in America, they must mean the anti-Semitism that disguises itself as anti-Zionism. And yet they continue to look for protection from the Left, which (to say yet again what cannot be said too often) has offered far less resistance than the Right to this latest mutation of what Ruth R. Wisse of Harvard rightly calls "the 20th century's most durable ideology."[2]

A second sociological factor often invoked is education. A very high proportion of Jews go to college, where the students are supposedly brought (in the words of Steven M. Cohen) "into contact with ideas different from their own, and calling into question previously accepted truths." But not Jewish students. The ideas with which they come into contact in college are in most cases the same as the liberal orthodoxies they have imbibed at home, so that instead of being called into ques-tion, these "previously accepted truths" are reinforced by an over-whelmingly liberal professoriate. This is confirmed by a survey summarized by Cohen that found that Jewish students become even more liberal on the economy, on the separation of church and state, and "on the social issues of abortion, gay rights and permitting pornography" than they were before going to college.*3

But why should people who are notorious for being exceptionally intelligent be incapable of taking a critical look at the ideas they have been saddled with and measuring those ideas against the realities of the world around them? As the philosopher Michael Walzer of the Institute for Advanced Study at Princeton sees it,

> The style of liberal politics is also a Jewish style: skeptical, questioning, inconclusive. Only liberalism guarantees the continuing openness necessary to arguments about, and now to differing versions of, a common Jewishness. While the Jewish tradition was not liberal in substance, it was (sometimes) close to liberal in cast of mind.4

This may in some sense be true of Abraham, Moses, Job, and some of the prophets, who dare to argue with God Himself, but how does it square with the "cast of mind" of the Jews of today, who cannot even bring themselves to argue with the dogmatic orthodoxies of contemporary liberalism?

After grappling with this puzzle for a long time, Irving Kristol—the author of the famous definition of a neoconservative as "a liberal who has been mugged by reality"—finally wrote an exasperated essay titled "On the Political Stupidity of the Jews." It opened with a story—long one of my own favorites as well—that the novelist Saul Bellow used to tell about his days as an undergraduate at the University of Chicago:

> [Bellow] and a group of highly intellectual and like-minded fellow students would meet frequently at his aunt's apartment, which was located next to the university. The meetings lasted long into the night, as abstract points of Marxism and Leninism

---

* The survey dated from 1988, but liberalism has become even more dominant on the campus since then.

agitated and excited these young intellectuals. . . . After the
meetings broke up in the early hours of the morning, Saul's aunt
would remark to him: "Your friends, they are so smart, so
smart. But stupid!"

Of course, Kristol said, the old "hard-core adherence to Marxist or
Leninist doctrines" no longer held sway, but he maintained that the
Jews had continued

to combine an almost pathologically intense concern for politics
with a seemingly equally intense inclination toward political
foolishness, often crossing over into the realm of the politically
suicidal. How is one to understand this very odd Jewish
condition—the political stupidity of Jews?[5]

Kristol's answer to his own question was a variant of the historical
theory: centuries of powerlessness had left the Jews bereft both of "the
skills necessary for astute statesmanship" and the experience that
makes for political wisdom, and this had turned them into an easy
prey for utopian fantasies.

There is surely some truth in Kristol's thesis, but it also overlooks
what Ruth Wisse describes as the "creative accommodation to local
political rule and socioeconomic opportunities" that kept the Jews of
the Diaspora going. "Look up the synonyms for *adaptation*," she
writes, "and you discover Jewish communities at work: elastic, flexi-
ble, pliable, and supple."[6] And this is not to mention the experience of
self-government acquired through the bodies (*kehillot*) into which
Jewish communities were organized throughout the Diaspora. If the
Jews of America are politically stupid, then, it cannot be for lack of
inherited political skills and experience.

A third sociological explanation is that most American Jews had
liberal parents ("political socialization" in the technical jargon). During the 1960s there was much talk of a "generation gap" between
young people and their parents, but all the evidence shows that political attitudes and affiliations are invariably transmitted from parent to
child. In fact, the "generation gap" was even a myth as applied to the

radical young of the '60s (and especially the Jews among them). Far from being rebels against the political views of their parents, they were (in the coinage of the sociologist Richard Flacks, himself a member of the New Left) "red-diaper babies"—that is, the children of left-wing parents. Many of these were Jewish and some went further to the Left than their parents had gone. But in time most whose parents had been Communists or socialists of some other stripe moved, as many of the parents themselves had already done, in the other direction— becoming not (God, so to speak, forbid!) conservatives but liberals.

But again, as with the historical theory (with which it overlaps) "political socialization" in this sense fails to answer the question of why these attitudes should have persisted in the face of a radically new set of circumstances. The same is true of the idea propounded by the highly esteemed sociologist Seymour Martin Lipset, writing in collaboration with Earl Raab, that Jews

> are more at ease with the kinds of people they find in the
> Democratic Party—their fellow ethnics with whom they grew
> up in America—than with the white Anglo-Saxon Protestants
> still predominant in the Republican Party.[7]

Still? Even when most Jews have so much less in common than they had with their fellow ethnics in what is by now a distant past? And even when so many of their old partners in the New Deal coalition have long since moved into the Republican Party?

So, too, with another kind of socialization—the kind that inculcates a fear of the punishment that will be exacted for dissent from the orthodoxies of the community. Friends will be lost, coveted invitations will stop coming, and one's good name will be besmirched.[8] These are certainly powerful incentives to continued conformity, but it is only in a more tightly closed community than the one in which most American Jews now live that the fear of being expelled can work as well as the threat of excommunication did for their forebears.

There is, however, yet another, hot-off-the-press, hypothesis that would, if true, explain why most Jews remain liberals even in the face of new circumstances that rob the old attitudes of the sense they once made. This hypothesis posits that there is an important genetic influence on our political beliefs. According to James Q. Wilson, no one argues for the existence of a Republican gene or a Democratic gene, but the available evidence (drawn, for example, from studies of identical twins) does show that "genes help us understand fundamental attitudes—that is, whether we are liberal or conservative."

It might seem, then, that Gilbert and Sullivan were right when they told us that "every little boy or girl / That's born into this world alive / Is either a little Liberal / Or else a little Conservative." The problem is that the beliefs held by Gilbert and Sullivan's liberal (limited government, free markets, and free trade) are what define a conservative in America today, while the American liberal of today takes positions that are nearly the opposite of what defined a liberal even as recently as 1960 (when John F. Kennedy ran for president on a platform calling for a stronger national defense, a tax cut to stimulate economic growth, and an end to discrimination against individuals as the path to racial justice). Not only that, but as Wilson himself says:

> One can be an economic liberal who favors a large state but a social conservative who opposes abortion. Or one can be an economic conservative who favors the free market but a social liberal who supports abortion and gay rights. If we add to this mix attitudes about foreign policy, the various combinations of liberals and conservatives double. Most tests used in genetic studies of our political views do not allow us to generate these important distinctions. As a result, we know that genes affect ideology but that knowledge is clumsy. In time, I suspect, we will learn more about these subtleties.[9]

If that time ever comes, the question of why Jews are still liberals will once again answer itself. But contrary to Wilson's suspicion, my own guess is that it never will.

In the meantime, we are left with the theory—the most popular by far—that traces Jewish liberalism all the way back to the "Jewish values" that are said to derive from the commandments of Judaism or, more broadly, the "spirit" of the Jewish "religious tradition." Lawrence H. Fuchs, an early exponent of this theory, focuses on *tzedakah* as the Jewish value with "the most relevance to the politics of our time."[10] *Tzedakah* is a Hebrew word for "charity" and the religious obligation to practice it, including by giving alms to the poor. However, recognizing that the word derives from the same root as the word for "justice," and can also signify "righteousness," Fuchs argues that its "real meaning" is what we know today as "social justice." He also contends that the reason it has so much relevance to contemporary politics is that it "deals with the distribution of power, which, after all, is what politics is about."[11]

This unwarranted leap from caring for the poor to giving them power having been made, it is but a short step to the assertion that *tzedakah* helped to

> promote Jewish sympathy for the Negro [as well as] a favorable attitude toward progressive taxation, Roosevelt's war on the economic royalists, social security, and most of the programs which constituted the New Deal.[12]

It is, Fuchs concedes,

> difficult to see the relevance of *tzedakah* to the silver-gold issue, . . . but how quickly *tzedakah* comes into play on such questions as unemployment compensation, shorter work, higher wages, relief . . . and so on.[13]

Trude Weiss-Rosmarin, longtime editor of the *Jewish Spectator,* not only agrees but, carrying the idea forward from Roosevelt's New Deal to Lyndon Johnson's Great Society, insists that even affirmative action (or "positive discrimination") for minorities and women is mandated by Jewish law:

> Jewish social law . . . demands not charity but *tzedakah* ("justice"): that is, compensation for the poverty caused by

ill-fortune or the lack of the ability to compete in the market-place. Jewish tradition is committed to [Johnson's] Great Society and to Roosevelt's Four Freedoms, especially "Freedom from Want."[14]

Two leading spokesmen for Reform Judaism (Albert Vorspan and David Saperstein) also see Jewish law as the source of Johnson's Great Society. "Indeed," they tell us, "many scholars believe that the first anti-poverty program in human history was spelled out in the Hebrew Bible and Talmud."[15] And in general, they declare:

> Jewish liberalism goes to the heart of our religious and historic heritage. Our Jewish ethical system *compels* us to be concerned with the unfortunate and the stranger in our midst, rejecting the [conservative] concept of "survival of the fittest."[16]

Jumping ahead all the way from the mid-'60s to 2008, we find Rabbi Sidney Schwartz of the Institute for Jewish Leadership and Values making the same point in a similar tone of moral self-gratulation:

> Isn't it obvious that social justice is the primary mandate of Judaism? Isn't it obvious that there is no attitude or behavior as universally shared by American Jews as their commitment to the ideals of tolerance, peace, and justice for all people?[17]

Finally, getting down from Rabbi Schwartz's lofty abstractions to the brass tacks of particular policies, Deborah E. Lipstadt, a professor of modern Jewish history at Emory University, explains why she could never have voted for John McCain in 2008:

> The Torah repeatedly instructs us to care for the "widow, orphan, poor, and the stranger." It is fundamental to Judaism that those who are blessed with "more" have an obligation—not a choice—to help those who have less. . . . How then could I support McCain, who has voted against the minimum wage at

least 10 times? How could I support someone who believes in the privatization of Social Security?[18]

But it is an intellectual absurdity to assume that the Torah actually endorses a specific policy like the minimum wage (which in any case has time and again been shown to do more harm than good to the poor). It is equally preposterous, as well as a piece of arrant chutzpah, to assert that Judaism takes a side in the technical debate over whether it would be better to give the individual some say in how his Social Security payments are invested than to go on letting the government make the entire decision for him.

But even apart from such considerations, there is a fatal flaw at the heart of the theory that the liberalism of American Jews stems from the teachings of Judaism—that is, from the Bible (especially the prophetic books) and the exegetical extrapolations from it in the Talmud and other rabbinical writings. If the theory were valid, the Orthodox would be the most liberal sector of the Jewish community. For it is they who are the most familiar with the Jewish religious tradition, who are the most deeply influenced by its holy books, and whose lives are the most shaped by its commandments.

Yet as we have repeatedly seen from the data, the Orthodox are the least liberal of all their fellow Jews. The Orthodox enclaves are the only Jewish neighborhoods where conservative candidates get any votes to speak of, and the Orthodox also support aid to parochial schools and the display of religious symbols in the "public square," which almost all their fellow Jews—like all other liberals—regard as serious breaches in the wall of separation between church and state. But even more telling is that on every one of the other issues involved in the culture war, the Orthodox oppose the politically correct liberal positions taken by most other American Jews—and precisely because these positions conflict with Jewish law. Jewish law forbids sex outside marriage and sex between men; it permits abortion only to protect the life of the mother; it takes a conservative view of the role of women; it prohibits suicide (except when the only alternatives are forced conversion and incest) and positive euthanasia.

Clever exponents of the religious theory acknowledge all this, but they then try to get around it through a shift of emphasis. A good example is the then executive director of the American Jewish Congress, Henry Siegman, who knows enough to know that "there is no basis for the notion that Jewish tradition is intrinsically liberal." He even admits that "a far better case can be made that, in important respects, it is intrinsically conservative." But this does not deter him from confidently conferring on liberalism a stamp of Jewish approval:

There is no question that the qualities of compassion and concern [of the liberal agenda] resonate with an authentic Jewish sensibility. There is something decidedly *"goyish"* about a Darwinian marketplace in which only the fittest survive.[19]

Michael Walzer, who also recognizes that "the Jewish tradition is not liberal in substance," nevertheless holds that

the Jewish commitment to justice is substantively connected to Jewish religious culture and to the experience of exile before as well as after emancipation. The connection goes all the way back to the first "exile," bondage in Egypt, and to the legal and moral code that came out of that experience. . . . The prophetic books reaffirm the values of the Exodus story: indeed, no other body of literature is so likely to press people who take it seriously toward an identification with the poor and oppressed.[20]

Yet even here "Jewish religious culture" is more out of tune with the liberal position than the likes of Walzer imagine. This is not to say that there is no congruence between Jewish tradition and the liberal ideal of social justice. As the former editor of *Commentary*, Neal Kozodoy, bitingly writes:

So instinctive and reflexive, by now, is the Jewish identification with this ideal of social obligation, so ingrained in habits of action and attitudes of mind, so in tune with long-sanctioned impulses and religious precept, that most Jews today would be hard-pressed even to conceive of any other model of civic virtue (there are a few!) than the model bodied forth by the catechism of liberal reform, any other definition of the good society than that epitomized by the commandment to do justice to the poor.[21]

Accurate as this most assuredly is, it is also true that the egalitarianism behind the liberal conception of social justice is altogether foreign to the Torah. Unlike the New Testament, which consistently favors the poor over the rich and sees money as the root of all evil, in the Hebrew Bible riches are just as consistently considered a blessing. Furthermore, as Steven H. Cohen and Charles S. Liebman take pains to point out, the poor to whom Jews are commanded to do justice "are primarily other Jews."[22] In other words, this commandment is, to use the standard technical term, "particularistic." *Pace* Walzer, particularism even informs the eschatological vision of the Hebrew prophets. They do indeed envisage the ultimate salvation of the whole world, but the redemption of the Children of Israel is the necessary precondition for this glorious future, which in any event will not be achieved until all nations cast away their idols and bow their knees to the one true God, the God of Israel.[23]

Clearly, then, the religious theory as usually expounded fails to answer our question. There is, however, another way of framing the religious theory that does, I believe, provide a solution to the last of the three great puzzles we have encountered in the story I have been telling in this book. The first, it will be recalled, was the failure to understand the significance of the hatred of the Jewish people that was built into the worldview of Voltaire and other major thinkers of the eighteenth-century Enlightenment. The second was the same blindness toward the anti-Semitism of Marx and other leaders of the nineteenth-century socialist movement. And the third, to which I now turn, is the continued commitment of Jews to liberalism in spite of the fact that the liberal community has since the last third of the twentieth century embraced several views that conflict with the teachings of Judaism and that are decidedly unfriendly to the things that they themselves profess to care about *as* Jews.

THE "TORAH" OF LIBERALISM

According to a well-known remark attributed to G. K. Chesterton, "When men stop believing in God they don't believe in nothing; they believe in anything." But this was not true of the Jewish immigrants who came to America from Eastern Europe. Almost all the young intellectuals and political leaders among them had stopped believing in the God of Judaism, but it was not "anything" they now believed—it was Marxism.

I said a long way back in this book that the Jews who became Marxists imagined that they were throwing off superstition and embracing a life guided entirely by reason and scientific truth (Marxism, remember, claimed to be scientific). But I also said that what they were actually doing was converting to a new religion in which Marx's *Capital* became (in the words of Paul Johnson) "a new kind of Torah" (which is precisely what Abraham Cahan, the very influential editor of the largest Yiddish daily, would later declare socialism to be, and also how I. J. Singer would characterize it in *The Brothers Ashkenazi*). To this new "Torah" they grew as stubbornly attached—both out of conviction and as a matter of honor—as their fathers and grandfathers had been to the Torah of Judaism itself. And as it was with their forebears in relation to Judaism, so it became with them in relation to Marxism: nothing could shake their faith in its doctrines. In spite of all the persecution they endured, the Jews of premodern times never stopped believing that they were God's chosen people; and in spite of the seemingly irrefutable case that could be made against His promise that fidelity to His commandments would bring them prosperity here on earth, they continued, like Job, to proclaim, "Though He slay me, yet will I trust in Him." The belief of the Jewish Marxists in the glorious promise of socialism was commensurately resistant to refutation by the horrors of "actually existing socialism" in the Soviet Union and other countries living under Communism.

In this, as both premodern Jews and the first two or three generations of Jewish Marxists would have been horrified to learn, they bore an uncannily close resemblance to the third-century Church Father Tertullian. It was he who said of one Christian doctrine that it was believable precisely because it was ridiculous (*credible est, quia ineptum est*) and of another that it was certain precisely because it was impossible (*certum est, quia impossibile*).* Like Tertullian's faith in the truth of Christianity, both the faith of premodern Jews in Judaism and the faith of their Marxist progeny in socialism were powerfully resistant to falsification either by reason or by facts unmistakably contradicting their respective claims.

As time went on, however, the intransigence of both the old Jewish faith in Judaism and the newer Jewish faith in Marxism became harder and harder for their adherents to sustain. Many dropped away. But many others who had also lost faith in the "old-time religion" felt that it would be dishonorable to desert it altogether. They therefore sought for a way to remain within the fold without being required to accept the dogmas that had, in their eyes at least, been discredited. It was out of this quest in the strictly religious sphere that Reform Judaism came into being; and it was out of an analogous feeling in the political sphere that "social democracy" (or "democratic socialism") was born.

We saw this process at work with David Dubinsky and other Jewish labor leaders. Having converted from Judaism to Marxism, they had then suffered another crisis of faith when they were forced to restrain

---

* Both of these statements are often misquoted as *credo quia absurdum* ("I believe because it is absurd").

their orthodox socialist convictions in order to engage in collective bargaining (for which adherents of the old-time Marxist religion accused them of collaborating with the capitalists). Then, going further, they decided to support Roosevelt and join the New Deal coalition (for which they were accused by the Communists of "preaching socialism while practicing fascism"). Nevertheless they would not and could not stop regarding themselves as socialists and they continued preaching it, albeit in increasingly attenuated versions.

Yet as still more time passed, it became difficult to sustain a faith even in those attenuated versions. After World War II, capitalism, instead of collapsing as the socialist faith had led its devotees to expect, began producing wealth on a previously unimaginable scale; not only that, but it made possible a level of prosperity for the poor that surpassed even the rosiest utopian dreams of Marxist theory (or, for that matter, of any other utopian fantasy of the past).

By 1989, moreover, any lingering illusions about Communism were smashed to smithereens by the collapse of the Soviet Union. More disillusioning yet, even the countries ruled by parties belonging to the social-democratic church were doing so much less well than the United States that most of them quietly began introducing elements of our wickedly capitalist system into their own economies.

In the face of these developments, the same process that had made social democracy into an acceptable refuge from orthodox Marxism now began making liberalism into an acceptable refuge from social democracy. This would have been impossible in the past, when all socialists had despised liberalism as the ideology of the bourgeoisie and as a cover for capitalist rapacity. But liberalism in America had steadily been moving to the Left and was looking more and more like European socialism and less and less like the American liberalism of an earlier day. This was why someone like Irving Howe, who had gone from Marxism (of the Trotskyite variety) to democratic socialism, could now describe liberalism as "our natural home" and as the " 'secular religion' of many American Jews."[1] Indeed it was; and the Jews of America were holding on to it for dear life because beyond the liberal faith there was nowhere to go but into the outright apostasy of conservatism. To them this was as deeply repugnant, and even horrifying, as conversion to Christianity had been to their grandparents in the shtetls of Eastern Europe, who had treated converted offspring as dead and had observed the prescribed rituals of mourning (*shivah*) for them.

To most American Jews, then, liberalism is not, as has often been said, merely a necessary component of Jewishness: it is the very essence of being a Jew. Nor is it a "substitute for religion": it is a religion in its own right, complete with its own catechism and its own dogmas and, Tertullian-like, obdurately resistant to facts that undermine its claims and promises. The talk-radio host and columnist Dennis Prager makes much the same point:

> Despite their secularism, Jews may be the most religious ethnic group in the world. The problem is that their religion is rarely Judaism; rather it is every "ism" of the Left. . . . It is therefore usually as hard to shake a liberal Jew's belief in the Left and in the Democratic Party as it is to shake an evangelical Christian's belief in Christianity. The big difference, however, is that the Christian believer acknowledges his Christianity is a belief, whereas the believer in liberalism views his belief as entirely the product of rational inquiry.[2]

The philosopher David Sidorsky of Columbia concurs: "An affinity for liberalism by Jews . . . cannot be abandoned when confronted by new events and circumstances."[3]

Sidorsky's statement comes from his contribution to "Liberalism and the Jews," a symposium published in *Commentary* (January 1980) when I was its editor and from which I have already quoted several times. It was made up of short pieces by fifty-two American Jews of varying political views who were asked whether they thought that a reconsideration of the traditional Jewish commitment to liberalism and to the Democratic Party was warranted by certain recent developments—namely,

the widespread support among liberals for quotas, the diminishing enthusiasm among liberals for Israel, the growing sympathy of liberals for the PLO, and the paucity of liberal protest against the anti-Semitism that had surfaced in the wake of Andrew Young's resignation [as Carter's ambassador to the United Nations].

In setting up this symposium, I hoped that it would force the participants to undertake such a reconsideration, and a few of them did. But what the symposium mainly accomplished was to show how Jewish liberals were managing then—and still manage today—to avoid a serious confrontation with the great political changes that had been taking place for some time and were now staring them right in the face.

One technique of avoidance, adopted by the prominent Jewish scholar Robert Alter of Berkeley, was to admit that the liberal community had in fact become hostile to Jewish interests, but then to absolve liberalism itself of any responsibility for the change:

> It hardly needs to be observed that when a liberal agenda begins to encourage discriminatory legislation and a species of racism at home, repressive and belligerent regimes abroad, it has come in its own circuitous way to espouse positions that have been traditionally associated with the political Right.[4]

But having acknowledged this phenomenon, Alter refused to recognize that a converse change had taken place on the political Right itself. Totally ignoring the conservative Christian community's fervent support for Israel, Alter insisted that the Republican Party was still no less hostile than the Democrats had become:

> One should remember that not only Jesse Jackson but John Connally is prepared to hand over the West Bank lock stock and barrel to the PLO with the demagogic claim that this will bring lasting peace to the region and give America cheap and abundant oil.

It was a symptom of intellectual desperation that Alter—and many other contributors to the symposium—should have seized upon John

Connally, a former Democrat who was then running in the Republican presidential primaries. Connally did indeed take the position on Israel that Alter ascribed to him, but so little appeal did he have for Republican voters that he wound up winning only one delegate at a cost of $13 million (a record at that time). About the candidate who did have great appeal to those voters, Alter had this to say:

> I suppose the one Republican candidate who is clearly a strong supporter of Israel is Ronald Reagan, but . . . his general views are so retrograde and his competence so questionable that I find it hard to imagine that sane liberals, whatever their concern for Israel, would want to contemplate voting for him.

And so, simply by waving aside the pro-Israel sentiment of the Republicans behind Reagan as of no account, Alter was able to argue that the only thing for "sane" Jews to do was to remain committed to "liberalism as a political orientation," to stick with the Democratic Party, and to hope that "polemical pressure" from within could recall "the liberal community as it [was] presently constituted" back to the true liberal principles it had betrayed but only (he also hoped) temporarily.

In one form or another, Alter's argument was adopted by several other contributors to the symposium, including the sociologist Daniel Bell of Harvard:

> [We] need to make clear distinctions. And the primary one is between liberalism and the liberals. Let us take back the one, and forgo the other.[5]

This way of thinking resembled nothing so much as the frantic efforts once made by certain devout members of the Marxist church to rescue the true faith by dissociating it from the "really existing socialism" and the really existing socialists of the Soviet Union and other Communist countries.

Instead of trying to dissociate the true liberal faith from "really existing liberalism" or to rescue liberalism from the liberals, a number of contributors to the symposium resorted to denial. That is, they insisted that no such dissociation or rescue was necessary because no such change had taken place within the liberal community.

Thus Rabbi Eugene B. Borowitz, the then editor of *Sh'ma,* "a journal of Jewish responsibility":

> I do not recognize the Jewish liberals the symposium statement mentions. I know Marxists, radicals, and pseudo-radicals who support quotas, turn from Israel, flirt with the PLO, and condone black anti-Semitism. Such views are generally anathema to the Jewish liberals I know.[6]

Thus, too, Leonard Fein, the then editor of the liberal Jewish magazine *Moment:*

> I do not recognize the "recent developments" which frame the symposium question. The "widespread support" among liberals for quotas? None at all for quotas. . . . The "diminishing enthusiasm among liberals for Israel"? Which liberals? . . . Where is the evidence that there is growing sympathy for the PLO among American liberals?[7]

And thus, too, Rabbi Alexander M. Schindler, then the president of the Reform movement's Union of American Hebrew Congregations:

> Just where . . . is there the wide support for quotas among liberals . . . ? I do not find it. . . . A diminishing support for Israel among liberals? Perhaps so. . . . Yet this adverse sentiment is fueled in no small measure by forces from the Right. . . . The paucity of liberal protest against post–Andrew Young anti-Semitism troubles me. . . . But let us note that . . . most of this anti-Semitism was given its most blatant expression in the camps of radicalism and reaction.[8]

Thirty years on, Jewish members of the liberal church like these are still relying on denial as a way to defend the faith against a mugging by reality. Others, however, following in the footsteps of the likes of

Michael Lerner, defend the liberal faith by claiming that it is indeed the new "Torah" of the Jews—and in the most literal sense of pursuing *tikkun olam,* the "repair of the world," a concept that (with the scantiest of justifications from the sacred texts) they have singled out as the essence of Judaism.

Here, for example, is the publisher's description of *Righteous Indignation,* a collection of essays that came out in 2008 and that addressed itself to the question, "Can the teachings of Judaism provide a sacred framework for repairing the world?":

> In this groundbreaking volume, leading rabbis, intellectuals, and activists explore the relationship between Judaism and social justice, drawing on ancient and modern sources of wisdom. The contributors argue that American Jewry must . . . dedicate itself to systemic change in the United States, Israel, and throughout the world.[9]

The specific "justice issues" on which the essays concentrate are without exception the ones that make up the current liberal agenda: "eradicating war, global warming, health care, gay rights and domestic violence"—and on each of these issues the "teachings of Judaism" always turn out to be identical with the "systemic changes" liberals are dedicated to making.

Someone once unkindly described the services in a Reform temple as "the Democratic Party at prayer," and Reform Judaism in general as "the Democratic Party platform with holidays thrown in." Even more unkindly, I have said that many Jews, insofar as they know anything about the Hebrew prophets at all, seem to think that they are high-class fund-raisers for the Democratic Party. A good recent example—to which I pointed earlier in another context—was the letter signed by three hundred rabbis endorsing Barack Obama's candidacy for president in 2008. By asserting that "he has been inspired by Jewish values such as *Tikkun Olam,*" and that his "deep and abiding spiritual faith" derives from "the teachings of the Hebrew prophets," the rabbis practically made it sound as though he was in effect being endorsed by Amos, Micah, Isaiah, and the rest.

But in *Righteous Indignation,* in addition to the usual verses from the prophets exhorting us to do justice and be merciful toward the poor, quotations from the Talmud are brought in to certify that every liberal jot and tittle of the moment carries a stamp of rabbinic approval as well.

Yet on the basis of a more thorough knowledge of and a much greater fidelity to the texts, Rabbi Seymour Siegel, then professor of ethics and theology at the Jewish Theological Seminary, pointed to the many ways in which the Torah of Judaism is at variance with the "Torah" of contemporary liberalism. Among those he listed were the following:

Judaism is law-oriented, tradition oriented, reverent of past usages. Liberalism celebrates the new and the novel. . . . Judaism insists on justice which is to be pursued . . . without "respect to persons."* Liberalism, for the moment at least, prefers to pursue justice with quotas and preferential treatment for favored minorities. Judaism [teaches] sexual restraint and the values of family and children. Liberalism favors permissive attitudes toward abortion, homosexuality, and unconventional family arrangements. . . . Judaism . . . does not disdain business or commerce. . . . Liberalism tends to be anti-business.[10]

Discussing the conception of Judaism pervading the forty essays in *Righteous Indignation,* Hillel Halkin is even more specific:

Health care, labor unions, public-school education, feminism, abortion rights, gay marriage, globalization, U.S. foreign policy, Darfur: on everything Judaism has a position—and, wondrously, this position just happens to coincide with that of the American liberal Left. . . . [These essays] treat Jewish tradition not as a body of teachings to be learned from but as one needing to be taught what it is about by those who know better than it does what it *should* be about.[11]

---

* This is an allusion to Deuteronomy 1:17, in which judges are exhorted to treat the "small" and "great" with impartiality.

What we see here, in short, is that liberalism has not only superseded socialism as the religion of most American Jews, it has even superseded Judaism itself among many Jewish liberals who presume to speak in its name. So far as they are concerned, where the Torah of contemporary liberalism conflicts with the Torah of Judaism, it is the Torah of liberalism that prevails and the Torah of Judaism that must give way. For, as Halkin rightly concludes,

> Judaism has value to such [liberal] Jews to the extent that it is useful, and it is useful to the extent that it can be made to conform to whatever beliefs and opinions they would have even if Judaism had never existed.

Most American Jews, however, do not speak in the name of Judaism or even think about it much. According to all the available survey data, says Steven M. Cohen, "religion per se is not all that important to many Jews." In this, they differ dramatically from American Christians:

> While almost half the non-Jews [in the sample] said that religion was "very important" in their own lives, only a quarter of the Jews made a similar claim. Proportionately three times as many white Christians go to church weekly as Jews who attend synagogue weekly. Most Jews attend synagogue four times a year or less.[12]

But, Cohen hastens to add, this does not mean that "being Jewish" is of no account to most American Jews:

> When asked, not about their religion, but about the importance of "being Jewish . . . in your own life," almost half say it is "very important," which is almost twice as many as those who have as much to say about "religion."[13]

In other words, for most American Jews, ethnic "Jewishness takes precedence over Judaism." But insofar as these ethnic Jews pay any mind to Judaism at all, they regard it as, in "essence," liberalism by another name. Hence in their eyes being "a liberal on political and economic issues" is equivalent to being "a good Jew."[14]

By this indirect route, these supposed secularists, no less than the Jewish liberals who speak in the name of Judaism, transfer and apply the faith that the Torah of Judaism inspired in their forebears to the Torah of liberalism, and to this new Torah they give a like measure of steadfast devotion and scrupulous obedience.

CONCLUSION

It is because liberalism has become the religion of American Jews that, Tertullian-like, they can remain loyal to it even though it conflicts in substance with the Torah of Judaism at so many points, and even though it is also at variance with the most basic of all Jewish interests—the survival of the Jewish people. Rabbi Seymour Siegel again:

> Judaism requires that the community protect its own interests and its own integrity, for only in this way can it survive. Liberalism expects Jews—especially Jews—to yield their own interests for the sake of "progress" and "justice."[1]

Let me state the same point more nakedly and more brutally: contemporary liberalism demands that, unlike any other people, Jews justify the space they take up on this earth. Furthermore, they must do so not, as they are commanded in the Bible, by loving God with all their hearts and all their souls and all their might,[2] but rather by clinging with the same intensity to certain currently fashionable conceptions of what constitutes progress and how to define justice—even if these conceptions are highly questionable, and even if, as most blatantly in the case of Israel, obedience to them could be tantamount to committing suicide. In this way, the Torah of liberalism puts itself radically at odds with the very commandment that comes closer than any other (certainly than *tikkun olam*) to encapsulating the essence of the Torah of Judaism, and the observance of which for more than three thousand years is probably the single best explanation of the mystery of Jewish survival:

> I have set before you life and death, blessing and cursing:
> therefore choose life, that both thou and thy seed may live.[3]

Rabbi Siegel stresses, as I have been doing throughout this book, that once upon a time what was known as liberalism *did* serve Jewish interests. Armed with this indisputable fact, members of the liberal church have tried to turn the tables on those of us who have called upon Jews to begin acting in their own self-interest. Naturally, being "universalists," these exponents of liberalism would rather not speak of self-interest at all since they think that such a call is tantamount to advocating a return to the "tribalism" and "parochialism" from which they have freed themselves. But if speak of it they must, they say that Jewish interests are still best served by an unwavering commitment to the liberal faith.

The problem is that the "really existing" liberalism that has become their religion, and that of most American Jews, is not (in the succinct formulation Gertrude Himmelfarb offers in her contribution to the *Commentary* symposium) "the liberalism that brought us into modernity, that gave us our freedom as individuals and tolerated us as Jews." For this old liberalism has been "replaced by a new liberalism that is inhospitable to us both as individuals and as Jews."

What, then, is to be done? Himmelfarb urges her fellow Jews to begin thinking more

> boldly about our real interests and principles—not only about
> [the] immediate and obvious ones (quotas, Israel, anti-
> Semitism) but also those which have a less direct but no less
> vital bearing upon us: a strong [American] military establish-

ment and a vigorous foreign policy without which the defense of Israel is empty rhetoric, and economic policies conducive to economic growth without which the future of Jews, like that of any other minority, is gravely imperiled.

But beyond these she sees a set of

more enduring interests and principles which we have given too little thought to during our long association with liberalism—the need for social attitudes and policies which will be favorable to (rather than, as is more often the case today, subversive of) family, community, tradition, morality, religion.[4]

Himmelfarb argues that the bold thinking she is calling for need not and should not lead to "conservatism as traditionally understood" or to an embrace of the Republican Party. The goal, rather, is "political independence." In my own view, even bolder thinking would reach the conclusion that it is long past time for the Jews of America to join the side that has come to side with them, and to stick with it unless and until this ceases to be the case.

In politics, to say it again and for the last time, this means the Republican rather than the Democratic Party. Admittedly, both parties are formally and officially friendly to Jewish interests, and most especially during campaigns for the presidency. Jewish support, in the form of money and in terms of votes in certain states, is still important enough to be courted by the Democratic and Republican candidates alike, and this still translates mainly and above all else into affirmations of commitment to the security and survival of Israel.

But more than money is involved here; and contrary to the allegations of undue and illegitimate influence by an all-powerful "Jewish lobby," the pro-Israel stand of most American politicians (as opposed to unelected officials) is, and has been since the establishment of the state in 1948, a faithful reflection of the sentiments of the vast majority of the people they represent. Of its position on Israel, writes Walter Russell Mead of the Council on Foreign Relations, the American public has few foreign policy preferences that are this marked, this deep, this enduring—and this much at odds with public opinion in other countries.[5]

There does, however, remain a difference here between the two parties, and it lies in the respective bases to which the two parties are tied and by which they are likely to be influenced when they are in power. For the Democrats, the tie is to the Left—and in that quarter (with some exceptions) attitudes toward Israel range from unsympathetic to passionately hostile. Conversely, on the Right—secular as well as religious—to which the Republicans are bound, support for Israel (also with some exceptions) runs from solid to fervent. To repeat: this was not true in the past, and it may not be true in the future, but it has most emphatically been true since the end of the Six-Day War of 1967.

Of course, when we speak of the conflict between Left and Right, or between liberals and conservatives, we are talking about a divide wider and deeper than electoral politics. The great issue between the two communities turns on how they feel about the nature of American society. Again with all exceptions duly noted, I think it fair to say that what the Left mainly sees when it looks at America is injustice and oppression of every kind—economic, social, and political. By sharp contrast, the Right sees a complex of traditions, principles, and institutions that have made it possible for more freedom and—even factoring in periodic economic downturns—more prosperity to be enjoyed by more of its citizens than in any other society known to human history. It follows that what liberals believe needs to be changed or discarded is precisely what conservatives are dedicated to preserving, reinvigorating, and defending against attack.

In this realm, too, American Jewry surely belongs with the conservatives rather than the liberals. For the social, political, and moral system that liberals wish to transform is the very system in and through which Jews found a home such as they had never discovered in all their forced wanderings throughout the centuries over the face of the earth. The Jewish immigrants who began coming here from Eastern Europe in the 1880s were right to call America *di goldene medineh,* "the golden land." Obviously there was no gold in the streets, as some of them may have imagined, and so they had to struggle and struggle hard. But there was another kind of gold in America, a more precious kind than the gold of coins. There was freedom and there was opportunity. Blessed with these conditions, and hampered by much less disabling forms of anti-Semitism and discrimination than Jews had previously grown accustomed to contending with, the children and grandchildren and great-grandchildren of these immigrants flourished—and not just in material terms—to an extent unprecedented in the history of their people.

Thus do we come full circle to the Augustinian idea of the Jew as "witness"—only in this case neither (as in the original form) to the truth of Christianity nor (as in the Voltairean inversion) to its lies and superstitions. This time, through the unique benignity of their experience in the United States, the Jewish people bear witness to the infinitely precious virtues of the traditional American system. Surely, then, we Jews have an obligation to join with the defenders of this system against those who are blind or indifferent or antagonistic to the philosophical principles, the moral values, and the socioeconomic institutions on whose health and vitality it depends.

It will be impossible for most of my fellow Jews to discharge that obligation so long as they remain caught in the Tertullian-like grip of the Torah of liberalism. As the story I have just told makes dishearteningly clear, there is no sign that this will change in the foreseeable future. Nevertheless, I cannot for the life of me give up the hope that the Jews of America will eventually break free of their political delusions, and that they will then begin to recognize where their interests and their ideals both as Jews and as Americans truly lie. But in the meantime they will continue to occupy the anomalous position in the political culture of America that has given rise in so many minds to the question I have tried to answer in this book.

NOTES

INTRODUCTION

1. Anna Greenberg and Kenneth D. Wald, "Still Liberal After All These Years?" in L. Sandy Maisel and Ira N. Forman (eds.), *Jews in American Politics* (Lanham, Md.: Rowman & Littlefield, 2001), pp. 173–74.
2. Ibid., pp. 169–70.
3. Ibid., p. 170.

CHAPTER ONE

1. Romans 11:1.
2. Romans 11:28.
3. Romans 7:6.
4. Romans 11:1–2.
5. Romans 8:6–7.
6. Matthew 27:15. But in 1965, at the Second Vatican Council, the Catholic Church formally and officially absolved the Jewish people of the crime of deicide. See chapter 22.
7. John 8:44.
8. R. J. Zwi Werblowski, "Christianity," in Geoffrey Wigoder (ed.), *Encyclopaedia Judaica*, CD Rom Edition, Version 1.0, 1997, Multimedia (Israel) Ltd. [henceforth EJ].
9. Léon Poliakov, "Anti-Semitism," in Geoffrey Wigoder (ed.), EJ.
10. Ibid.
11. Paul Johnson, *A History of the Jews* (New York: Harper & Row, 1987), p. 208.

12. David Berger, "The Attitude of St. Bernard of Clairvaux to the Jews," *Proceedings of the American Academy for Jewish Research*, 40, 1972.

13. I should note that, according to at least one scholarly authority, Paula Fredericksen of Boston University, Augustine's view of Judaism was more positive than has generally been thought and that the idea of keeping the Jews in a state of misery came later. But it remains to be seen whether this revisionist interpretation will achieve widespread acceptance.

14. Quoted in H. H. Ben-Sasson, "The Middle Ages," in H. H. Ben-Sasson (ed.), *A History of the Jewish People* (Cambridge, Mass.: Harvard University Press, 1976), p. 474.

15. Quoted in Robert Seltzer, *Jewish People, Jewish Thought* (New York: Macmillan, 1980), p. 359.

16. Quoted in H. H. Ben-Sasson, "Blood Libel," in Geoffrey Wigoder (ed.), EJ.

17. Ibid.

18. Ibid.

19. Ibid.

20. Quoted in H. H. Ben-Sasson, "Black Death," in Geoffrey Wigoder (ed.), EJ.

21. Ibid.

22. Quoted in P. Johnson, *A History of the Jews*, p. 216.

23. Genesis 4:12.

CHAPTER TWO

1. Quoted in *The Jewish Encyclopedia* [henceforth JE] (New York: Funk & Wagnalls, 1901–6), vol. X, p. 564; also available online without charge at www.jewishencyclopedia.com.

2. H. H. Ben-Sasson, "Poland," in Geoffrey Wigoder (ed.), EJ.

3. Herman Rosenthal, "Russia," in JE, vol. X, p. 566.

4. Shmuel Ettinger, "The Modern Period," in H. H. Ben-Sasson (ed.), *A History of the Jewish People* (Cambridge, Mass.: Harvard University Press, 1976), p. 752.

5. Rosenthal, "Russia," p. 564.

6. Léon Poliakov, "Official Anti-Semitism in Old Russia," *Commentary*, July 1956.

7. Quoted in Rosenthal, JE, p. 564.

8. Poliakov, "Official Anti-Semitism in Old Russia."

9. Quoted in Poliakov, "Official Anti-Semitism in Old Russia."

10. Poliakov, "Official Anti-Semitism in Old Russia."

11. Ibid.

12. Paul Johnson, *A History of the Jews* (New York: Harper & Row, 1987), pp. 241–43.

13. Quoted in Ronald H. Bainton, *Here I Stand: A Life of Martin Luther* (New York: Mentor Paperback, 1955), p. 297.

14. Martin Luther, "Concerning the Jews and Their Lies," quoted in H. H. Ben-Sasson (ed.), *A History of the Jewish People* (Cambridge, Mass.: Harvard University Press, 1976), p. 650.

15. P. Johnson, *A History of the Jews*, p. 242.

16. Quoted in Poliakov, "Anti-Semitism."

CHAPTER THREE

1. Hillel Halkin, "Hebrew Poets in Old Spain," *Commentary*, July/August 2007.

2. Deuteronomy 11:19.

3. Quoted in H. H. Ben-Sasson, "The Middle Ages," in H. H. Ben-Sasson (ed.), *A History of the Jewish People* (Cambridge, Mass.: Harvard University Press, 1976), p. 522.

4. Ibid., p. 524.

CHAPTER FOUR

1. The editors of the *Encyclopaedia Judaica* designate 1740–89 as the first period, but I see it as beginning a century earlier. Otherwise, I will be following the periodization they use in their lengthy article on "Emancipation."

2. http://www.reformedreader.org/rbb/williams/btp.htm.

3. http://www.constitution.org/jl/tolerati.htm.

4. Book XXV:9. (http://www.constitution.org/cm/sol_25.htm#009).

5. Quoted in Haim Herman Cohen, "Usury," in Geoffrey Wigoder (ed.), EJ.

6. Quoted in Shmuel Ettinger, "The Modern Period," in H. H. Ben-Sasson (ed.), *A History of the Jewish People* (Cambridge, Mass.: Harvard University Press, 1976), p. 743.

7. http://www.jewish-history.com/Occident/volume3/aug1845/menasseh.html.

8. Book XXI:20 (http://www.constitution.org/cm/sol_21.htm#020).

9. Ettinger, "The Modern Period," p. 743.

10. Quoted in Arthur John Sargent, *The Economic Policy of Colbert* (London and New York: Longmans, Green, 1899), p. 36 (socserv.mcmaster.ca/econ/ugcm/3113/sargent/EconomicPolicyColbert.pdf).

11. Ettinger, "The Modern Period," p. 754.

12. In recent years, scholars like Peter Gay have cast doubt on the validity of this concept, but in my opinion it can still serve a useful purpose in connection with the history of Jewish emancipation.

13. Robert Seltzer, *Jewish People, Jewish Thought* (New York: Macmillan, 1980), pp. 518–19.

14. Quoted in Ettinger, "The Modern Period," p. 756.
15. Ibid.
16. Quoted in Gotthard Deutsch, "Joseph II," JE, vol. VII, p. 253.

CHAPTER FIVE

1. Some historians, most notably Gertrude Himmelfarb, distinguish between the French Enlightenment, "which was antireligious and anticlerical," and the variant that developed in England, "where even deists were tolerant of the established church" (*One Nation, Two Cultures*, Knopf, 1999, p. 88). But whenever I use the term here, it refers only to the French Enlightenment. In any case, while the deists may have been tolerant toward the Church of England, they were at least as hostile to Judaism and the Jewish people as most of the French *philosophes*. Indeed, Voltaire himself went to school with them on this issue (see below in this chapter).

2. Paul Weissman, "Anti-Semitism: The Enlightenment," in Geoffrey Wigoder (ed.), EJ.

3. Quoted in Paul Johnson, *A History of the Jews* (New York: Harper & Row, 1987), p. 309.

4. Quoted in Shmuel Ettinger, "The Modern Period," in H. H. Ben-Sasson (ed.), *A History of the Jewish People* (Cambridge, Mass.: Harvard University Press, 1976), p. 745.

5. Quoted in P. Johnson, p. 309.

6. Quoted in Adam Sutcliffe, "Can a Jew Be a Philosophe?" *Jewish Social Studies*, March 22, 2000 (http://www.accessmylibrary.com/coms2/sum mary_0286-28739189_ITM).

7. Shmuel Ettinger, "The Modern Period," in H. H. Ben-Sasson (ed.), *A History of the Jewish People* (Cambridge, Mass.: Harvard University Press, 1976), pp. 744–45.

8. Ibid., p. 745.

9. P. Johnson, p. 308.

10. Ibid., p. 309.

11. Sutcliffe, "Can a Jew Be a Philosophe?"

12. Jacob Katz, *From Prejudice to Destruction: Anti-Semitism, 1700–1933* (Cambridge, Mass.: Harvard University Press, 1980), p. 34.

13. Zalkind Hourwitz, quoted in Léon Poliakov, "Voltaire," in Geoffrey Wigoder (ed.), EJ.

14. Quoted in Salo W. Baron, "The Impact of the Revolution of 1848 on Jewish Emancipation," *Jewish Social Studies*, July 1949, p. 228.

CHAPTER SIX

1. Quoted in Salo W. Baron, "The Modern Age," in Leo W. Schwarz (ed.), *Great Ages and Ideas of the Jewish People* (New York: Random House, 1956), p. 380. On the same page, Baron also quotes a waggish reply: "The wise believe 'cause Moses taught it; / From Mendelssohn but fools have caught it."

2. Quoted in Robert Seltzer, *Jewish People, Jewish Thought* (New York: Macmillan, 1980), p. 563.

3. Ibid, pp. 563–64.

4. Ibid., p. 564.

5. Sol Liptzin, "Schlegel, Dorothea Von," in Geoffrey Wigoder (ed.), EJ.

6. Quoted in Ruth R. Wisse, *Jews and Power* (New York: Schocken Nextbook, 2007), p. 74.

7. Baron, "The Modern Age," p. 381.

8. Arthur Hertzberg, *The French Enlightenment and the Jews* (New York: Schocken Paperback, 1970), p. 10.

CHAPTER SEVEN

1. Quoted in Benzion Dinur, "Emancipation," in Geoffrey Wigoder (ed.), EJ.

2. Quoted in Arthur Hertzberg, *The French Enlightenment and the Jews* (New York: Schocken Paperback, 1970), p. 265.

3. Quoted in Shmuel Ettinger, "The Modern Period," in H. H. Ben-Sasson (ed.), *A History of the Jewish People* (Cambridge, Mass.: Harvard University Press, 1976), p. 760.

4. Quoted in Paul Johnson, *A History of the Jews* (New York: Harper & Row, 1987), p. 306.

5. Salo W. Baron, "The Modern Age," in Leo W. Schwarz (ed.), *Great Ages and Ideas of the Jewish People* (New York: Random House, 1956), p. 324.

6. Quoted in Léon Poliakov, "Voltaire," in Geoffrey Wigoder (ed.), EJ.

7. Ibid.

8. Ibid.

9. Quoted in Ettinger, "The Modern Period," p. 804.

10. Ibid., p. 805.

11. Isaiah 49:17.

12. Ed. Staff, "Stahl, Friedrich Julius," in Geoffrey Wigoder (ed.), EJ.

13. Shmuel Ettinger, "The Modern Period," in H. H. Ben-Sasson (ed.), *A History of the Jewish People* (Cambridge, Mass.: Harvard University Press, 1976), p. 808.

14. Ibid., p. 809.

15. Dinur, "Emancipation."

16. Salo W. Baron, "The Impact of the Revolution of 1848 on Jewish Emancipation," *Jewish Social Studies*, July 1949, p. 228.
17. Ibid.
18. Quoted in Salo W. Baron, "The Impact of the Revolution of 1848 on Jewish Emancipation," *Jewish Social Studies*, July 1949, pp. 220–21.
19. Ibid., p. 217.
20. Ibid., p. 199.
21. Ibid., p. 223n.

CHAPTER EIGHT

1. Karl Marx, "On the Jewish Question," http://www.marxists.org/archive/marx/works/1844/jewish-question/index.htm. The italics are in the original.
2. Ibid. The italics are in the original.
3. Both quoted in George Lichtheim, "Socialism and the Jews," in *Collected Essays* (New York: Viking Press, 1973), pp. 420, 425.
4. I quoted this passage, which comes from a letter to Mathilda Wurm, in "A Certain Anxiety," *Commentary*, August 1971. It can also be found in a slightly different translation at http://archives.econ.utah.edu/archives/marxism/1995-08-14.000/msg00118.htm.
5. Arthur Hertzberg, *The French Enlightenment and the Jews* (New York: Schocken Paperback, 1970), p. 4.
6. Paul Johnson, *A History of the Jews* (New York: Harper & Row, 1987), p. 354.
7. I. J. Singer, *The Brothers Ashkenazi* (New York: Atheneum, 1980), p. 184.
8. Ibid., p. 250.
9. Galatians 3:28.
10. Singer, p. 341.
11. Ibid, p. 267.
12. Shmuel Ettinger, "The Modern Period," in H. H. Ben-Sasson (ed.), *A History of the Jewish People* (Cambridge, Mass.: Harvard University Press, 1976), p. 810.
13. Quoted in http://www.aish.com/literacy/jewishhistory/ Crash_Course_in_Jewish_History_Part_57_-_The_Czars_and_the_Jews.asp.
14. Ibid.
15. The exchange was recorded by Herzl in his diary, and is reproduced in this form by P. Johnson, *A History of the Jews*, p. 364.
16. Quoted in Salo W. Baron, "The Modern Age," in Leo W. Schwartz, ed., *Great Ages and Ideas of the Jewish People* (New York: Random House, 1956), pp. 332–33.
17. Cecil Roth, *A Short History of the Jewish People* (London: East and West Library, 1969), pp. 356–57.

18. Baron, "The Modern Age," p. 418.

19. Ibid.

CHAPTER NINE

1. Cecil Roth, *History of the Jews in England,* quoted in Edmund Wilson, *A Piece of My Mind: Reflections at Sixty* (New York: Farrar, Straus and Cudahy, 1956), p. 91.

2. P. Masserman and M. Baker, "The Jews Come to America," quoted in Abraham I. Katsh, "United States of America: Colonial American Jewry," in Geoffrey Wigoder (ed.), EJ.

3. From *A Life of Roger Williams* written in verse, and also Abraham I. Katsh, "United States of America: Colonial American Jewry," in Geoffrey Wigoder (ed.), EJ.

4. Quoted in Abraham I. Katsh, "United States of America: Colonial American Jewry," in Geoffrey Wigoder (ed.), EJ.

5. Ibid.

6. Ibid.

7. Ibid.

8. Ibid.

9. Perry Miller (ed.), *The American Puritans: Their Prose and Poetry* (New York: Columbia University Press, 1982), p. ix.

10. Quoted in Edmund Wilson, *A Piece of My Mind: Reflections at Sixty* (New York: Farrar, Straus and Cudahy, 1956), p. 92.

11. Ibid., p. 93.

12. Ibid., p. 92.

13. Ibid., p. 93.

14. Abraham I. Katsh, "United States of America: Colonial American Jewry," in Geoffrey Wigoder (ed.), EJ.

15. Quoted in E. Wilson, p. 97.

16. Ibid., pp. 94–95.

17. Ibid, pp. 95–96.

18. Ibid., p. 98.

CHAPTER TEN

1. Lloyd P. Gartner, "United States of America: 1820–1880," in Geoffrey Wigoder (ed.), EJ.

2. Quoted in Nathaniel Weyl, *The Jew in American Politics* (New Rochelle, N.Y.: Arlington House, 1968), p. 40.

3. Quoted in Paul Johnson, *A History of the Jews* (New York: Harper & Row, 1987), pp. 366–67.

4. Louis Berg, "Founders and Fur Traders," *Commentary,* May 1971.

5. Louis Berg, "Peddlers in El Dorado," *Commentary*, July 1965.

6. Berg, "Founders and Fur Traders."

7. Gartner, "United States of America: 1820–1880."

8. Ibid.

9. Ibid.

CHAPTER ELEVEN

1. Quoted in Lloyd P. Gartner, "United States of America: 1820–1880," in Geoffrey Wigoder (ed.), EJ.

2. Quoted in George Weigel, "The New Anti-Catholicism," *Commentary*, June 1992.

3. Quoted in Paul Johnson, *A History of the Jews* (New York: Harper & Row, 1987), pp. 373–74.

4. Jakob J. Petuchowski, "Reform Judaism," in Geoffrey Wigoder (ed.), EJ.

5. "The Pittsburgh Platform," in Geoffrey Wigoder (ed.), EJ.

6. Quoted in Edmund Wilson, *A Piece of My Mind: Reflections at Sixty* (New York: Farrar, Straus and Cudahy, 1956), pp. 96–97.

7. Edmund Wilson, *A Piece of My Mind: Reflections at Sixty* (New York: Farrar, Straus and Cudahy, 1956), p. 97.

8. Quoted in Ibid., pp. 99–100.

9. E. Wilson, p. 100.

10. Quoted in my book *The Bloody Crossroads: Where Literature and Politics Meet* (New York: Simon & Schuster, 1986), p. 196.

11. Quoted in Bruce J. Schulman, *Business History Review*, http://www.hbs.edu/bhr/archives/bookreviews/79/bschulman.pdf

12. Quoted in Robert Michael, *A Concise History of American Antisemitism* (Lanham, MD: Rowman & Littlefield, 2005), p. 116.

13. Quoted in Ernest Samuels, *Henry Adams: The Middle Years* (Cambridge, Mass: Belknap Press, 1958), p. 129.

14. Quoted in *The Bloody Crossroads*, p. 110.

CHAPTER TWELVE

1. Quoted in my book *The Bloody Crossroads: Where Literature and Politics Meet* (New York: Simon & Schuster, 1986), p. 200.

2. Quoted in Howard M. Sachar, *A History of the Jews in America* (New York: Vintage Books, 1993), p. 281.

3. Henry James, "The American Scene," in *Collected Travel Writings: Great Britain and America* (New York: Library of America, 1993) p. 464.

4. Ibid., p. 471.

5. Ibid., p. 468.

6. Edmund Wilson, *A Piece of My Mind: Reflections at Sixty* (New York: Farrar, Straus and Cudahy, 1956), pp. 213–14.

7. Oscar Handlin, quoted in Irving Howe, *World of Our Fathers* (New York: New York University Press, 2005), pp. 39–40.

8. Quoted in Irving Howe, *World of Our Fathers* (New York: New York University Press, 2005), p. 88.

9. Ibid., p. 81.

10. Paul Johnson, *A History of the Jews* (New York: Harper & Row, 1987), p. 372.

11. Irving Howe, *World of Our Fathers* (New York: New York University Press, 2004), pp. 113, 139.

12. Ibid., p. 325.

13. Ibid., p. 329.

14. Ibid., p. 349.

CHAPTER THIRTEEN

1. Shmuel Ettinger, "The Modern Period," in H. H. Ben-Sasson (ed.), *A History of the Jewish People* (Cambridge, Mass.: Harvard University Press, 1976), p. 874; "Duehring, Karl Eugen," in Geoffrey Wigoder (ed.), EJ.

2. Quoted in Ettinger, "The Modern Period," p. 875.

3. Ibid.

4. Ettinger, p. 877.

5. Quoted in Ettinger, "The Modern Period," p. 876.

6. Ettinger, "The Modern Period," pp. 876–78.

7. Quoted in Paul Johnson, *A History of the Jews* (New York: Harper & Row, 1987), p. 381.

8. Paul Johnson, *A History of the Jews* (New York: Harper & Row, 1987), p. 381.

9. Quoted in P. Johnson, *A History of the Jews*, p. 381.

10. Ibid.

11. Ibid., p. 382.

12. Arthur Hertzberg, "Anti-Semitism: Emancipation and Reaction," in Geoffrey Wigoder (ed.), EJ.

13. P. Johnson, *A History of the Jews*, p. 383.

14. Quoted in P. Johnson, *A History of the Jews*, p. 380.

15. Ibid., p. 386.

16. Ibid., p. 387.

CHAPTER FOURTEEN

1. Shmuel Ettinger, "The Modern Period," in H. H. Ben-Sasson (ed.), *A History of the Jewish People* (Cambridge, Mass.: Harvard University Press, 1976), p. 878. The italics are in the original.
2. Quoted in Paul Johnson, *A History of the Jews* (New York: Harper & Row, 1987), p. 391.
3. Ibid., p. 394.
4. Paul Johnson, *A History of the Jews* (New York: Harper & Row, 1987), p. 482.
5. Quoted in P. Johnson, *A History of the Jews,* p. 473.
6. Ibid., p. 474.

CHAPTER FIFTEEN

1. Quoted in Howard M. Sachar, *A History of the Jews in America* (New York: Vintage Books, 1993), p. 282.
2. Howard M. Sachar, *A History of the Jews in America* (New York: Vintage Books, 1993), p. 282.
3. Quoted in Sachar, *A History of the Jews in America,* p. 321.
4. Ibid., p. 280.
5. Ibid.
6. Ibid., pp. 280, 286.
7. William Z. Ripley, *The Races of Europe: A Sociological Study* (New York: D. Appelton, 1899), quoted in Howard M. Sachar, *A History of the Jews in America* (New York: Vintage Books, 1993), p. 283.
8. Quoted in Sachar, *A History of the Jews in America,* p. 324.
9. Ibid., p. 455.
10. Ibid., p. 454.
11. David S. Wyman, "Why Auschwitz Was Never Bombed," *Commentary,* May 1978.
12. Quoted in Sachar, *A History of the Jews in America,* p. 521.

CHAPTER SIXTEEN

1. Irving Howe, *World of Our Fathers* (New York: New York University Press, 2005), p. 392.
2. "Herb London's Shanda," *Forward,* March 1, 1991.
3. Lawrence H. Fuchs, *The Political Behavior of American Jews* (Glencoe, Ill.: Free Press, 1956), p. 100.
4. Ibid., p. 160; and the following account of the 1945 mayoral race in New York City leans heavily on Fuchs as well.
5. Daniel P. Moynihan, " 'Bosses' and 'Reformers,' " *Commentary,* June 1961.

6. Quoted in Irving Howe, *World of Our Fathers* (New York: New York University Press, 2005), p. 393.

7. I quote here from memory of a talk given by Peretz. The allusion is to Psalms 137:5.

8. David Evanier, *FrontPage* magazine, April 2008.

9. Joseph Epstein, "Thinking Outside the Lox," *Wall Street Journal*, September 15, 2008.

10. Quoted in Howard M. Sachar, *A History of the Jews in America* (New York: Vintage Books, 1993), p. 603.

11. *Memoirs by Harry S. Truman*, vol. 2 (New York: Doubleday, 1955), pp. 162, 164.

12. Quoted in Richard Holbrooke, "Washington's Battle over Israel's Birth," *Washington Post*, May 7, 2008.

13. Ibid.

14. Howard M. Sachar, *A History of the Jews in America* (New York: Vintage Books, 1993), p. 612.

15. Ibid., p. 612.

16. Quoted in http://www.scribd.com/word/full/2883677?accesskey=key-lrzl pjmzdq29z8nnfly312.

17. Richard Holbrooke, "Washington's Battle over Israel's Birth," *Washington Post*, May 7, 2008.

18. Fuchs, *The Political Behavior of American Jews*, p. 81.

CHAPTER SEVENTEEN

1. Quoted in David Tal (ed.), *The 1956 War: Collusion and Rivalry in the Middle East* (London, UK, and Portland, Ore.: Frank Cass, 2001), p. 28 (http://books.google.com/books?id=DJVK9RfMEJAC&pg=PA28&lpg= PA28&dq=Jewish+vote+for+president+1956&source=web&ots=k7veD sCZ9W&sig=Ckq0qMZhEPuy0rxqUOgw4UA-tNQ&hl=en&sa=X&oi= book_result&resnum=4&ct=result#PPA28,M1).

2. *RN: The Memoirs of Richard Nixon* (New York: Grosset & Dunlap, 1978), p. 44.

3. Ibid., p. 179.

4. Hans J. Morgenthau, "Goldwater—The Romantic Regression," *Commentary*, September 1964.

5. Lyndon Baines Johnson, *The Vantage Point: Perspectives of the Presidency, 1963–1969* (New York: Holt, Rinehart and Winston, 1971), p. 70.

6. Anna Greenberg and Kenneth D. Wald, "Still Liberal After All These Years?" in L. Sandy Maisel and Ira N. Forman (eds.), *Jews in American Politics* (Lanham, Md.: Rowman & Littlefield, 2001), pp. 172–74.

CHAPTER EIGHTEEN

1. The full text can be found at http://www.sdsrebels.com/oglesby.htm.
2. *Julius Caesar,* Act 3, Scene 2.
3. Joseph J. Zasloff, "The Problem of South Vietnam," *Commentary,* February 1962.
4. Hans J. Morgenthau, "Vietnam—Another Korea?" *Commentary,* May 1962.
5. Oscar Gass, "Political Economy and the New Administration," *Commentary,* April 1961, and "The New Frontier Fulfilled," *Commentary,* December 1961. The quotation is from the latter piece.
6. Norman Podhoretz, "My Negro Problem—and Ours," *Commentary,* February 1963.
7. David Danzig, "The Radical Right and the Rise of the Fundamentalist Minority," *Commentary,* April 1962.

CHAPTER NINETEEN

1. This was the title under which the talk would be published, in the August 1971 issue of *Commentary.*
2. See footnote, p. 159.
3. Quoted in Howard M. Sachar, *A History of the Jews in America* (New York: Vintage Books, 1993), p. 814.

CHAPTER TWENTY

1. Norman Podhoretz, "Is It Good for the Jews?" *Commentary,* February 1972.
2. Quoted in Stephen D. Isaacs, *Jews and American Politics* (Garden City, N.Y.: Doubleday, 1974), p. 248.
3. Ibid., p. 249.
4. Sefton D. Temkin, "United States of America," in Geoffrey Wigoder (ed.), EJ.
5. Melvin M. Tumin, quoted in Milton Himmelfarb, *The Jews of Modernity* (Philadelphia: Jewish Publication Society of America, 1973), p. 65.
6. Quoted in Isaacs, *Jews and American Politics,* p. 192.
7. Ibid.
8. Earl Raab, "Quotas by Any Other Name," *Commentary,* January 1972.
9. Quoted in Isaacs, *Jews and American Politics,* p. 194.
10. Ibid., pp. 196–97.
11. Isaacs, *Jews and American Politics,* p. 196.
12. *RN: The Memoirs of Richard Nixon* (New York: Grosset & Dunlap, 1978), p. 924.
13. Ibid.; Henry Kissinger, *Years of Upheaval* (Boston: Little, Brown, 1982), p. 515.

14. *RN: The Memoirs of Richard Nixon,* p. 927.
15. Ibid., p. 924.

CHAPTER TWENTY-ONE

1. Milton Himmelfarb, "Are Jews Becoming Republican?" *Commentary,* August 1981.
2. Quoted in Carl Gershman, "The Andrew Young Affair," *Commentary,* November 1979.
3. Daniel P. Moynihan, "Joining the Jackals: The U.S. at the U.N. 1977–1980," *Commentary,* February 1981.
4. Ibid.

CHAPTER TWENTY-TWO

1. This was the title of an article I wrote for the January 1981 issue of *Commentary.*
2. Milton Himmelfarb, "Are Jews Becoming Republican?" *Commentary,* August 1981.
3. Ibid.
4. "Now, Instant Zionism," *New York Times Magazine,* February 3, 1974.
5. Howard M. Sachar, *A History of the Jews in America* (New York: Vintage Books, 1993), p. 825.
6. "Declaration on the Relationship of the Church to Non-Christian Religions," http://www.vatican.va/archive/hist_councils/ii_vatican_council/documents/vat-ii_decl_19651028_nostra-aetate_en.html.
7. Genesis 12:2–3. "Within the pro-Israeli Protestant camp," says David R. Parsons, media director for the International Christian Embassy in Jerusalem, "there are two major theological schools. The first is covenantal Christian theology, which . . . is based on the belief that God eternally keeps his covenantal promises made through Abraham, Moses, David, and Jesus. . . . The other pro-Israeli Christian theology is dispensationalism. . . . Dispensationalism says that Israel was temporarily replaced by the church but—at the end of days—Israel will once again be the main redemptive agent for God in the world for a short season. This happens when the true church is 'raptured' or caught up into heaven at the start of the seven-year Tribulation. Then, during this time of great turmoil on earth, two-thirds of the Jews in the Land of Israel will die and the other one-third, through their conversion, will bring back Christ. . . . Still, even with these interpretations, most adherents of dispensationalism have a deep, abiding love for Israel. And it is not they who would be forcing Israel into some last, grand, convert-or-die scenario, since they would already be in heaven."

As to "Israel's Christian foes," their main theology, Parsons continues, is "replacement [or fulfillment] theology, also called supersessionism. . . . Under this covenant the church replaces Israel as God's main redemptive agent in the world. . . . Liberation theology is one more Christian theology that is hostile to Israel. . . . Adherents use Jesus as a historic role model, considering him the 'first Palestinian revolutionary.' . . . I have seen so-called study missions from the [mainstream] World Council of Churches coming to Israel and using liberation-theology arguments. . . . to justify Palestinians blowing themselves up to kill the 'oppressors' " (David R. Parsons, Interview with Manfred Gerstenfeld, http://www.jcpa.org/JCPA/Templates/ShowPage.asp?DRIT=3&DBID=1&LNGID=1&TMID=111&FID=610&PID=0&IID=2877&TTL=Christian_Friends_and_Foes_of_Israel).

8. Quoted by Jonathan Gurwitz in "Friends in Deed," Books in Review, *Commentary,* March 2009.

9. Howard M. Sachar, *A History of the Jews in America* (New York: Vintage Books, 1993), p. 825.

10. Himmelfarb, "Are Jews Becoming Republican?"

11. Quoted in my article "In the Matter of Pat Robertson," *Commentary,* August 1995.

CHAPTER TWENTY-THREE

1. Ronald Reagan, *An American Life* (New York: Simon & Schuster, 1990), p. 410.

2. Ibid.

3. Ibid.

4. Ibid., p. 411.

5. *New York Times Magazine,* May 2, 1982.

6. Reagan, *An American Life,* p. 412.

7. Jeane J. Kirkpatrick, "Dictatorships and Double Standards," *Commentary,* November 1979.

8. Lou Cannon, *President Reagan: The Role of a Lifetime* (New York: Simon & Schuster, 1991), p. 197n.

9. Reagan, *An American Life,* p. 413.

10. Ibid., p. 423.

11. Ibid., p. 428.

12. Quoted in my article "J'Accuse," *Commentary,* September 1982.

13. Ibid.

14. Ibid.

CHAPTER TWENTY-FOUR

1. Henry Kissinger, quoted in Mitchell G. Bard, Myths and Facts Online, http://www.jewishvirtuallibrary.org/jsource/myths/mf11.html#a.
2. Ronald Reagan, *An American Life* (New York: Simon & Schuster, 1990), p. 428.
3. Lou Cannon, *President Reagan: The Role of a Lifetime* (New York: Simon & Schuster, 1991), p. 391.
4. Quoted in Deborah Hart Strober and Gerald S. Strober, *Reagan: The Man and His Presidency* (Boston: Houghton Mifflin, 1998), p. 189.
5. Ibid.
6. Cannon, *President Reagan*, p. 391.
7. Ibid., p. 401.

CHAPTER TWENTY-FIVE

1. *The Nation*, March 22, 1986.
2. Ibid. All subsequent quotations from Vidal come from the same article.
3. "The Hate That Dare Not Speak Its Name," *Commentary*, November 1986. The account that follows draws on this piece, and all the quotes from other writers are also taken from it.

CHAPTER TWENTY-SIX

1. This and all subsequent quotations in chapter 26 come from "The Hate That Dare Not Speak Its Name," *Commentary*, November 1986.

CHAPTER TWENTY-SEVEN

1. Milton Himmelfarb, "Another Look at the Jewish Vote," *Commentary*, December 1985.
2. Quoted in Deborah Hart Strober and Gerald S. Strober, *Reagan: The Man and His Presidency* (Boston: Houghton Mifflin, 1998), p. 349.
3. Jay Lefkowitz, "Jewish Voters and the Democrats," *Commentary*, April 1993.
4. Lou Cannon, *President Reagan: The Role of a Lifetime* (New York: Simon & Schuster, 1991), p. 583.
5. Quoted in my article "America and Israel: An Ominous Change," *Commentary*, January 1992.

CHAPTER TWENTY-EIGHT

1. Quoted in my article "Buchanan and the Conservative Crackup," *Commentary*, May 1992.
2. Quoted in Joshua Muravchik, "Patrick J. Buchanan and the Jews," *Commentary*, January 1991.

3. Ibid.
4. Ibid.
5. "Buchanan and the Conservative Crackup."
6. "Buchanan and Anti-Semitism," *Wall Street Journal*, October 25, 1999.
7. For the record, they were, in alphabetical order: Peter L. Berger, Walter Berns, Robert H. Bork, Terry Eastland, Patrick Glynn, Michael Joyce, Harvey C. Mansfield Jr., Richard John Neuhaus, Michael Novak, James Nuechterlein, Thomas L. Pangle, R. Emmett Tyrrell Jr., and George Weigel.
8. Quoted in "Buchanan and the Conservative Crackup."
9. William F. Buckley Jr., "In Search of Anti-Semitism," *National Review*, December 30, 1991.
10. "What Is Anti-Semitism?: An Open Letter to William F. Buckley, Jr.," *Commentary*, February 1992.
11. Ibid.
12. Buckley, "In Search of Anti-Semitism."

CHAPTER TWENTY-NINE

1. Quoted in Joshua Muravchik, "Lament of a Clinton Supporter," *Commentary*, August 1993.
2. Quoted in my article "In the Matter of Pat Robertson," *Commentary*, August 1995.
3. Martin Peretz, "There Are Reasons Why There Are So Few Jewish Republicans," *Jerusalem Post*, October 7, 2008.
4. James Q. Wilson, "Liberalism vs. Liberal Education," *Commentary*, June 1972.
5. James Q. Wilson, "The DNA of Politics," *City Journal*, Winter 2009.
6. Peretz, "There Are Reasons Why There Are So Few Jewish Republicans."
7. "In the Matter of Pat Robertson," *Commentary*, August 1995.
8. Letters from Readers, *Commentary*, January 1996.

CHAPTER THIRTY

1. *New York Times*, March 1, 2000.
2. Ibid.
3. Quoted in my book *World War IV* (New York: Doubleday, 2007), p. 65.
4. Robert Satloff and David Makovsky, quoted in my article "Israel and the Palestinians: Has Bush Reneged?" *Commentary*, April 2008.
5. Ibid., in a paraphrase of Satloff by Joshua Muravchik.

CHAPTER THIRTY-ONE

1. Alan Dershowitz, "Why I Support Israel and Obama," *Jerusalem Post* ("Double Standard Watch" Blog), October 15, 2008.

2. Marty Peretz, "Biden Is More Than Just 'A Friend of Israel,' " *Jerusalem Post*, September 5, 2008.

3. Martin Indyk, "Obama Passes the *Kishke* Test," *Jerusalem Post*, November 2, 2008.

4. Eric Fingerhut, "Some Stats on the Orthodox Jewish Vote," Jewish Telegraphic Agency, November 25, 2008.

5. The 78 percent figure was based on the national exit poll. A tally of state polls yielded an average of 76 percent.

6. Brett Lieberman, "Sarah Silverman Was Wrong: Older Jews More Likely to Vote Obama," *Haaretz*, November 3, 2008.

7. Mark Mellman and Michael Bloomfield, "Israel and the Jewish Vote," *Jerusalem Post*, November 13, 2008.

8. Ibid.

9. Steven M. Cohen and Samuel J. Abrams, "The Diminished Place of Israel in the Political Thinking of Young Jews," quoted by Shmuel Rosner, "Jews and the 2008 Election," *Commentary*, February 2009.

10. http://www.rasmussenreports.com/public_content/politics/general_politics/americans_closely_divided_over_israels_gaza_attacks.

11. http://pewresearch.org/pubs/1076/modest-backing-for-israel-in-gaza-crisis-no-desire-for-greater-us-role. But as evidenced by the nearly unanimous support for Israel in Congress, the politicians were more evenly matched than their constituents. See Conclusion.

12. It was even worse with the European Left (and not just its Jewish members). Thus, in the wake of Gaza, the British sociologist Frank Furedi, while attacking the "defenders of Zionism" for what he called their "habit" of "labeling criticisms of Israel as a form of anti-Semitism," nevertheless acknowledged "the absorption of anti-Semitic sentiments by Europeans who politically identify themselves as left-wing." Even more worrisome, Furedi added, was "the new culture of accommodation to anti-Semitism." Many or most of those shouting "Death to the Jews" or "Hamas, Hamas, Jews to the gas" at demonstrations protesting the Israeli incursion into Gaza were Muslims, but Furedi sees "the emergence [on the secular Left] of a slightly embarrassed 'see nothing, hear nothing' attitude that shows far too much 'understanding' towards expressions of anti-Semitism" (www.spiked-online.com, January 19, 2009). Added testimony comes from the Irish writer Dennis MacEion, editor of the *Middle East Quarterly*: "In a bizarre reversal of all their commitment to human rights and the struggle of men and women for independence and self-determination, the European Left has chosen again and again to side with [Hamas] and to condemn a small nation struggling to survive in a hostile neighborhood" ("Marching for Hamas," *Jerusalem Post*, January 24, 2009).

Nor is it only in relation to Israel or Jews in general that the European Left has undergone this "bizarre reversal." Thierry Chervel, editor of the online German magazine *Perlentaucher*, writes: "In the confrontation with Islamism, the Left has abandoned its principles. In the past it stood for cutting the ties to convention and tradition, but in the case of Islam it reinstates them in the name of multiculturalism. It is proud to have fought for women's rights, but in Islam it tolerates head scarves, arranged marriages, and wife-beating. It once stood for equal rights, now it preaches a right to difference—and thus different rights. It proclaims freedom of speech, but when it comes to Islam it coughs in embarrassment. It once supported gay rights, but now keeps silent about Islam's taboo on homosexuality. The West's long-due process of self-relativization at the end of the colonial era, which was promoted by postmodernist and structuralist ideas, has led to cultural relativism and the loss of criteria." (SightandSound.com, Feb. 16, 2009).

CHAPTER THIRTY-TWO

1. The phrase is from Edward Shapiro, "Right Turn?" in L. Sandy Maisel and Ira N. Forman (eds.), *Jews in American Politics* (Lanham, Md.: Rowman & Littlefield, 2001), p. 211.

2. George Nash, "Joining the Ranks," in Murray Friedman (ed.), *Commentary in American Life* (Philadelphia: Temple University Press, 2005), p. 173.

3. Anna Greenberg and Kenneth D. Wald, "Still Liberal After All These Years?" in L. Sandy Maisel and Ira N. Forman (eds.), *Jews in American Politics* (Lanham, Md.: Rowman & Littlefield, 2001), p. 171.

4. Ibid., p. 174.

5. Ibid., p. 175.

6. Earl Raab, "Are American Jews Still Liberal?" *Commentary*, February 1996.

7. Murray Friedman, "Are American Jews Moving to the Right?" *Commentary*, April 2000.

8. Lawrence H. Fuchs, *The Political Behavior of American Jews* (Glencoe, Ill.: Free Press, 1956), p. 132.

9. Ibid., p. 131.

10. Ibid., p. 133.

11. Steven M. Cohen and Charles S. Liebman, "American Jewish Liberalism: Unraveling the Strands," *Public Opinion Quarterly*, vol. 61 (1997), 405–30.

12. Ibid., pp. 425–26.

13. Nathan Glazer in "Liberalism and the Jews," *Commentary*, January 1980.

14. "American Jewish Liberalism," pp. 417–18.

15. Charles S. Liebman and Steven M. Cohen, "Jewish Liberalism Revisited," *Commentary*, November 1996.

16. Greenberg and Wald, "Still Liberal After All These Years?" p. 177.

17. Tom Smith, *Jewish Distinctiveness in America* (New York: American Jewish Committee, 2005), p. 11.

18. Ibid., p. 24.

19. Ibid., p. 45.

20. The data also defeat two other challenges to the thesis of this book—one from Marc Dollinger's *Quest for Inclusion: Jews and Liberalism in Modern America* (Princeton University Press, 2000), and the other from Michael E. Staub's *Torn at the Roots: The Crisis of Jewish Liberalism in Postwar America* (Columbia University Press, 2002). Staub argues that the American Jewish community has not been monolithically liberal, while according to Dollinger, the need to fit in ("acculturation") has invariably taken precedence among American Jews over their commitment to liberalism. There is something to both of these arguments, but in the end they are trumped by the surveys and the voting behavior cited here.

CHAPTER THIRTY-THREE

1. Steven M. Cohen, *The Dimensions of American Jewish Liberalism* (New York: American Jewish Committee, Institute of Human Relations, 1989), p. 36.

2. Ruth R. Wisse, *If I Am Not for Myself: The Liberal Betrayal of the Jews* (New York: Free Press, 1992), p. 43.

3. S. M. Cohen, *The Dimensions of American Jewish Liberalism*, p. 28.

4. Quoted in Cohen and Liebman, "American Jewish Liberalism," *Public Opinion Quarterly*, vol. 61 (1997), p. 408.

5. Irving Kristol, "On the Political Stupidity of the Jews," *Azure*, Autumn 1999.

6. Ruth R. Wisse, *Jews and Power* (New York: Schocken Nextbook, 2007), p. 31.

7. Seymour Martin Lipset and Earl Raab, *Jews and the New American Scene* (Cambridge, Mass.: Harvard University Press, 1995), p. 170.

8. In *Breaking Ranks: A Political Memoir* (New York: Harper & Row, 1979) and *Ex-Friends: Falling Out with Allen Ginsberg, Lionel & Diana Trilling, Lillian Hellman, Hannah Arendt, and Norman Mailer* (New York: Free Press, 1999), I have written about my own experience as a dissenter from the orthodoxies of the intellectual community in which I had spent my entire adult life, but much of it would apply to the Jewish community as well.

9. James Q. Wilson, "The DNA of Politics," *City Journal*, Winter 2009.

10. Lawrence H. Fuchs, *The Political Behavior of American Jews* (Glencoe, Ill.: Free Press, 1956), p. 180.

11. Ibid., p. 187. Fuchs's transliteration (*Zedakeh*) is inaccurate, and I have therefore corrected it here and below.

12. Ibid., p. 188.

13. Ibid., pp. 188–89.

14. Letters from Readers, *Commentary*, October 1984.

15. Albert Vorspan and David Saperstein, *Jewish Dimensions of Social Justice: Tough Moral Choices of Our Time* (New York: UAHC Press, 1998), pp. 84–85.

16. Ibid., p. 84. The italics are in the original.

17. Sidney Schwartz, Or N. Rose, Jo Ellen Green Kaiser, and Margie Klein (eds.), *Righteous Indignation: A Jewish Call for Justice* (Woodstock, Vt.: Jewish Lights, 2008), p. 3.

18. Deborah E. Lipstadt, "Obama: A National Perspective," Chicago Jewish News Online, October 31, 2008.

19. "Liberalism and the Jews," *Commentary*, January 1980.

20. Michael Walzer, quoted in Cohen and Liebman, *Public Opinion Quarterly*, p. 408.

21. "Liberalism and the Jews," *Commentary*, January 1980.

22. Cohen and Liebman, *Public Opinion Quarterly*, p. 407.

23. I provide extensive documentation of this point in my book *The Prophets: Who They Were, What They Are* (New York: Free Press, 2002).

CHAPTER THIRTY-FOUR

1. "Liberalism and the Jews," *Commentary*, January 1980.

2. Townhall.com, April 25, 2006.

3. "Liberalism and the Jews."

4. Ibid.

5. Ibid.

6. Ibid.

7. Ibid.

8. Ibid.

9. Or N. Rose, Jo Ellen Green Kaiser, and Margie Klein (eds.), *Righteous Indignation: A Jewish Call for Justice* (Woodstock, Vt.: Jewish Lights, 2008), jacket copy.

10. "Liberalism and the Jews."

11. Hillel Halkin, "How Not to Repair the World," *Commentary*, July/August 2008.

12. Steven M. Cohen, *The Dimensions of American Jewish Liberalism* (New

York: American Jewish Committee, Institute of Human Relations, 1989), p. 31.
13. Ibid., pp. 31–32.
14. Ibid., p. 2.

CONCLUSION

1. "Liberalism and the Jews," *Commentary,* January 1980.
2. Deuteronomy 6:5.
3. Ibid., 30:19.
4. "Liberalism and the Jews."
5. Walter Russell Mead, "The New Israel and the Old," *Foreign Affairs,* July/August 2008.

BIBLIOGRAPHICAL NOTE

Of the many books and articles I consulted in writing Part One, I relied most heavily on one of the great works of twentieth-century Jewish scholarship, the *Encyclopaedia Judaica* (EJ in the endnotes). The seventeen-volume edition of EJ was originally published by Macmillan in 1972, but I used the CD-ROM edition put out in 1997 by Judaica Multimedia (Israel) Ltd., which has additional material but does not contain either volume numbers or page numbers.

Books that proved equally indispensable included *A History of the Jews* by Paul Johnson; *A History of the Jewish People* edited by H. H. Ben-Sasson (and especially the section on "The Modern Period" by Shmuel Ettinger); *Great Ages and Ideas of the Jewish People* edited by Leo W. Schwarz (and especially the section on "The Modern Age" by Salo W. Baron); *Jewish People, Jewish Thought* by Robert M. Seltzer; *A Short History of the Jewish People* by Cecil Roth; *The French Enlightenment and the Jews* by Arthur Hertzberg; *A History of the Jews in America* by Howard M. Sachar; and *World of Our Fathers* by Irving Howe. (Bibliographical information on all these books can be found in the endnotes.)

In writing Part Two, I relied mainly on the following books (bibliographical information on which can also be found in the endnotes): *The Political Behavior of American Jews* by Lawrence H. Fuchs; *Jews in American Politics* edited by L. Sandy Maisel and Ira N. Forman; *The Jews of Modernity* by Milton Himmelfarb; *Jews and American Politics* by Stephen D. Isaacs; *Jews and the New American Scene* by Seymour Martin Lipset and Earl Raab; *If I Am Not for Myself* and *Jews and Power* by Ruth R. Wisse; and *Jewish Dimensions of Social Justice* by Albert Vorspan and David Saperstein.

For Part Two, as detailed in the endnotes, the Annual Surveys of American Jewish Opinion sponsored by the American Jewish Committee, and various scholarly papers by Steven M. Cohen (either writing alone or in collaboration with Charles Liebman) and Tom Smith proved equally invaluable. Then there was *Commentary,* whose archives contain many of the best analyses ever done of the political attitudes of American Jews.

Finally, I also adapted and drew freely on several of my own past writings, most of them articles originally published in *Commentary.*

INDEX

Aaron (Bible), 90
Abbas, Mahmoud, 250
Abel (Bible), 17
Abelard, Peter, 28
abortion, 3, 185, 238, 252, 262, 265,
    271, 274, 277, 288
Abraham (Bible), 48, 187, 200, 271,
    309n
Abrams, Elliott, 194
Abrams, Samuel J., 256
Abzug, Bella, 182
Acheson, Dean, 138
Action Française, 112
Act to Disestablish the Anglican
    Church (1786), 72
Adams, Brooks, 92
Adams, Henry, 92, 93, 94, 204–5
Adams, John, 92
Adams, John Quincy, 92
affirmative action, 152, 163, 170,
    171, 172, 176, 228, 235, 261,
    264–65, 275, 283, 286, 288,
    292
Afghanistan, 177, 183–84
African Americans, 85, 131, 151–52,
    157, 161–66, 168, 169, 170, 171,
    172, 176, 217, 228, 229, 235,
    254, 255, 261, 264–65, 275, 283,
    286, 288, 292
Agobard, Archbishop of Lyon, 12,
    20

Ahmadinejad, Mahmoud, 253
Aksakov, Ivan, 108
Alexander II, Czar of Russia, 65
Alexander III, Czar of Russia, 67
Al Khet prayer, 234–35
Alter, Robert, 284–85
Alternative The (magazine), 165
Amalgamated Clothing Workers of
    America, 123
America First Committee, 126
American Christian Defenders, 121
American Civil Liberties Union
    (ACLU), 185, 260–61
American Conservative Union (ACU),
    229
American Federation of Labor (AFL),
    100, 120
American Jewish Committee (AJC), 1,
    147–48, 152, 154, 157, 158,
    159–66, 167, 170, 253, 256, 260,
    261, 266, 267–68, 270
"American Jewish Liberalism" (Cohen
    and Liebman), 262–64
American Jewish Yearbook, 121
American Jews:
  assimilation of, 83–89, 156, 183,
    272–73, 315n
  author's experiences as, 2, 4–5, 131,
    135–36, 140, 142–43, 147, 233–
    34, 238
  beliefs of, 88–90

Jewish Socialist Party, 69
Jews, 35–36, 74–75, 134, 278
  Ashkenazi, 25, 27–29, 71
  assimilation of, 43–52, 57–59, 62,
      83–89, 105–6, 107, 109–10,
      113–14, 156, 183, 272–73, 315n
  blood libel against, 14–15
  children of, 35, 109–10, 116
  as chosen people, 9–10, 63–64, 69,
      75, 76–79, 128, 134, 200, 279,
      280–81
  as "Christ-killers," 11–12, 13, 17,
      186–87
  citizenship acquired by, 43, 49, 51–
      54, 57–59, 71–73, 105–6, 125
  civil rights of, 30–37, 47, 49–54, 57–
      59, 65, 71–73, 85–86, 88, 105–
      12, 125, 142, 147, 263
  collective guilt of, 22–23, 186–87
  conservatism as viewed by, 1, 2, 34–
      35, 52n, 59, 61, 102–3, 108,
      113–14, 117, 120, 122, 128–30,
      137, 142, 166, 169–72, 180,
      181–90, 217–19, 224–32, 260–
      64, 268, 269–74, 283–84, 285,
      293, 294
  conversions of, 16–17, 23, 27, 28,
      36, 47–50, 52–53, 56, 60–61, 62,
      64, 67, 83, 106, 111, 187, 213,
      277, 283–84, 309n
  culture of, 26–29, 36–37, 40, 43–44,
      45, 47, 49–50, 56, 79–80, 88–90,
      94–97, 106, 113–20
  Diaspora of, 17, 125, 133–34, 198,
      272, 274, 294
  dietary (kosher) laws of, 82–83, 89,
      130–31
  discrimination against, 18–19, 35–
      36, 49, 53–54, 57, 66, 71–73, 90,
      119–21, 125, 154–56, 163, 166,
      167, 171, 264–65; see also anti-
      Semitism
  from Eastern Europe, 64–65, 71, 81,
      94–103, 105, 119, 280, 283–84,
      294–95
  economic status of, 1, 2, 32, 34, 39,
      53, 61, 65, 71, 81–86, 91, 94–
      103, 107–8, 131, 134, 142, 157,
      170, 171, 259, 263–64, 293,
      294–95
  education of, 1, 28–29, 35, 36, 39,
      45–46, 49, 50, 53, 61, 88, 90,
      120–21, 136, 155–56, 157, 270–
      72

  emancipation of, 30–37, 42, 44, 45–
      59, 96, 105–6, 108, 113–14, 117,
      142
  emigration of, 25–26, 64–86, 118–
      20, 125, 126, 133–34, 156, 227–
      28, 280, 294–95
  Ethiopian, 218
  ethnic identity of, 89–90, 105–12,
      116, 118–20, 182, 270, 273–90
  expulsions of, 17, 23–24, 25n, 34,
      56–57, 64–70, 90, 107–8, 109,
      213
  French, 2, 15, 23, 25n, 34, 37, 41,
      51–54, 58, 59, 68, 92n, 105,
      109–15, 124, 136, 160, 300n
  German, 12, 15, 23–24, 25n, 34, 37,
      48, 49, 54–57, 62, 66, 81–86,
      104–8, 110, 114–17, 120, 121,
      122, 124–26, 135, 140, 153,
      196–97, 198, 200, 201, 219, 226,
      227, 256–57
  ghettos for, 19, 20, 24, 57, 62, 65,
      98, 167
  as intellectuals, 69–70, 101, 147–48,
      161, 182, 241, 270–72, 287
  intermarriage of, 83–84
  "international conspiracy" of, 90–
      93, 121, 126, 204–5, 241–42
  liberal support for, 34–35, 36, 39,
      41–42, 52n, 53, 56–59, 68, 69–
      70, 108, 113–14, 117, 142, 166
  literature of, 28–29, 56, 114–15
  loyalty of, 71–73, 88, 137, 182–83
  in medieval period, 11–22, 25–26,
      29, 32, 34, 43, 49, 55, 56, 79,
      103, 106, 212–13
  as merchants, 32, 35, 39, 53, 61
  as "nation within a nation," 43, 49,
      51–52, 54, 71–73, 105–6
  as neoconservatives, 187–90, 194–
      95, 226, 247, 258
  non-Jews compared with, 1–2, 63–
      64, 69, 106–10, 116–17
  Orthodox, 47–48, 68–69, 82–83,
      168, 182, 193, 255, 256, 259, 277
  pogroms against, 21, 65–66, 213
  political influence of, 57–59, 66–70,
      90–93, 105–6, 222–23
  Reform, 45–50, 88–90, 182, 276,
      281, 287
  as religious community, 89–90, 105–
      6, 182
  as revolutionaries, 54–57, 58, 60,
      64–67, 69, 119, 153, 241–42

Printed in the United States
by Baker & Taylor Publisher Services